Paths in a Working Life
Charting Your 21st Century Career

DeVry University Press
July 2007

The authors and editor would like to thank DeVry University students, faculty, and administrators for supporting the Career Development course (CARD-205/405) and the development of this textbook, whose purpose is to help graduating students assess their academic achievements and their professional interests and goals in preparation for launching or enhancing their careers.

Special thanks to the staff of DeVry's Career Services departments, who have embraced the mission of helping all DeVry students gain the most from their education and helping students translate an education into a productive career.

Thanks also to Daniel Hamburger, Chief Executive Officer of DeVry Inc., and to David Pauldine, President; Donna Loraine, Vice President for Academic Affairs; and David Overbye, Dean of Curriculum for DeVry University, for their support of this initiative.

ISBN: 978-0-9777951-2-3

To the Career Development faculty
and
Career Services staff
of
DeVry University

and to
their productive collaboration

Preface

This text embodies the conviction that career entry and career progression arc aspects of the same continual process and share the same ideas, strategies, and methods. We further believe that colleges and universities serve their students well by offering upper-division courses that help students take stock of their educational attainments, prior work experience, and their goals – in the context of a post-graduation job search or planned career progression.[1] Such courses must treat both the immediate needs of career entry and the long-term needs of career development with equal seriousness, or they will end up short-changing both aspects.

If we apply one of Franklin Covey's principles to this challenge, we would recognize that a career search must *begin with the end in mind.* It may be true, increasingly, that few of us can foresee the ends of our careers, both in the kinds of work we will do and the fields in which we will labor. Nevertheless, it is still clearly true that we do best to begin our career journey with a plan in mind and a prospective path laid out in some detail. One of the advantages of having done the self-assessments and investigations that lead to our plan is that these provide a solid base for later adjustments and mid-course corrections.

Al Barbaro, one of the illustrative "characters" we use in this book, is represented as a worker in mid-career whose industry declines and whose company outsources his job, among others. By returning to college to earn a degree in a different field, Al is able to launch a new career in a new profession. His career change also illustrates the value of planning, of self-assessment, and of the skills and experience gained in the previous career. Al is able to build on a base of steady work habits, analytical ability, teamwork, and supervisory experience – what we would recognize as *transferable skills* – to restart his career journey from an advanced position, rather than starting from scratch again.

The Plan of Paths in a Working Life

This book is organized into three major sections, each with its own rationale and internal logic. Part I includes the first four chapters that start with a look at the realities of today's workplace and employer needs and desires. This reality check is followed by a pair of chapters that explore the career planner's motivations and interests in a framework of self-reflection and self-discovery. The fourth chapter, on the vital role of communication skills and including practical suggestions for improving these skills, is a recognition of the critical importance of communication in careers. As we point out throughout the book, communication is equally relevant as a skill needed for career entry and for successful career development.

Part II of the book – Chapters 5 through 10 – addresses the practical needs of the job search. These six chapters may be seen as themselves subdivided into two parts. Chapters 5-7 focus on preparation for the job search through company and industry research; development of resumes, cover letters, and related documents; and the fashioning of a self-marketing plan that includes

---

[1] DeVry University offers a Career Development course (CARD-205/405) to all upper-division undergraduate students in their next-to-last term. The course combines the practical requirements of the job search with consideration of the long-term needs of professional growth and career advancement.

getting organized and also preparing brief self-presentations called "commercials" and "elevator pitches."

The research chapter (Chapter 5) offers suggestions in several non-traditional areas, in addition to company and industry research. These are the exploration of career tracks associated with focused academic programs, and the investigation of press releases, new-product announcements, and other information available on company Web pages.

The second half of Part II – Chapters 8-10 – provides guidance for *using* the preparation of the prior chapters. Here we guide the applicant in launching the search, networking, participating in interviews, and, in the positive case, evaluating job offers and compensation packages.

Part III of the text once again presents a short- and long-term perspective by exploring the immediate needs of adjusting to a new position and learning the corporate culture, and then taking a career-long view of a current position and occupational category. As you will see, Chapter 12 presents suggestions for planning an entire career through many of the methods and means suggested earlier for the career preparation and job search campaigns. These include self-assessment, research, learning new skills, networking, developing contingency plans, and other such activities.

Characters in Search of a Career

A feature of the book that we believe will help students apply these concepts to their own circumstances is the use of three job-searching, career planning "characters" – 19-year-old Mark, 33-year-old Margaret, and 45-year-old Al. These characters represent the circumstances and the needs of (a) the traditional career launcher, (b) the returning adult student seeking to upgrade a career through education, and (c) the mid-life career changer. Their differing circumstances illustrate the different choices that must be made in light of a person's total situation. To an equal extent, these characters show us the common needs and requirements of the career entry and career development processes.

Our Developers

A primary source for the balanced view of career development presented in this book is the accomplished and experienced group of authors responsible for the ideas, exposition, and supporting evidence presented in our chapters. Most of these authors have taught the subject of career development, either at DeVry University or elsewhere. Many of them have also worked in the Career Services end of the spectrum with the challenges of helping graduates enter new careers or enhance existing ones.

To ensure that the plan for the book would draw on the rich experience of our authors, we worked in a collaborative way to define the contents and strategies for the book. We also shared content outlines and initial drafts of chapters within this group to gain feedback and suggestions for improvement. In addition to designating chapter authors, we asked one member of the group to develop case materials that we could apply across the chapters to illustrate key aspects of the career planning and development cycle. Adena Johnston took on this responsibility and gave us vivid accounts of the characters we call Mark, Margaret, and Al.

Here are the brief and current career profiles of the authors of this text.

- **Debra Hartman** is a Career Education Consultant based in Chicago.

- **Janice Hinds** is an Occupational Therapist, Registered, for the Colorado Mental Health Institute.

- **Louise Bishop** is Senior Career Advisor, DeVry University-Phoenix.

- **Mark Hinrichs** is Dean of Business Programs, DeVry University-Pennsylvania.

- **Thomas Allen** is Director of Career Services, Security, and Student Services, DeVry University-Atlanta.

- **Kim Brandt** is Associate Director of Alumni and Graduate Career Services, DeVry University-Chicago

- **Corey Vigdor** is Manager of Instructional Technology, Georgian Court University (NJ).

- **Linda Dobbs Willis** is a Senior Professor in Liberal Arts and Sciences, DeVry University-Dallas.

- **Kirsten Nicholas** is Program Coordinator and Career Advisor for the Master's of Engineering Management Program at Duke University.

- **Barbara Yetman** is Dean of Assessment and Evaluation, DeVry University-North Brunswick, NJ.

- **Karen Hanes** is a former Assistant Professor of General Education and Business, DeVry University-South Florida.

- **Monty Stanford** is Vice President and Managing Partner of Cardinal and Gold Inc., a California-based consulting firm.

- **Adena Johnston** is Center Dean for the Valley Forge (PA) DeVry University Center.

Thanks to this talented group. Thanks also to Susan Chang and David Crawford of DeVry University-DuPage for assistance in readying the manuscript.

Maris Roze
Executive Editor
DeVry University Press

July 2007

Table of Contents

CHAPTER ONE
Understanding Today's Workplace
Debra Hartman

The only place where success comes before work is in the dictionary.

– Vince Lombardi

Chapter Goal:

The purpose of this chapter is to provide a launch for the chapters that follow, which discuss the work associated with job searching and career management. This chapter will help you see the job search process through the eyes of the employer, providing a valuable perspective that can give you a competitive edge in the job market.

And Who Are You?

Before we look at what employers want, let's consider your own situation first. This is something everyone must do, even if the goal is to understand and respond to what employers are looking for. Knowing who you are as a prospective entrant into the job market will help you develop a strategy for responding to employer needs and desires. In that sense, it will be useful to explore some of the structural factors that you bring to the job search and career development process – your age, gender, family status, schooling, and prior experience. You may not be able to change these factors, but you can certainly use your understanding of them to your advantage.

The next several chapters will help you think about who you are in a broader way – by assessing your own motivation for work and for a career, by thinking about the concept of success, and by clarifying your values, priorities, and goals. Chapter Four will help you take a closer look at the most important job qualification of all – oral and written communication skills. The chapter will also suggest some strategies for improving this vital skill.

What Is Your Situation?

One of the assumptions of this book is that you are or have been a student at the college level, and that you are interested in linking your studies with the career you are planning to enter – or the career you want to enhance. Here are some typical considerations related to education and careers.

- You are a post-high school student (age 18-22) who recognizes the career value of an education and wants to apply that education to a new career.
- You started college many years ago but did not successfully finish.
- You are a woman who left the workforce to raise a family and now wants to return.
- You are a laborer who has been steadily employed but no longer wants to rely on physical work for your livelihood.
- You are a technical or business professional who has been consistently overlooked for promotions, simply because you don't have a degree.

To show how such factors can affect the planning to be done for a job search or career change, this text will introduce you to three characters whose differing circumstances will demonstrate application of the concepts you will be learning. Even if your situation differs from some or all of these folks, you will find that they provide lessons for you as well.

Meet Mark, Margaret, and Al.

The Traditional Student

Mark, age 19, graduated from high school last June with a general diploma but no plans for college. He was a solid student earning mostly Bs with an occasional C, but he didn't really excel in any one area of the curriculum, although the thought of going into business seemed appealing. After graduation, Mark moved into an apartment with his girlfriend Ginger and got a job at the local supermarket with the idea that he would soon be promoted to assistant manager. The promotions were passing him by and when he asked why, he was told that promotion would require a college degree. His parents had never attended college, but Ginger's father steered him to a good local university, where he enrolled as a business major.

Mark took some time getting back into the habit of studying while working full-time, but after his second term he decided to cut back to part-time hours at the supermarket and focus on finishing school. With the help of his Career Services Advisor, Mark got a Co-op position at an auto parts plant and is now getting his resume updated for the job search campaign he is planning at graduation. His background looks like this.

Mark Staples	markgodaddy@hotmail.com

436 Indiana Blvd, Apt. 6-A
Cremoc, Ohio, 44139
416-695-2096

Goal: a co-op position in business where there is opportunity to learn new skills and gain valuable experience.

Education:
Walsh University, 9/2005-present
BS in Business Administration (in progress)
GPA: 3.0
Expected graduation 9/2008

Cremoc High School
Diploma awarded 6/2004
GPA: 2.75

Experience:
Speedy Auto Parts, Cremoc, Ohio   4/2006-present
Student Co-Op in the Business Office

IGA Supermarket, Cremoc, Ohio   6/2004 - present
Cashier and Meat Department Associate

Camp Hawatonga, Elyria, Ohio   Summers 2001 – 2004
Counselor

YMCA, Cremoc, Ohio   2001-2004
Assistant Coach, Youth Softball League

Interests:
Sports, wreck diving, video games

The Adult Learner

Margaret, age 33, graduated from high school 15 years ago and although she took a few courses at her local community college, she never completed her degree. She has two children, ages 9 and 12, and was divorced four years ago, at which point she enrolled in a certificate program for legal assisting. She has been working as a legal assistant full-time in a small law office for three years. Her supervisor has told her she must earn a degree before she can advance in their firm. Even then, her possibilities would be limited without a law degree. Margaret decided to attend Rubicon University because they were receptive to her community college credits and because she could take courses part-time and on-line. In addition, she knows that to advance she must enter a new field since she has no desire to go on for a law degree.

Now at the end of her studies at Rubicon, Margaret is trying to pull her experience together, begin working with the Career Services office, and juggle her family situation and bills. She's trying to determine how much she needs to earn in a new job to leave her present position, which pays $29,000 per year. Her background looks like this:

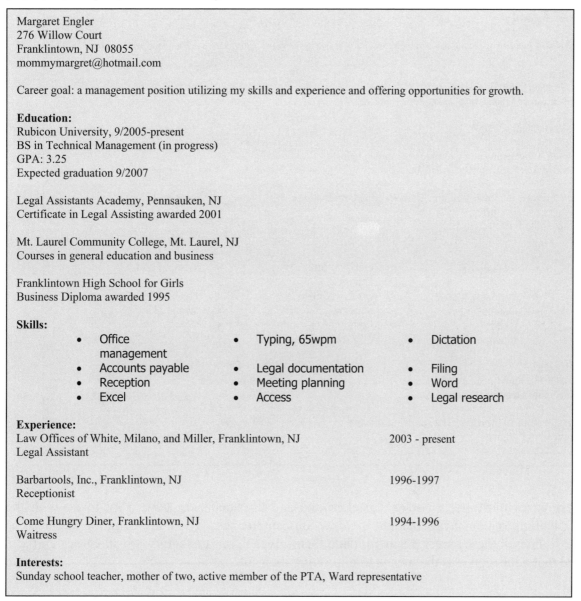

Margaret Engler
276 Willow Court
Franklintown, NJ 08055
mommymargret@hotmail.com

Career goal: a management position utilizing my skills and experience and offering opportunities for growth.

Education:
Rubicon University, 9/2005-present
BS in Technical Management (in progress)
GPA: 3.25
Expected graduation 9/2007

Legal Assistants Academy, Pennsauken, NJ
Certificate in Legal Assisting awarded 2001

Mt. Laurel Community College, Mt. Laurel, NJ
Courses in general education and business

Franklintown High School for Girls
Business Diploma awarded 1995

Skills:

- Office management
- Accounts payable
- Reception
- Excel

- Typing, 65wpm
- Legal documentation
- Meeting planning
- Access

- Dictation
- Filing
- Word
- Legal research

Experience:
Law Offices of White, Milano, and Miller, Franklintown, NJ   2003 - present
Legal Assistant

Barbartools, Inc., Franklintown, NJ   1996-1997
Receptionist

Come Hungry Diner, Franklintown, NJ   1994-1996
Waitress

Interests:
Sunday school teacher, mother of two, active member of the PTA, Ward representative

Mid-Life Career Changer

Al, age 45, was laid off four months ago from his machinist's position after his shop closed its doors and relocated its services abroad. After careful consideration, Al decided to remain in his area of residence, take advantage of some local retraining dollars, and enroll in Union College in an engineering technology program. Al already had an associate degree and had completed an apprenticeship program as a machinist. His manufacturing sector had changed dramatically, however, and offered few job prospects in the future. He had been earning $47,000 per year and had a family to support, but with the retraining award and his unemployment benefits he was able to return to school full-time, although his wife had to pick up extra hours with her employer. Al is nearing the end of his studies at Union College and his unemployment is about to expire. Al's background looks like this:

Alphonse Barbaro
7613 Fort Manow Drive
Uniontown, IN 46241
260-795-2343
barcutter@hotmail.com

Career goal: a position as an electronics technologist in a stable company where there is room for advancement.

Education:
Union College, 9/2005-present
BS in Electronics Engineering Technology (in progress)
GPA: 3.6
Expected graduation 9/2007

Uniontown Area Community College, Uniontown, Indiana
Associate of Science Degree awarded 5/1982

National Institute for Metal Working Skills (NIMS) Certification
Machining Level I earned 1986
Metal Stamping II earned 1991

Skills:

- Manual drill press
- Parts inspection
- Die making
- Reading blueprints

- Grinding and chucking
- Quality control
- Molding
- Computer Numerical Controls

- Turning and milling
- Machine building
- Welding
- CAD

Experience:
Hubmonell Machine Company, Uniontown, Indiana   9/1984 - present
Machine Shop Supervisor

Carversville Tool and Die Shop, Indianapolis, Indiana   1983
Apprenticeship Program

As these cases illustrate, a person's background and circumstances have a lot to do with the career planning options available and the decisions one makes. There are common elements as well. All three of these career planners found themselves in unsatisfactory job situations and decided that education was the means to improving their lot.

Earning a degree certainly opens doors that were previously closed. It does not mean that employers will now come knocking, of course. The doors will open wider, but it is still up to you to find the right ones and knock on those you want to enter. Once you are inside, it is up to you to present yourself in such a way that you are asked to stay.

You can improve your chances both of getting inside those doors and being asked to stay, if you develop a better understanding of today's workplace and match that understanding with a clearer idea of your own goals, skills, and capabilities. Knowing the job market and knowing yourself will help you tailor your approach to career planning and development.

What Employers Want

Your goals in the job search process are to get the employer to really read your resume, bring you in for an interview, bring you back for a series of follow-ups, and make the decision to offer you a job. To help make this scenario happen, view your job search through the eyes of the employer.

Why Employers Are in Business

It would be nice to think that employers are primarily interested in giving you an opportunity to gain experience, use your education, add to your skills, pay off your student loans, and fulfill your career goals. In reality, these are largely side effects resulting from an employer's primary motivation – to achieve success in an enterprise for which he has a significant responsibility. His interest in you will be greater to the extent that he believes you can contribute to that success – his success.

One of the common ways of measuring the success of an organization is to measure its ability to increase its revenues and profits, if it is a profit-seeking organization such as a business. Many not-for-profit organizations that employ people would define success in other ways than making money. But both kinds of organizations are interested in employing people they believe can help them achieve success as they define it. Here are some examples of the goals of organizations, and of the "employers" in their ranks who make the hiring decisions.

- Create new products and services
- Improve existing products and services
- Grow the size of the organization
- Improve efficiency and productivity
- Help grow one's industry
- Capture new markets
- Expand market share in an existing market
- Help develop new technologies
- Invest in a local community or region
- Contribute to the alleviation of social problems
- Influence civic and political affairs

To get a clearer idea of the particular goals of an organization, you might look at the words that serve as the foundation for a company's purpose – the mission statement. A mission statement

5

describes the organization's reasons for being and identifies its clients and some of its planned activities.

Mission statements can be broad and sweeping:

3M	To solve unsolved problems innovatively
Merck	To preserve and improve human life
Wal-Mart	To give ordinary folk the chance to buy the same thing as rich people
Walt Disney	To make people happy
Microsoft	To help people and businesses throughout the world realize their potential

In these cases, the broad vision of the mission statement will usually be accompanied by a more specific set of purposes and by statements of the organization's values. Here are Microsoft's values:

- Integrity and honesty
- Passion for customers, for our partners, and for technology
- Openness and respectfulness
- Taking on big challenges and seeing them through
- Constructive self-criticism, self-improvement, and personal excellence
- Accountability to customers, shareholders, partners, and employees for commitment and quality

Mission statements can also be quite specific and focused:

> FedEx will produce superior financial returns for shareowners by providing high value-added supply chain, transportation, business and related information services through focused operating companies. Customer requirements will be met in the highest quality manner appropriate to each market segment served. FedEx will strive to develop mutually rewarding relationships with its employees, partners and suppliers. Safety will be the first consideration in all operations. Corporate activities will be conducted to the highest ethical and professional standards.

One of the lessons provided by these kinds of statements is that companies are not just interested in making money, but in providing their products or services in the right ways. For example:

- Through innovation
- With integrity and honesty
- Through high quality
- Safely
- To meet a social need

As your job search progresses and you identify particular companies you want to apply to, take a few moments to access the company's mission statement – either on the Web or in a printed brochure – and think about the *ways* this company wants to do its business, and how you might contribute to them.

Your Contributions to an Employer

Demonstrating to an employer how you can contribute to achievement of her goals – from the broad perspective of the mission to the narrowest perspective on a balance sheet – is a high priority in all phases of your job search and career management process. If you can do this, you will ensure your own success in the organization.

If you are a salesperson, your contributions to a bottom line can be readily seen – bringing in customers, increasing sales, securing repeat business. What if you work as a database administrator, health services coordinator, computer programmer, network analyst, or project manager? And how could you demonstrate your potential impact if you have little or no work experience in your field? Here is one perspective on this issue:

> *In the eyes of the employer, saving money and saving time are
> the same as making money.*

- As a database administrator, you might streamline a process to be more efficient.
- As a health services coordinator, you might apply your organizational skills to produce more efficient or more effective patient care.
- As a computer programmer, you might write code or user instructions to improve the functioning of a consumer product.
- As a network analyst, your decision to upgrade a system to track important data might provide insight to product development specialists.
- As a project manager, you might solve problems and coordinate efforts to complete a project on time and under budget.

Even when you have limited work experience in your field, you can communicate your orientation toward efficiency, innovation, and problem solving through the examples you present:

- As a store clerk, you used your conflict management skills to resolve an issue for an angry customer.
- In your job at a garage, you spotted a safety hazard and made a point to get it removed.
- As a waiter, you helped other servers during the evening rush and on non-scheduled weekends to ensure that patrons received good service.

In linking past accomplishments to potential applications in the future, you are relying on the employer's acceptance of the concept of *transferable skills*. The fact that you lack the specific experience to do a job for the employer may be viewed as a training issue. Your lack of transferable skills – such as problem-solving ability or interpersonal and communication skills – may also be viewed as a deficiency that is harder to overcome.

When employers are trying to determine how you will help them succeed, they look for three general categories of skills:

1. Your ability to do a certain job – your work skills.
2. Your ability to solve problems – your critical thinking skills.
3. Your ability to fit within the culture of the organization – your interpersonal and communication skills.

Most candidates consider the first of these to be most important. From an employer's perspective, however, the first skill may be the least important, simply because it is most amenable to training or on-the-job learning. Assuming a general background of education and experience in the computer field, which of the following do you think would be the easiest to teach a new employee?

1. How to re-image a laptop
2. How to solve problems efficiently
3. How to communicate effectively with customers and manage conflict in the workplace.

To help answer this question, consider the impact of a lack of skills in each of these areas. Not knowing how to re-image the laptop is certainly a problem if this is one of the essential functions of the job. However, the inability to solve problems or relate to others can have a much greater impact on the bottom line.

An example: Imagine you are the network administrator in charge when the server crashes. Every minute the server is down is a minute during which hundreds of people cannot do their jobs. What should you do if an immediate fix is not possible? How do you effectively communicate the problem to your internal and external customers? Compare the following messages.

A. You have realized I am sure by now that the Titan server has crashed. It was inevitable this server would eventually crash and burn and take us all down with it. The IT department has tried to get management to upgrade this hardware for more than a year, to avoid a situation like this, but we were unsuccessful. We are doing everything we can to get you up and running again as soon as possible. For now, think of the Titan as the Titanic. Thanks for your patience.

B. To all Titan users: The IT department is aware that the server has crashed, and we are working diligently to identify and correct the problem for you as soon as possible. We recognize the impact of this failure on your ability to do your job. If we are unable to resolve the problem by 10:00 a.m. CST, we will activate the back-up server and provide you with specific login instructions. Aside from a change in login procedures, the use of the backup server would be virtually seamless to you. It is our goal, however, to have the Titan running efficiently by 10:00 a.m. CST. We will continue to communicate with you regarding our progress. Thanks for your patience.

Perhaps these two IT spokespersons are of equal ability in diagnosing and helping fix the failed server. What of their differing approaches, however, to fixing the problems of network users depending on the server? What of their skills in communicating with the users to reassure them and give them useful information? And what does the strategy of blaming senior management for the problem say about speaker A's maturity, team spirit, and basic good sense?

We can see from these examples why employers value certain kinds of transferable skills. Let's take a closer look at these skills and how they weigh in an employer's decision making about job candidates.

Skills in Demand

According to the National Association of Colleges and Employers (NACE) 2007 Job Outlook annual employer survey, the following qualities and skills rank as the most sought-after by employers in job applicants[2]. As a prospective job applicant, you can improve your chances by recognizing the value of these attributes to an employer and by providing evidence of your strengths in these areas.

Figure 9	Employers rate the importance of candidate skills/qualities
Communication skills (verbal and written)	4.7
Honesty/integrity	4.7
Interpersonal skills (relates well to others)	4.5
Motivation/Initiative	4.5
Strong work ethic	4.5
Teamwork skills (works well with others)	4.5
Computer skills	4.4
Analytical skills	4.3
Flexibility/adaptability	4.3
Detail-oriented	4.2
Organizational skills	4.0
Leadership skills	4.0
Self-confidence	4.0
Friendly/outgoing personality	3.9
Tactfulness	3.9
Well-mannered/polite	3.8
Creativity	3.7
GPA (3.0 or better)	3.6
Entrepreneurial skills/risk-taker	3.3
Sense of humor	3.2
Bilingual skills	2.3

(5-point scale, where 1=not important, 2=not very important, 3=somewhat important, 4=very important, and 5=extremely important)

Communication skills: Oral and written communication skills rank at the top of the list because they are the basis of teamwork within the organization and essential to good relations with customers. A well-written cover letter and well-organized resume are keys to gaining an interview. Speaking clearly, accurately, and concisely in the interview process is the key to demonstrating your good communication skills. The key to being able to speak well is an understanding of the interview process along with preparation and practice.

Honesty and integrity: This quality is also at the top of the list for employers because they need to know they can rely on you in multiple circumstances. Given this self-evident principle, how should you respond in an interview? Probably the most basic point here is that you should tell the truth and comment accurately about the equally true information in your resume. This doesn't mean that you can't "sell" yourself, but that you should not claim abilities and accomplishments that are not true for you. You can say that you work well with others; this is a subjective evaluation. Don't claim, however, that you have a driver's license, C++ certification, or a degree from Yale if these things are not true.

---

[2] Chart reprinted from the NACE 2007 Job Outlook, with permission of the National Association of Colleges and Employers, the copyright holder.

Motivation/initiative: "What motivates you?" is a typical interview question and often difficult for people to answer. Knowing that you are willing to take initiative versus waiting until you are told to do something is important to an employer.

Strong work ethic: Are you willing to go beyond the "required" aspects of a job? Would you be willing to work beyond your job requirements when needed and work earlier or later than scheduled when necessary? If so, let the employer know that your orientation is toward getting the job done, not just meeting the requirements of the position description.

Teamwork: What would happen if Republicans and Democrats worked together in policy making for the country, rather than against each other? Do you think the country would gain better education, a stronger economy, and perhaps social security and healthcare reform? In business, effective teamwork usually stimulates good morale, higher productivity, and more revenue. Use the interview to describe your teamwork experience and demonstrate how your participation contributed to the team's success.

Analytical skills: Showing the employer how you solved a problem is just as important as achieving the solution itself. Employers value people who take an analytical approach and a systematic follow-through to solving problems, as opposed to those who make quick decisions without investigation. Despite the possibilities of success from some quick decisions, employers realize that the analytical approach will serve them best in the long run.

Flexibility/adaptability: Employers want to know if you are willing to adapt when their own needs change – as is common in business and other dynamic environments. Show the employer that you are willing to work at the times you are needed and adjust your way of doing things to benefit the company.

Computer skills: In today's world, very few professional jobs remain in which some form of technology is not used. Feature your training and experience with software and hardware specialties during the interview, and show these skills on your resume.

Detail orientation: If you are *not* a person who attends to the specifics of a job, the interviewer may conclude that you would need close supervision, or micro-managing. Such relationships are usually fraught with problems for both parties. In addition, managers are responsible for the overall quality of departmental operations and results. Having people on their team who attend to details and work accurately helps them get the work done with less management oversight. Use examples from previous work or school experience to demonstrate your attention to details.

Organizational skills: Managers also want to know how you organize information physically. Telling an interviewer that you typically have a large pile of papers on your desk but always know where to find something is not the best strategy. You should be able to reference an example of how you keep things organized. This could be as simple as personal experience with monthly bills or as complex as having created a filing system with detailed cataloging and referencing processes.

Leadership skills: While this is a lower-rated ability than teamwork skills, it is a natural counterpart of teamwork, and a quality valued in its own right. You can show a hiring manager you are a leader by describing situations where you have lead a team or taken the initiative to facilitate change in a process. Work, school, and volunteer activity provide occasions from which you may be able to pull experiences to cite.

Self-confidence: Observe the fine line here between confidence and arrogance. An arrogant comment is likely to leave an employer feeling that you would not be a good fit for the team. Proclaiming your superior knowledge level or mastery of your specialty areas could be a mistake, because you are likely to be compared to people who have many accomplishments and many years of experience. Managers want people who are confident in their abilities but still willing to learn from their peers and co-workers.

Human Resources and the Hiring Manager

Now that you have the general perspective of the employer, let's take a closer look and examine the differences between the perspective of the Human Resources department compared to that of the hiring manager.

A Human Resources department can serve a number of important functions, including these typical activities: recruiting and staffing, job/market analysis, compensation and benefits, training and education, union and labor relations, policy interpretation, performance review standardization, workplace safety, and equal employment opportunity issues.

Focusing on just the recruiting and staffing function, here are some of the tasks associated with this area:

1. Advertise available employment opportunities
2. Receive, organize, and sort resumes; maintain a resume database
3. Track candidates as they move through the hiring process
4. Screen resumes and/or conduct the first interviews of candidates
5. Perform pre-employment testing
6. Complete background checks, reference checks, drug screening, etc.
7. Formally extend offers of employment that are decided by hiring managers
8. Discuss employee benefits with candidates
9. Assist with salary negotiation
10. Process new-hire paperwork

Perhaps number 7 above comes as a surprise, since many job seekers believe that the HR department actually makes the hiring decisions. In fact, while they do hire their own staff, they generally play only a secondary role in hiring for other departments.

Does this mean that you don't need to be concerned with tailoring your approach to this audience? Absolutely not. Though it is secondary in the hiring decision, HR is the first level of contact with an organization for most candidates. Their impressions can play a major role in helping or hindering a candidacy.

The HR Screen

Human Resources employees are generalists, and hiring managers are specialists. Human resources employees know a little bit about many jobs. Hiring managers know a lot about just a few jobs. As a result, Human Resources measures your quality as a candidate using very different criteria than a hiring manager might use.

When looking at your resume, for example, Human Resources needs to be able to quickly ascertain whether you have the minimal skills to fill a position. Your resume may never be seen by the hiring manager if HR is unable to determine that you meet these qualifying criteria. For the HR staff person, such criteria will be closely linked to the requirements and preferences listed in the job posting. These might include degree requirements, years of experience, and similar factors.

Remember that the role of Human Resources in the hiring process is not to find the best person for the job. Their purpose is to screen applicants, weed out those who are obviously not qualified, and present the remaining candidates to the hiring manager. Essentially, Human Resources is working to reduce the *unqualified* applicant load.

To improve your chances of inclusion in the list of surviving applicants, do your best to avoid mistakes and errors that call attention to you in a negative way. These might include misspellings, typos, or incongruent use of dates on your resume. Similarly, arriving late or dressed too casually for the first HR interview may detract from your chances of meeting the hiring manager, even if you test well and answer screening questions effectively.

The Perspective of the Hiring Manager

Because the hiring manager – the person you would work for if hired – has most to do with the decision to offer you a job, it should be your goal from the start of the process to reach this person and to convey a strong positive impression of your candidacy to her. In addition to HR, other managers and perhaps senior executives may contribute to your evaluation. Hence, you should do your best to present yourself not only in the strongest terms but also in a consistent way that helps build the consensus for a positive decision. Other things being equal, however, the deciding vote in the process rests with the hiring manager.

As suggested earlier, the hiring manager is a specialist with a better grasp of the particular skills and qualities necessary to effectively perform the job. This person understands the challenges of the position and can gauge the problem solving skills necessary to do the job well. He wants the person he hires to do well in the position, because that will make his job easier and will reflect favorably on him.

Beyond that, the hiring manager is interested in whether the other members of the department will be able to work harmoniously and productively with the new hire. On one level, this is an issue of "fitting in" with an established culture – a way of doing things (see Chapter 11 for more on this). Fitting in may also mean that you relate to established members of the department in a way that creates *synergies*, or improved outcomes resulting from the combination of inputs. In addition to looking for ways to demonstrate that you would fit in, therefore, you might look for ways to indicate that your contributions could be complementary or might stimulate productivity in others. Opportunities of this kind may arise during the interview stages of the process, as you will learn in Chapter 9.

Career Trends

Let's broaden the focus now from analyzing an employer's perspective to looking at some of the forces shaping careers and job markets today. While Chapters 11 and 12 of this book will help you with plans and strategies for the longer-term development of your career, some of these considerations should be part of your analysis at the time you are prospecting for specific jobs and job opportunities.

Change

In today's employment market, change is inevitable and constant. Companies and organizations change in response to problems and issues that arise both internally and externally. In addition, companies make proactive changes in an effort to remain competitive. Such changes often become the cornerstone for an emerging direction that a team, business unit, or entire company must follow. As an employee, you may be faced with changes in process, procedure, or philosophy. How you respond will be a determining factor in your success. Are you open to change?

Many people find change unnerving and respond with fear and resistance. They react to new ideas by finding reasons why they can't instead of reasons why they can. They talk to others about the way things were and should continue to be, rather than embracing a planned change and responding to the way things are.

Change resisters provide real challenges for an employer trying to stay competitive and maintain a productive work environment. A hiring manager who is aware of the *need* for change in his industry will be wary of candidates who convey their reluctance or mistrust of change.

Beyond accepting and implementing change, consider whether you have potential for acting as a change agent. Because the success of a company or organization depends on its ability to adapt to an evolving, globally competitive market, change agents are vital members of the organization. Think about your potential in these ways:

- Can you think of a more efficient process for accomplishing a familiar daily task?
- Do you know how your company might use its particular strengths – expertise, good will, distribution networks, etc. – to increase its market share?
- Can you identify new opportunities in a market, consistent with current business objectives?
- Have you identified an emerging trend that poses a risk to your organization?
- Can you see how a new technology could simplify or enhance some of the ways your company does business?
- Are you able to create contingency plans to respond to threats or risks?
- Can you lead others in the implementation of change initiatives?

Keep in mind also that a fine line exists between acting as a change agent and being perceived as a malcontent. Positive proponents of change make clear their interest in the long-term health and growth of an organization. In contrast, malcontents tend to see problems largely from their own narrower perspective and promote changes that are good mostly for themselves or some subset of the organization.

Remember also that once you have entered a new career and established yourself, you will likely be in a changing environment. A key strategy for your continued growth and development will be to stay up to date with the technologies associated with your field. Technology is a component of almost all professional positions today, and it is here to stay. Demonstrate your commitment to technology to a potential employer and to your colleagues on the job.

The Team Emphasis

In the workplace of today, everyone is a leader. Companies and organizations are more horizontal in structure than before, eliminating the many layers of management used in the past. This horizontal structure disperses leadership and places an emphasis on teamwork to achieve organizational goals. This workplace trend empowers teams to make important decisions and to do so quickly in an effort to stay competitive.

To be successful in today's workplace, candidates need to be able to lead others, follow others, and work beside others. It is quite likely that you will find yourself working in a team, even leading a team, with people from a variety of levels within an organization. It may be your job to motivate others, including those who stand higher than you in the corporate hierarchy. You may also need to take direction from a teammate who ranks below you. The goal in these cases is effective collaboration, regardless of the team members' status.

Good interpersonal communication is essential to success in leadership and teamwork. When communication functions poorly, redundancy occurs, conflicts arise, deadlines pass, and relationships suffer. These problems bear a cost in time and money. How will you show the employer that you are not likely to contribute to such problems, but rather to their solution?

Successful teams focus on accomplishing two general objectives – their assigned tasks and the strengthening of the team itself. When a team chooses to focus only on task goals and ignores team maintenance, team issues often get in the way of accomplishing the tasks. Here are some strategies for building the team, which should then be in a better position to get its tasks completed.

- Take the time to interact socially upon formation of the team. Determine what is important to each team member.
- Exchange schedules and contact information, and discuss outside commitments; this will help set reasonable goals.
- Consider cultural issues that might impact the team.
- Discuss strengths and weaknesses related to teamwork from the start; this will help the team work together to overcome these issues, before they get in the way of task completion.
- Establish how and when to communicate. Choosing a channel of communication and a schedule that works for everyone will help maintain the team's effectiveness.
- Resolve to treat all team members with respect.

Perhaps some of these principles reflect your own experience with teams, either in school or on the job. In the job search process, you can expect scrutiny of your potential for teamwork and for contributing to the maintenance of a strong team. Your understanding of the role of teams in today's organizations, along with the ability to demonstrate successful participation in teams, will help you gain favorable consideration by employers.

Offshoring, Outsourcing, and Consulting

Companies and organizations are no longer situated in a single primary location. Operations may be spread across separate buildings, cities, and states. A company's operations may also be conducted in other countries, or *offshored*. Employees may work from home, as telecommuters, and external vendors may perform functions *outsourced* by the company. Independent contractors or *consultants* fill in gaps in a company's operations. These conditions have changed the ways companies operate and employees function as a team.

Geographically dispersed employees create the need for teams that use technology to collaborate but also require frequent travel. Time zone differences, cultural variations, and differing styles and norms all complicate communication within teams in these complex organizations. Manufacturing operations for many U.S. companies, for example, have been moved entirely overseas. Because products are launched on factory lines thousands of miles away, using both generalist and specialist workers from a variety of backgrounds, sensitivity to the cultural preferences of others is essential (more on this in Chapter 11).

Perhaps your job as a software engineer requires you to work with overseas staff to modify product software prior to a product launch. Whether your teammates are actual employees of your company, contracted to perform a function, or outside consultants working on a specific task, it remains your responsibility to hold such a team together to ensure you meet the end goal.

When functions are outsourced, employees work for one company but are often housed at another. This can blur the lines of loyalty creating ethical concerns and uninvited conflicts of interest. Contractors and consultants work with companies to provide expertise of significant depth, but work for themselves.

It is not unusual today, for example, in the field of information technology for IT workers at a company to experience the outsourcing of their jobs. This trend is supported by the belief that outsourcing non-core functions offers cost savings to an employer. In this case, the IT worker might work in the same physical location, at the same company, with the same job title, and with the same people, but for the outsourcing or contract firm.

The IT worker's prior experience with the client company gives her valuable insight that serves both the client and the contract firm. It also creates unique challenges as the employee makes decisions for one company as an employee of another. She may be asked by the contract firm to perform a task that she knows is in conflict with the desires of the client company. Where should her loyalties lie?

Offshoring, outsourcing, and the use of consultants are all helping businesses take better advantage of worldwide labor and capital. Technology has made much of this possible.

Employers seek candidates who understand and have the ability to successfully navigate these complex structures of today's organizations. Can you?

This complex, shifting job environment also makes it important that you think about the long-term implications of your career choices. Above all, it means that you must act decisively now to maximize your chances for future advancement and growth.

Making Choices

Often students make the decision to delay entry into a new career field – waiting until the market seems right, the timing seems right, when life's challenges seem right. If you view your career this way, there will always be a better time sometime in the future. Fast-forward ten years and you will likely find yourself in the same place, facing the same challenges, but with credentials that may have lost some of their currency and value.

If you are at the point of completing your education to help you enter a new career, the best time to make this move is *now*. Your new degree credential will have the greatest impact on your earning potential today. Every year that you delay entering the new field dilutes the career value of your education.

Let's take another look at the students in the profiles described earlier in the chapter and consider how their choices are likely to impact their futures.

Mark Staples

At age 19, Mark has already discovered that making a "career" in just about any industry will be a challenge without a degree – this is why he returned to school. Now that he is completing his degree in business administration, he has a choice to make.

Life Choice A: Mark can stay in his job as a cashier at the grocery store, where he has gotten comfortable in the last couple of years, waiting for the store manager to recognize his potential; after all, he is making more money now as a result of two 3% annual increases. In addition, he really likes the people he works with and the added benefit of priority scheduling due to his seniority. He also likes the opportunity he has to earn overtime pay; he and his girlfriend are saving for a down payment on a townhouse and the extra cash will really help.

Life Choice B: Mark can take that recent degree and fresh co-op experience and transition to a new job that requires his educational background. The new position will likely pay the equivalent of his current salary at the grocery. He may no longer earn overtime pay, but his opportunity for promotions will be better than he is likely to see at the grocery store. While he will be the new member of a department, he will be in a professional job with a good future. His co-op experience, though not extensive, helps demonstrate his commitment to making a career change. He is excited about what he has learned.

Which life choice would you make in Mark's case, or in circumstances similar to his? While the ability to earn overtime pay might help accelerate his townhouse purchase by a year or two, imagine the long-term impact of working in a job that is not satisfying. What motivates Mark today might be very different from his motivation five, ten, or fifteen years in the future. It would be great if he had also learned to look ahead, to anticipate and plan for the next phase of his life.

Margaret Engler

In her mid-30s, Margaret is no stranger to hard work. As a single mom going to school and working full time, she has not had an easy road to completing her degree. Her studies were also a considerable monetary investment, even with financial aid. Now that she is graduating, she has some choices to make.

Life Choice A: Margaret can continue working at her law firm. Her degree will likely lead to a promotion to Executive Legal Assistant and a 5% raise. She finds the law really fascinating and is good at what she does, though most of her responsibilities are clerical in nature. While the stress level at the firm can be high, the lawyers generally treat her with respect. Margaret usually earns a bonus of about $1,000 at the end of the year, which comes in handy for holiday presents for her kids. In addition, the firm has been accommodating when she has needed to leave early or take a day off to be with her kids.

Life Choice B: Margaret has significant experience in clerical work, understands how to prioritize office tasks, and is well versed in legal terminology and procedure. These skills, combined with her new degree, qualify her for positions such as Office Manager or Management Trainee in any number of industries that utilize contract law. Combining her experience and education is a good strategy for adding value to her qualifications. She can market her clerical skills as an added benefit to any organization and is in a good position now to emphasize her management potential.

If you were in Margaret's shoes, which life choice would you make? Continuing to work in a clerical position after earning her degree would certainly send a message to an employer that she lacks confidence in her education and in her own potential. In addition, continuing to perform clerical work will not add to Margaret's skill set, nor will it give her the opportunity to put into practice what she has learned in college. Without practice and application, any skills will diminish, along with her confidence in making a change later.

While the job at the law firm is interesting, she has been told that without a law degree, which she does not intend to pursue, her long-term growth potential is limited. Making the change now, before her salary begins to approach its ceiling, will position her to make a painless transition into a new career that will offer dividends beyond an annual increase and a modest bonus.

Alphonse Barbaro

Al has been forced to make a career change in his mid-40s as a result of a layoff, which was initially a worrisome prospect. He really knew only the tool-and-die industry, which had provided him with a good living for more than two decades with the same employer. With the help of outplacement training provided by the employer and the resources of unemployment insurance, Al chose to go back to school for a technical degree to improve his employability.

Life Choice A: While Al has enjoyed returning to school, he feels a bit intimidated by his classmates, who are younger and seemingly more confident and carefree. Al would like to use his new electronics engineering technology degree, but feels uncomfortable selling himself to an employer. He is not sure that he is quite what employers are looking for. He is also not sure he wants to take orders in a new job from someone ten years younger than him. His job at the machine shop paid a nice salary, one that he won't likely get as an entry-level engineering technologist. Al could decide to stay in his comfort zone, and look for a job as a machinist, hoping that such a job lasts long enough to get him through to retirement.

Life Choice B: Al accepts that the tool-and-die industry is no longer a viable field and recognizes that he is only halfway through his working years. His new degree provides an opportunity to establish himself in a field that is growing. It also gives him a chance to use his supervisory skills while developing his technical skills. While Al knows that he may have to make a lateral move on the pay scale, or even take a step back, he recognizes that these moves could still be taking him forward. Believing in the solid supervisory skills that he offers and practicing his proof stories, Al knows that his move from a job to a career will offer long-term benefits for him.

Which life choice would you make in Al's circumstances? It is easy to fall into the trap of taking a layoff personally, which can lead to a lack of confidence in selling your skills and education to an employer. Al felt good about himself as a machinist prior to the layoff and wanted that feeling back again. When an industry is in decline, it is important to recognize that staying in that industry is only setting oneself up for a cycle of disappointments.

Even if Al were to successfully find another job as a machinist, he may find himself in a similar position just a couple of years later with a technical degree that is now a couple of years older. Focusing on industries that are viable today, with good future potential, helps ensure that Al's efforts to re-tool will offer stable work opportunities for the second half of his career.

One of the most difficult things in making a career change is to move to a new career and a new industry at the same time, particularly if you are concerned about salary. Changing only one of these at a time will likely minimize the pay cut and maximize the focus on added value. Fortunately for Al, his job as a machinist involved making jigs for the production of medical equipment. Since the healthcare field is a rapidly expanding one, it makes sense for Al to place emphasis on the medical equipment knowledge he has gathered over the years as he transitions into an electronics engineering technology position in a healthcare related field.

Choices for Life

Note that we called the decisions faced by Mark, Margaret, and Al _life choices_ and not simply job or career choices. The choices we make regarding our careers have a major impact on our lives, our relationships with others, and our self-concept. These consequences reach far beyond the routines associated with getting up and going to work each day. Estimates are that we spend more than 40% of our waking hours in the workplace. Many of us extend our working hours beyond the time we spend in the workplace, and our friends and acquaintances may well be our co-workers. Our career choices become choices of the kinds of lives we lead.

Chapter Exercise:

In later sections of this text you will learn in some detail how to analyze your capabilities and market these effectively. The focus will emerge from these general competencies:

1. Your ability to do a job – your work skills.
2. Your ability to solve problems – your critical thinking skills.
3. Your ability to fit into the culture of the organization – your interpersonal and communication skills.

Get started now on this important journey by completing the following exercise. Take into consideration the general things employers are seeking as well as the results of the NACE survey presented earlier in this chapter. Include technical skills as well as general abilities. Then, take a few minutes to study the list and prioritize the items according to their value to an employer. (Indicate the perceived priority order by changing the numbers in the left column.)

Keep this list with you as you move forward in your job search and career development activities.

	15 things I want an employer to know about me:	One or more instances when I have demonstrated this quality or skill:
1		
2		
3		
4		
5		
6		
7		
8		
9		
10		
11		
12		
13		
14		
15		

CHAPTER TWO
Motivation for a Career
Janice Hinds

Winners simply keep falling forward. When there is a setback they are not hard on others; rather, they are hard on themselves, asking, "What can I do to learn from this experience and move toward excellence in my life?"

– John G. Miller

Chapter Goals:

- To introduce concepts and strategies that can increase the chances of successful outcomes in your job search
- To clarify theories of motivation related to career planning and development
- To help you formulate a personal philosophy of motivation for your job search and career development activities
- To provide suggestions for both getting started in the job search and sustaining momentum at a high level to maximize results
- To challenge you into letting go of what doesn't work and replacing it with more effective approaches.

Consider this simple philosophy of motivation: As you know from experience, if you give average effort, you reap average results. When you work harder, as well as smarter, you achieve better outcomes. Now apply this truism to your job search options. If you settle for whatever comes along, if you choose the easiest search methods, if you send out only a few resumes and then sit back to wait for the results – you are setting yourself up for the likelihood of fewer, less appropriate, and lower-paying job offers.

On the other hand, if you apply yourself, plan for the long haul, use a variety of methods and resources, stay resourceful, and sustain your momentum, you will likely learn from and enjoy the process. You will also feel empowered in your newfound abilities, and you will almost certainly earn more and better job offers.

Motivation

If motivation is "the will to act," what is your motivation to build the best career you can? Career building starts with your education and preparatory work experience, includes the job search process, and then plays out over the career track itself. These are activities that require goal setting and planning, along with sustained effort to realize your potential. Your efforts are likely to take you further to the extent that your motivation for building a career is strong.

Motivating factors can be both internal and external. Self-esteem is internal power, for example, that can set a foundation for self-discipline and determination. It can fashion a desire to learn from mistakes and to persevere. Motivation can also be external. The guidance and example of parents, teachers, and respected authorities can add to our motivation in specific ways. Whether these external factors support positive and rewarding actions or detrimental ones depends on the influences themselves and on our ways of integrating them.

If an admired and respected person tells us, "You can do it," we might take it as encouragement and respond positively, because we want to please that person and earn his respect. If we perceive this statement as a directive uttered by an overbearing superior who is trying to put us down, we might respond grudgingly at best.

Whether motivation is internal or external, it is generally more productive when its influence is positive rather than negative. We are likely to work harder and achieve better results when we see the value of the outcomes we strive for, and when these outcomes produce positive regard from ourselves and from respected others. We are likely to work less productively toward certain ends when the motivating factors are negative – fear, insecurity, self-doubt, and similar emotions.

Seeing a value in the work we do is one of the most powerful of career motivators. The belief that what they do is significant and makes a positive difference has motivated many teachers, artists, writers, nurses, social workers, counselors, and public defenders. This belief is not necessarily altruistic only, because it has a strong component of professional pride in the quality of the work done. Thus, many business and technical professionals, scientists, doctors, civil servants, librarians, farmers, and others achieve superior results in large part because they value the achievements they are able to produce. To these workers, doing the job just to get by is unacceptable.

Inspiration
This quality is something that can also encourage people to generate greater and more productive effort. Inspiration is bolstered by enthusiasm and associated with creativity. In the process of formulating job search strategies and conducting a job search campaign, inspiration might be the added motivational factor that can produce superior results. What will it take to mobilize your efforts in the job search? An inspired effort would include a positive attitude (such as enthusiasm or quiet confidence), initiative, innovative approaches, and a series of connections with people. These connections might include people who are part of your networking activities, as well as those associated with potential employment opportunities – the hiring manager, Human Resources staff, receptionists, potential co-workers.

Knowing and Doing
We hope that one of the sources of motivation and inspiration for your job search efforts will be this text, which will present the best possible advice and strategy, and explain why and how this advice is worth following. This text, along with other sources, will thus tell you what you need to do to be successful in your job search and career development efforts. The additional requirement is that you must *apply* what you know.

This is where motivation comes in. If you lack the desire to maximize your career possibilities, your results will likely not reach their potential – either now or later. If you only go through the motions of reading this text and doing the assignments for a course grade, you will predictably underachieve. If you integrate and apply this knowledge, you may be able to reach the higher and better outcomes you desire.

To make the better results possible, you will need to *internalize* the external motivation provided by books, mentors, career advisors, parents, and significant others. These external forces can tell you, and some can show you, what to do. To make it happen, you have to want the outcome and then go get it.

Sustaining the Effort

One of the measures of your motivation is the effort you put into carrying out a plan or an intention. In the job search process, this idea can be expressed as the challenge of sustaining momentum toward your goals. Can you conceive of the possibility that your search gets interrupted or stalled – you are not getting interviews or offers, for example? This can be a discouraging kind of feedback, and it may have the even more negative effect of stalling your efforts.

Consider another scenario, one in which you do get an interview at a company, but your response is to stop sending out resumes or engaging in networking activities while you go through several interview rounds, hoping this opportunity will prove out. If it does not, you have no other inquiries in the pipeline and must start prospecting anew.

As a final example, imagine that you see an attractive position listed in your local Sunday paper, and you plan to respond, but put it off from early in the week to later, and then perhaps conclude that "it's too late by now anyway."

As we will show in Chapters 7 and 8 of this text, you can sustain momentum in your job search campaign in a very practical way – by developing a systematic approach and a schedule of activities. Using such a system, you would not suspend efforts while waiting to see if something else works out, and you wouldn't delay submitting an application to a posted job, and you wouldn't stop networking or researching companies just because you hadn't been summoned to an interview yet. But, most importantly, your systematic process would carry you through the lulls and low spots because of your strong motivation to ensure the best possible outcomes.

A Personal Philosophy

Consider the following statement a suggested step toward developing your own philosophy of motivation in the career development process.

> I am motivated to be successful in my job search and career development activities by the following factors: _____. These factors inspire me to search for the best job I can find that will use my abilities and stretch me in preparation for advancement in my career. As I learn and grow professionally, I will review this philosophy of success and amend it as necessary to sustain my progress.

Motivation Theories

At this point, it will help to examine some of the classic theories of motivation to see what they contribute to understanding the needs of the job search and career building processes.

Maslow's Hierarchy of Needs

The human needs identified by Abraham Maslow exist in a hierarchy that requires lower needs to be satisfied before higher ones may be achieved. As shown in the pyramid below, fulfillment of the lower-level physiological and safety needs supports our attempts to meet the needs for love and belonging and self-esteem. Only when these "lower" needs are satisfied, do we move to the higher stages. The highest stage of motivation – one less often reached – addresses the need for self-actualization, or fulfillment of our potential.

In more detail:

- Physiological needs: for food, water, shelter, and warmth
- Safety needs: for security, stability, freedom from fear
- Love and belonging needs: to be accepted, to be needed, to give and receive friendship
- Self-esteem needs: for achievement, recognition, and a sense of mastery
- Self-actualization needs: for self-fulfillment, creativity, meeting our potential.

Maslow's Hierarchy of Needs

Maslow felt that very few of us reach the stage of self-actualization, and so made it the narrow tip of his broad-based pyramid. This may be a fair assessment, given the unlimited upside suggested by the term *potential.* Perhaps none of us, not even the most accomplished and successful of us, ever reaches our full potential. Nevertheless, all of us are capable of achieving more than we imagined when we set out on our journey, thus fulfilling more of our potential than we thought possible. Make this highest stage your goal too, and you will undoubtedly come closer to it than if you set your sights lower.

Herzberg's Two-Factor Theory

The social scientist Frederick Herzberg developed a theory that relates workplace factors and job satisfaction. Herzberg concluded that some features of a job were merely "hygiene factors" while others were "motivators." Hygiene factors do not contribute to job satisfaction or higher levels of motivation. If these factors are inadequate, however, they will cause dissatisfaction with the job.

Consider a few examples from the chart below. If my compensation falls below levels needed to support me adequately, I will be dissatisfied with the job and may seek to change it. If my salary rises beyond adequate levels, however, perhaps to levels that make me very well compensated, I will not therefore become satisfied with my job, says Herzberg. (This may capture the thought behind the adage, "Money does not buy happiness.") Consider the hygiene factor of job security. If I am unsure that my job will last, I will likely be dissatisfied with the position; when I am assured that my job and my tenure in it are secure, I do not therefore become satisfied with the position – just not dissatisfied.

Herzberg's Two-Factor Theory

Hygiene Factors	Definitions, Examples
Company policies, procedures; Standard Operating Procedures	Formal and informal governing rules and regulations
Salary and benefits	Basic income, bonuses, fringe benefits, vacation time, and the like
Working conditions	Working hours, equipment, facility layout and upkeep
Job security	Level of confidence regarding continued employment; contract work; at-will employment laws
Supervision, degree of autonomy	External and internal control over job-related tasks, professional involvement

For Herzberg, motivators are based on what people actually do while working, and directly contribute to job satisfaction. These include challenging work, achievement, recognition, and advancement.

Motivators	Definitions, Examples
Challenging work	Potential for realistically possible tasks; energizing, thought-provoking work; networking opportunities
Achievement	Sense of satisfaction in reaching or exceeding objectives
Advancement	Belief that advancement is possible; progress, promotion, endorsement
Responsibility	Potential for decision making authority, leadership, risk-taking

Maslow and Herzberg Reconsidered

The relationship between Maslow's Hierarchy of Needs and Herzberg's Two-Factor Theory can be shown in the example of a student launching a job search campaign as she nears graduation.

If a career-entering or career-changing student is focused on basic physiological needs such as providing food and shelter, along with a sense of security in the new position, these "lower" requirements will likely take precedence. Motivating factors such as challenging work, opportunities for achievement and recognition, and the potential for advancement might receive secondary consideration, particularly if the student is low on confidence and self-esteem. She may focus primarily on the hygiene factors of salary and benefits to fulfill the need for food, shelter, and basic security.

A more confident student might consider the basic needs, but also evaluate positions from the standpoint of their potential to provide job satisfaction through challenging work that can lead to professional growth and advancement. She may also look for an organization whose culture seems to offer a good fit and good prospects for meeting her needs for belonging.

Mark, Margaret, and Al Revisited:
Review the information provided in Chapter One on these typical career planners as they near graduation and face career choices that can alter their lives (pages 16-18). How would you rank them in the hierarchy suggested by Maslow and Herzberg? Which of them is most likely to emphasize the basic physiological needs (or hygiene factors), and who is most tuned into the higher-order concerns? Explain your rankings.

Covey's Seven Habits

Stephen Covey's *Seven Habits of Highly Effective People* (1990) offers recommended ways of looking at ourselves and at how we operate in the world. These outlooks, or paradigms, lead to habits that are consistently practiced. Here is Covey's set of desirable outlooks/habits:

Habit	Explanation
1. Be proactive	Take the initiative and assume the responsibility to make things happen.
2. Begin with the end in mind	Understand where you are now, where you're going, and what you value.
3. Put first things first	Set priorities and manage yourself.
4. Think win-win	Seek cooperation that allows everyone to win.
5. Seek first to understand, then to be understood	Be empathetic in your communication.
6. Synergize	Seek the additional value that cooperation creates.
7. Sharpen the saw	Renew yourself.

The first three habits in Covey's theory – the habits of Private Victory – focus on individual self-awareness and developing a sense of self-confidence based on one's own values. The next three – the habits of Public Victory – center on desires and resources necessary for building and maintaining productive relationships. The seventh habit is a cycle of continual renewal resulting from living the first six.

A study of Covey's concepts may lead you to explore and implement habits that contribute to your definition of success. By way of illustration, consider Covey's paradigms – the Circle of Concern and the Circle of Influence. The outer Circle of Concern includes matters that concern us but do not particularly involve us emotionally or mentally. We also have little or no control over them. Within this wider sphere is a smaller circle, known as the Circle of Influence. In this smaller circle are the matters over which we have some control, including ourselves.

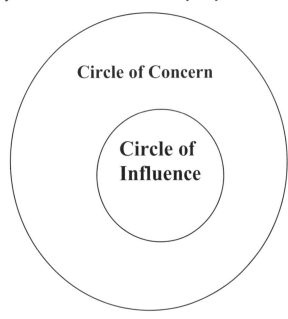

To be effective, Covey suggests, we need to focus our efforts on what we can control. If we try to control circumstances and people beyond our Circle of Influence, we create conflict and expend negative energy, ineffectively. When we focus on ourselves, we are able to proactively affect change. Working within our Circle of Influence may be a practical strategy for success.

Goal Setting

Before considering specific strategies for goal setting, review the key questions regarding motivation, success, and inspiration. What is your definition of success? What are your incentives for applying yourself to the job search with determination and dedication ? Write these in the form of goals, and then use the goals to help you achieve the best results possible.

Setting a goal is declaring an intention.

If you set a goal, and don't meet it, either because you didn't attempt it or you tried and failed, you end up with a negative outcome that hampers your next efforts. You feel badly, and it is hard to declare the next intention.

Success comes from action – from goal attainment or progress toward meeting goals. Success can also derive from adversity, assuming that our response to it is positive. We can allow adversity to defeat us, or we can use it to strengthen our dedication and commitment, to change our perspectives on the task, and perhaps to adjust our goals.

Setting SMART Goals

SMART is an acronym for a method of creating goals that are attainable. This approach was developed from Paul J. Meyer's work on attitude and motivation. In the SMART framework advocated by Meyer, goals should be:

Specific – they should include answers to the questions *who, what, where, when, which,* and *why*
Measurable – address questions such as how many, how much, how will we know when the goal is achieved?
Attainable – opportunities and necessary resources to meet the goals are available
Realistic – goals take into account the difficulties and the competing priorities
Tangible – achievement or progress on the goal is perceived through the senses – we can "see" it, we "hear" information about progress, for example.

The SMART approach suggests that goals have a greater chance of being met if you write them down, and if your written statement recognizes how progress will be measured and considers factors such as time, cost, and your personal characteristics.

For example, one of your job-search goals might be to "get an interview." While this might be measurable in a bottom-line way, it is too vague in other ways. Consider this restatement:

> By the end of the week, research the entry-level technical support position
> at XYZ Company; if it meets my previously defined criteria, secure a job
> interview with Mr. Widget, head of the RST department.

A goal written like this takes the SMART factors into consideration. It also tells you what you need to do first to fulfill the end goal of securing the interview: research the position and the company to compare the job description with your qualifications, review the hygiene and motivating factors, and ensure that your resume is tailored for this particular position. When you meet a goal that is set in the specific ways suggested by the SMART approach, you recognize your abilities, which are reinforced and celebrated via goal attainment. Carrying out a job search strategy – or other worthy goals – spurs motivation and contributes to building your commitment and enhancing self-confidence.

Not meeting a goal stated in the SMART format can also provide an opportunity to review your objectives in general. Did you write the goal at a higher level than your education and abilities can support? If so, you might decide to address the gap through continued education. Or, did you fail to achieve the goal because it was intangible and abstract? If so, rewrite to make it more specific, measurable, and tangible.

Writing SMART goals may also help you to address what your *value-added* contribution is to a prospective employer. Define the specifics of your knowledge, skills, and abilities (among the "tangibles" of the method), identify your network of connections (e.g., professional associations and membership in professional organizations), and list your valuable personal qualities (such as enthusiasm, dedication, and creativity). You can then use these attributes help you write a cover letter and resume. It is also great preparation for answering those challenging interview questions.

Chapter Exercises:

1. Write a reflection paper describing a recent college or work related event that illustrates a successful experience of yours. Based on your own definition of success, describe the context (situation, environment), the relationship (e.g., with teammates, instructors, or supervisors), the experience (i.e., the achievement), and the sense of mastery over obstacles you overcame.

2. Review the academic mission statement you created in the Critical Thinking and Problem Solving course (COLL-148). Using a similar format and content ideas, update the personal mission statement for a job search situation. Turn your plan of study into a job search plan of action. Create a professional development plan, and include areas/skills you want to improve (e.g., investigate resources for professional speaking and writing, negotiation strategies, interviewing). Identify resources readily available to you (e.g., the Career Services office, textbooks, professional organizations, journals, user support groups).

3. Conduct an informational interview with someone in your current or planned field of practice whom you consider to be successful. Include questions from which you will be able to glean the motivational level and the motivational strategies used by the person.

4. Develop a list of your own motivating factors. Create another list for your success statements. Link the two lists by showing the relationship between the two sets of components – either through graphic presentation or through a verbal explanation.

5. Conduct a self-esteem profile. Heim offers one beginning on page 39 of *In the Company of Women*. Refer also to assessment tools found on www.queendom.com. Use the results of the profile to assess your strategies for a job search or career change campaign.

Chapter Mini-Cases:

1. Mark has the option of (a) going to a late night networking party on Tuesday night with a friend who is employed or (b) going to a career fair that starts at 8 a.m. the next day. Mark knows that the networking party will be attended primarily by people who work in fields unrelated to his program of study, and that his college is sponsoring the career fair the next day. In order to balance his work with his studies he can only attend one event. Which one should he choose and why?

2. Margaret's classmate Mary spends her evenings hanging out with friends and watching late-night television. She does not take morning classes. Recently Mary had the opportunity to interview for a job that was right down her intended career path and offering good growth potential. The job would start at 7 a.m., however, which would be a poor fit with her lifestyle. Additionally, Mary's boyfriend works evenings while he is finishing school, and they have limited time to spend together. What would you advise Mary to do and why?

Works Consulted

General Works:

Arden, Paul. *It's Not How Good You Are, It's How Good You Want to Be.* New York: Phaidon Press Limited, 2003.

Johnson, Spencer. *One Minute for Myself.* New York: William Morrow and Company, 1985.

--------------------. *Who Moved My Cheese?* New York: G.P. Putnam's Sons, 1998.

Niven, David. *The 100 Simple Secrets of Successful People.* New York: HarperCollins, 2002.

Nelson, Bob. *1001 Ways to Take Initiative at Work.* New York: Workman Publishing, 1999.

Positive Attitude and Success:

Heller, Robert & Hindle, Tim. *Essential Manager's Manual.* New York: DK Publishing, 1998.

Meyer, Paul J. *Attitude is Everything*, 1997; www.pauljmeyer.com

Sanders, Tim. *Love is the Killer App.* New York: Three Rivers Press, 2002.

Theories:

Covey, Stephen. *Seven Habits of Highly Effective People.* New York: Simon & Schuster, 1989.

-------------------. *The Eighth Habit.* New York: Free Press, 2004.

Miller, John. G. *QBQ! The Question Behind the Question.* Denver: Denver Press, 2001.

-------------------. *Flipping The Switch.* New York: The Penguin Group, 2006.

Gender issues:

Heim, Pat. *Hardball for Women.* New York: Plume, 2005.

Heim, Pat, and Susan Murphy. *In the Company of Women.* New York: Tarcher/Putnam, 2001.

www.heimgroup.com

Inspiration and Creativity:

SARK. *Inspiration Sandwich.* Berkeley, CA: Celestial Arts, 1992.

--------. *Make Your Creative Dreams Real.* New York: Simon & Schuster, 2004.

www.planetsark.com

CHAPTER THREE
Self-Assessment
Louise Bishop

I always wanted to be somebody, but now I realize I should have been more specific.

–Lily Tomlin

Chapter Objectives:
- To help you conduct an inventory of your skill set.
- To help you identify strengths and weaknesses.
- To clarify why self-assessment is important in the career planning process.
- To help you apply self-assessment results to the job search and to career development.

The Role of Self-Assessment

A person of college age, having begun a focused program of study, has probably reached this stage, in part, by formulating some ideas about who she is and what she likes and dislikes. Despite such general self-awareness, there are a number of good reasons to go through a targeted self-assessment process that can focus the answers and relate them to goals and aspirations.

For one, it's important to convey to others what you know about yourself, which is not always easy. Because we think mostly without using grammar, syntax, or precise vocabulary, we may find it difficult to articulate our self-awareness and self-knowledge. We all have a general sense of "what I'm good at" and "what I'd like to do in the ideal job," but only a few people can articulate these concepts in a first attempt, clearly and concisely.

When an employer asks the inevitable question, "What are some of your strengths?" that should not be the first time you give the answer some thought. Even if you are a more seasoned candidate, perhaps looking within your own organization for a new position or a promotion, you must be able to lay before the employer a clear set of strengths and a definitive set of examples of using these strengths to better the company.

Self-assessment is an important process to the employer as well, and can be used in hiring, managing, career evaluation and growth, team building, and better communication overall.

Self-assessment is not all about strengths either. Whether in the interview for a new job, or in the yearly performance evaluation, it's important to be able to offer a balanced view of your capabilities and achievements. Including the areas where you fall short helps set up improvement plans. Any self-assessment that omits weaknesses and spotlights only strengths is likely to be perceived as unbalanced and self-serving. As a result, employers and peers are likely to discount some of the strengths as well.

Additionally, the value of a structured self-assessment process is that it can clarify the status of your "transferable" skills. These are the abilities you have developed in college and in prior jobs that you can also apply to new positions you may be interested in. While you may again have a general sense of your abilities and traits, you may not be recognizing their potential in different applications areas.

Job-Specific and Transferable Skills

The university experience, like life, teaches or enhances two main categories of skills. The first category includes skills that pertain specifically to a discipline or profession. These vary by curriculum area, with some opportunity for overlap.

For those studying business or accounting, the program-specific skills include knowledge of basic accounting and GAAP; the ability to analyze data and forecast trends; understanding of the business life cycle; and the ability to use spreadsheets, databases, and word processing tools. For computer systems majors, the field-specific skills include the ability to write, code, debug, test, and design software; design and develop Web pages; provide user support and security; and manage databases. Electronics engineering technology students learn the basics of electronics, including the use of digital multimeters, oscilloscopes, function generators, and other test equipment; reading schematics; and operating, maintaining, and repairing semiconductor capital and biomedical equipment.

By contrast, transferable skills are more general and for that reason more widely applicable. These are skills learned in the general education areas of the curriculum, but they can also be developed through everyday life and family experience. They include the skills of communication, problem solving, critical thinking, conflict resolution, time management, teamwork, leadership, attention to detail, and other skills applicable in many situations.

As a caveat, it should be recognized that transferable skills are learned in the curriculum-major areas as well, and in significant ways. A general problem-solving model might teach me how to approach problems systematically, but until I am able to apply this model to my area of specialization, I may not have a very solid grasp of the problem-solving idea. In other words, both the general skill and its specific applications help me understand how a skill can be applied to different areas of practice.

Recognizing Your Skills

As you will see, a formal self-assessment procedure can help you identify both transferable and job-specific skills. Furthermore, the clear recognition of these skills serves both you and your employer. If you feel that communication is one of your transferable skills, you can give an employer an example of how you used that skill to resolve a customer satisfaction issue. If you recognize that communication is one of your weak points, you can give the employer examples of what you are doing to improve it. (See Chapter 4 for more on this topic, by the way.)

Among the general ways we can try to identify our strengths and weaknesses is through feedback from others and from ourselves. How do you know if communication is one of your strengths? Perhaps you think so because you've been told you're good at it. This kind of feedback may come from your written and oral presentations in school, which are evaluated by knowledgeable instructors and by your peers. You may also have been able to demonstrate your interpersonal communication and team skills to co-workers and supervisors. Another source of feedback might be your own sense of enjoyment of the communication process, and your understanding of its value in informing and motivating others.

A clearer recognition of your job-specific skills can also help you see their potential for transferability. As an accounting student, for example, you might enjoy the details required to successfully balance a ledger or reconcile financial statements. And you might feel that your own enjoyment of the process and your good grades indicate that you are proficient in this kind of work. On further reflection, you might begin to see that your skill in balancing and reconciling financial statements represents a broader ability, or a transferable set of skills: quantitative ability, a detail orientation, and an analytical mind.

Inventorying your skills can be quite a challenge. By thinking back to what you've been told you're good at, and thinking about what kinds of things you like to do, you should be able to put together a provisional list of your skills. It can help, too, to have a teacher, classmate, co-worker, parent, or friend tell you what they think you're good at. You can also consider evaluations by your employers, recent training or education, and feedback from clients and colleagues.

An additional source of insight into your skills, abilities, styles, and preferences is the use of a formal self-assessment instrument. Such a tool can provide qualitative and quantitative information to individuals planning career search or enhancement activities. Such instruments produce results in a form that helps you to not only know, but also articulate your strengths and preferences.

Self-Assessment Tools

There are numerous helpful assessment tools available on-line. Just Googling "self-assessment" will bring up more than 57 million entries! "Personality test" returns well over 9 million hits. Narrowing the search to "personality types" reduces the total to about 3 million.

Many of these sites lead to organizations that will develop and interpret your personality profile, once you've taken the test. An important consideration should be which method of self-assessment to use: one that requires analysis by a professional, or one that can be taken and interpreted by the user. Here's the range of possibilities for most students and/or employees:

- If you are enrolled in a college course that includes a unit on self-assessment, a simple tool that helps identify or further define already-known personality traits might work best.
- If money is not a limitation (perhaps the employer is paying for tools used in the course of outplacement services), you might choose to take one of the tests that requires professional evaluation, which allows for a more in-depth look at the results.
- Another possibility is to take advantage of a well-staffed Career Services office at your college or university. This office may be able to guide your choice of instruments, and to provide help in interpreting the results.

Personality Profiles

An example of a self-assessment instrument that looks more broadly at behavioral styles and preferences is the DISC Personality Profile (http://www.inscapepublishing.com/prod_disc.asp).

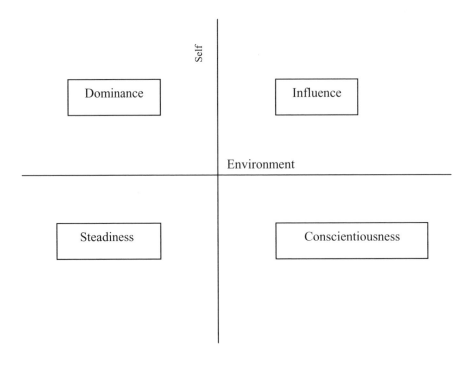

The Personality Field in DISC

DISC measures the types, patterns, and styles of behavior and personality as "high" or "low" across four different dimensions: *D*ominance, which relates to control; *I*nfluence, which relates to communication; *S*teadiness, which relates to patience and persistence; and *C*onscientiousness, which relates to structure or organization. In the above grid, the top row represents the extroverted facets of the personality and the bottom row the introverted aspects. The left column represents task-focused aspects, and the right social aspects. The DISC assessment can be a bit pricey, and its guidance for a career searcher remains somewhat general.

The Myers-Briggs Type Indicator (MBTI), using theories developed from the works of Carl Jung, is arguably one of the most accurate personality classifiers. It also bears a cost if you take the full version, and should be administered and evaluated by a trained professional to be fully appreciated. The MBTI uses 93 questions allowing only two answers each, and results in a classification of 16 different "preferred" types. The types include Introverts and Extroverts (how your energy is directed and received); Sensors and Intuitives (how data are perceived); Thinkers and Feelers (how you make decisions); and Judgers and Perceivers (what kind of environment makes you most comfortable).

Many of the same purposes can be achieved without spending money. Many short, free, and, arguably, equally valuable tools are available on-line on a self-check basis.

Arizona State University's "Arizona Career Information Systems" provides tools to help you choose a college or program of study, explore occupations, and get or change jobs, among other options. It is available at http://www.azcis.intocareers.org

The University of Chicago offers a self-assessment exercise that begins by asking you to identify your interests: (http://caps.uchicago.edu/resources/pdfs/Self-Assessment.pdf). You are led then to inventory your skills, define your values, and finally to decide what kind of working conditions you would prefer. After completing all the exercises, you are asked to look for patterns.

A site at www.queendom.com offers tests on leadership styles and skills and on career advancement potential. It also adds a few twists, including "Sensitivity to Criticism," "Accident Proneness," and "Success Likelihood." A profile or "snapshot" of the outcome is presented and you are given an opportunity to purchase a full report.

The "personality type" quiz at www.personalitytype.com is simple and self-scoreable. Instead of wading through 60-plus questions to determine 16 personality types, you start with four easy questions. For instance, the question "Where is your energy naturally directed?" is followed by descriptions of Extroverts and Introverts and allows you to select your type based on what you already know. Generally, people in college will know whether they tend to "talk more than listen" or "listen more than talk" and whether they "think out loud" or "think inside [their] head." Another question, "What kind of information do you naturally notice and remember?" differentiates between Sensors and Intuitives. "How do you decide or come to conclusions" describes Thinkers and Feelers; and "What kind of environment makes you the most comfortable" gives a name to the qualities of Judgers or Perceivers.

The student who tests as an Introvert will be happiest in a position where contact with other people is limited to the 40-hour work week. (This does not preclude jobs that require more than 40 hours per week, of course, especially if the extra hours are worked in the quiet of a home or office.) Since Introverts' energy is directed inwardly, they typically look to refresh themselves at the end of a long week by being alone or with family. On the other hand, an Extrovert, whose energy is directed outwardly, would enjoy a position that requires a lot of social interaction with clients, perhaps in such areas as public relations, marketing, selling, and consulting.

The Sensor is going to be happiest in a job where he can use black-vs.-white information to create an outcome. The Sensor can also team successfully with an Intuitive in creative endeavors. For example, the Intuitive, whose thought processes are not limited by things that already exist, might conceptualize a computer program that allows a busy parent to create a week's menu for her family. The Sensor could take that concept and create a database or spread sheet that displays a personalized menu and generates a customized shopping list.

Thinkers "go by the book," whereas Feelers consider options. There are arguments for and against each of these types being good managers. A Thinker will usually be quite consistent in following procedures and applying rules. You rarely have to guess how your Thinker boss will act in a given situation. The Feeler, on the other hand, is less predictable. An ideal manager demonstrates traits of both Thinker and Feeler. She goes by company policy, but will not be so rigid as to be unconscious of the human element involved.

Judgers keep their days organized, relying on planners, calendars, and lists. A Judger will probably not be comfortable in a position that requires a lot of flexibility and change. For example, a Judger could be a very good teacher – of the organized type. While classroom interaction is not always precise and structured, a Judger could work well from a teaching plan, and can implement a consistent class focus. The Perceiver, who by nature avoids making concrete plans, will enjoy working in an ever-changing environment. The Perceiver will be comfortable going to a different workplace every day, working with different clients, using different tools, and solving new problems.

How would these "personality types" apply to several of our career-searching characters?

In a job interview, Mark is asked a routine question: "Give me an example of how you prioritize daily tasks." Mark begins describing in great detail a day at the supermarket, where he was told to build a new product display, to off-load a pallet of dry goods, and to spell the cashiers at their breaks. He talks about his enthusiasm for building the display, and how he spent a couple of hours making it look just right, when a co-worker reminded him to start relieving the checkers. He mentions that at the end of the day, he hadn't gotten to off-loading the pallet, so he stayed an extra two hours to help the next shift complete that task.

When he's finished answering, it occurs to Mark that he may not have answered the question as well as he could have, and he hopes that the interviewer doesn't ask him to expand on the answer. He remembers that his employer complimented him on the look of the floor display, but also reprimanded him for not completing all of the tasks set before him.

Based on the four personality types (see www.personalitytype.com/quiz), Mark appears to be primarily an Extrovert, who tends to think out loud and to act before thinking. He also demonstrates the quality of an Intuitive, in that he is inventive and likes to figure things out for himself. While these are not negative qualities, Mark has not yet learned the possible downsides of his enthusiasm. It has only just occurred to him that he was told by his boss that he needed to learn to prioritize.

Knowing that his personality type shows his preference *for acting in certain ways, could Mark sell his traits as skills in an interview?*

Al interviews for a job at a local manufacturer of electronics equipment for "smart houses" The position is Line Supervisor, which requires the technical knowledge Al has gained through his degree program, as well as his experience in machining. The interviewer asks Al to describe a situation where he disagreed with his boss. Al reflects that he learned a little about personality types in one of his management courses, and that his long work history has given him experience in making his preferences work with both his co-workers and his boss.

He remembers the day he came into work to find two machines that he operated set up differently than he was used to. As a Thinker, Al often takes joy in arguing just for the intellectual exercise. He also has a tendency to point out flaws that he sees regardless of other people's feelings.

He described the scenario to the interviewer and explained the downsides he saw in the new machine arrangement. However, he says, he kept his comments to himself. While Al doesn't remember the specific terminology from his class, he had learned that his boss is the opposite of himself (a Feeler), and dislikes conflict. As Al told the interviewer, "While I had my own opinions, I also needed to consider my boss's preferences." Instead of being blunt and direct, Al learned to discuss changes with his boss and tempered his Thinker's outspoken honesty with respect for a Feeler's values of diplomacy and harmony.

How do you think this example worked for Al in the interview? Did he earn credibility as a candidate, or did his example raise concerns for the interviewer?

While we may typically act in a certain way according to our personality "type," we can and will have to use other traits to be successful in a chosen profession. The types of tests that are most helpful in this regard (e.g., DISC, MBTI, the quiz at www.personalitytype.com) indicate a *preference* for a certain behavioral style, not a locked-in mode. Most of us, for any number of reasons, can act in a way that is not typical for us, but is in our repertoires. It is helpful to know in what settings we'll be most comfortable, but also to know that we can do what it takes to get the job done in a variety of situations.

Two other sites worth checking include www.actualme.com and www.personalitypathways.com. These instruments are designed to help you articulate what you already know about yourself, which makes them fun. They are also free. Be wary, however, of their request for personal information, which may be sold to advertisers. As you should do for any Website, read the "Terms and Agreements" disclaimer.

The book *Do What You Are* (Tieger, 2001) is an excellent supplement to using and interpreting personality inventories.

Vocational Interest Inventories

In addition to working on defining your personality type, you might find it valuable to use tools that help you identify and articulate your interests. Knowing that you have Introverted tendencies might not be as useful to you if you don't know whether you want to be a forest ranger or a computer programmer.

The Strong Interest Inventory (SII) provides feedback on an individual's interests in a wide range of areas, including occupations, hobbies, and people. This tool bases its outcomes on the assumption that people who are successful in particular occupations share common traits and skills, and that they are more likely to be successful in an occupation if its day-to-day activities are of interest to them. As an alternate, the free career test at www.projectcareer.org helps "identify careers that match your personality and define potential career fields and trends."

Some instructions common to most personality tests and self-assessment tools:

- Give answers based on how you really act, not how you'd like to act.
- Don't over-think the answers; your first impulse is usually the most accurate.
- There are no right or wrong answers.

Conceptualizing Your Preferences

A self-assessment you can do without the aid of formal instruments is to imagine different aspects of the day-to-day job and workplace. Imagine your first day on that job you worked so hard to get: this is your *ideal* job, with the features that would make you most comfortable and satisfied. Now, answer the following questions.

- Where do I work every day?
- Do I work in a different place every day?
- Am I meeting new people at work all the time?
- Would I be more comfortable going to work at the same place every day?
- Do I work with my hands, using tools to build or repair things?
- Do I build or repair units, or do I do research and develop new ideas?
- What kind of clothes am I wearing? Is it a uniform? A suit and tie? A "space suit" worn in a clean-room environment? (If you're in the clean room, consider that it takes a certain type of individual to be able to work eight, ten, or even twelve hours at a time in a highly sterile room, while wearing layers of protective gear. If you are claustrophobic, or need a high level of interaction with people, this would most likely be difficult.)
- Is my clothing business casual, or maybe even more casual than that? Maybe I'm wearing sweat pants, or even pajamas, because I work from home. (Are you disciplined enough to work from home?)
- What does my work environment include? Am I in an office, with a desk and bookshelf full of reference books? Am I at a repair-depot bench, with equipment and tools on the shelves? (Do you prefer to work with the theory or to apply theory to practice?)

Those are some examples of the evidence from which the personality tests might define your personality type. Perhaps you can reach some of the same conclusions yourself by thinking about the kind of job you would prefer.

Keep in mind also that the personality inventories tell you how you *typically* act under certain conditions, how you *usually* respond to different circumstances and input. On the other hand, to be successful in any business, you will need to be flexible in how you act and respond. The Introverts, for example, might be called upon to give a presentation to investors or training colleagues; the Extroverts might need to work alone in a closed room to finish a project plan by a due date.

Informational Interviews for Job Assessment

Another way of exploring your own fit and comfort level for particular kinds of jobs is to conduct a second-person assessment instead of a self-assessment. An informational interview (more on these in Chapter 8) can help you see what qualities or personality traits might work best in certain situations and jobs. For example, by interviewing a successful manager, you might learn that one of the most useful management skills is listening, rather than directing. Talking to a person who works in a staff support role, you might find that organizational skills come in second to the ability to be aware of and act on others' unspoken needs. Sometimes the strengths needed to be successful in a position are counter-intuitive to its description or title.

Use your networking contacts (also in Chapter 8) to help you locate people who are currently doing the kind of work you are trained to do and want to be doing when you graduate.

When you conduct an informational interview, remember that you're not in a job-seeking mode, so make your questions count. Be mindful also of the time of the person who has agreed to talk to you. Try to limit the interview to 20-30 minutes.

Get a brief description of the job duties, and the skills required to perform them. Ask your contact what he likes most about the job. Try to get him to be specific about the job, as opposed to discussing the company in general. You can even ask some of the questions provided in www.personalitytypes.com. Ask him what personality traits make him successful in this job, and what personality traits allow him to enjoy the job (if he does). Ask what he doesn't like about the job, and what he'd change if he could.

You can find value in almost anything you're told. If your interview subject is unlike you in personality, you can evaluate whether or not she feels she's a good match for that job, and then extrapolate whether or not you would be.

You can also ask the people in your personal job search network to talk about their jobs. This will help you get an idea of some of the personality types in relation to their jobs. You will be able to see if they are in a good fit at their current jobs.

A Personal Mission Statement

As you saw in Chapter 1, successful companies create mission statements that define their goals as well as their values. They describe what is important to them, in other words, and this approach can also work for individuals.

In determining what is important to you, you can describe the kind of organization and employer you are seeking, and how you expect your goals to mesh with theirs. If you are unsure how to go about creating such a statement, make use of some of the many good tools on the Internet. One of the best is the Franklin Covey Mission Builder, available at the following site: www.franklincovey.com/fc/library_and_resources/mission_statement_builder. The site Wizard will walk you through defining your values and using them to create a personal mission statement. As the site will remind you, defining your personal mission statement should be an ongoing process, as life goes on and changes.

Identifying your values and determining if those values are personal or career-related is an important part of your self-assessment. As an example, some college recruiters represent defense contractors and research labs whose businesses may involve the manufacture and sale of weaponry. Some people may find this conflicting with their personal values to the degree that they would choose not to work there. Some companies and positions require travel. An individual whose values require her to spend regular time with her family will probably not want to travel regularly. She may also find it difficult to work a lot of overtime, as it could require additional child or adult day care.

As a reader of this textbook, one of your personal values almost certainly involves continuing your personal growth and education. You will want to evaluate whether a company promotes (and possibly even pays for) ongoing career development and education.

Chapter Summary

Self-assessment is a process that can be helpful at career entry, and at any stage of a career. If the professional workplace will be a new experience, self-assessment can help us articulate our skills, possibly for the first time. The process allows us to inventory our technical and transferable skills. If we're entering a new field, we need to look at how our personality traits might allow us to become successful, or how they can prevent us from doing our best work. Self-assessment helps us achieve the highest possible career growth, and grounds us by showing us where we need to improve.

There are various means of performing self-assessment: Tools like the MBTI and the DISC Profiles go into some depth in categorizing personalities, but can require professional assistance and cost money both to take and to interpret. While the results obtained are more broad and provisional, there are free and easy ways of assessing one's personality traits. These include conceptualizing the elements of the ideal job environment and the qualities needed to succeed there; informational interviewing of people working in a selected field; developing a personal mission statement and comparing it with job requirements; and identifying values to match against prospective employers and organizations.

Chapter Exercises:

1. Go to one of the sites mentioned in this chapter, or find one on your own that provides a free personality assessment. Take the assessment and use the results to develop a personal mission statement. You can use the Covey free personal mission statement tool, or any other method of creating a personal mission statement.

2. Go to one of the sites mentioned in this chapter, or find one on your own that provides a free personality assessment. Based on what you find, or what you already know about your personality type, describe your ideal supervisor's personality type, and why your personality types would work together well.

3. Brainstorm, in essay form, your ideal job situation once you've graduated. Consider everything, in as much detail as you can. Where will you be working? (City, State, Company.) What will you do every day? (Job duties and skills.) What tools will you use? (Hand tools, electronic tools, computers, software.) How will you be dressed? (Casually, in a suit, a uniform.) Who are your customers? (Internal or external.) Do you report to the same place every day, or do you go to different sites? Do you travel and, if so, how much? How much of your education are you using? How much past-life experience? What new educational opportunities are available, and which ones are you taking advantage of? What do you do to keep your skills updated? Once you've come up with this situation, write another paragraph describing which of these elements you would consider doing without, and which you *must* have to accept an offer.

Works Consulted

Beatty, Richard H. *The Interview Kit.* 3rd ed. Hoboken, NJ: John Wiley & Sons, 2003.

Covey, Stephen R. *The Seven Habits of Highly Effective People*. New York: Free Press, 2004.

"Mission Statement Builder." Franklin Covey. 19 June 2007
    http://www.franklincovey.com/fc/library_and_resources/mission_statement_builder.

Taylor, Emerson. *Graduates' Guide to Business Success.* Hollywood: Biography for Everyone, 1997.

Tieger, Paul, and B. Barron Tieger. *Do What You Are*. New York: Little, Brown, 2001.

CHAPTER FOUR
Doing Something About Communication
Mark Hinrichs

It usually takes me more than three weeks to prepare a good impromptu speech.
— Mark Twain

Chapter Goal:

This chapter provides practical suggestions for improving writing and speaking skills essential to the immediate job search, such as developing and revising your resume and preparing for an interview. The chapter also notes the importance of communications skills to career progress and promotion, and suggests strategies to ensure continued development and improvement in your writing and presentation skills.

Improvement as a Process

Whether you have limited work experience or are changing careers, you may be tempted to look outside yourself for ways to improve your chances of success. Many self-help books are devoted to uncommon or sophisticated strategies for getting hired. Amid this glut of advice, there is much to recommend a more common-sense approach. Writing and speaking at a professionally competent level is a process that requires continuous application and adjustment.

The job search and later career development require:

- Honest self-exploration and self-evaluation
- Research, planning, and networking
- Above all, a *commitment* to professional communication.

As previous chapters have emphasized, communication skills are both the most important skills sought by employers and the skill set that candidates are least likely to have, at least to the standards that employers desire. This finding is not new. Communications skills, along with honesty and integrity, have ranked at the top of employers' wish lists for the last decade. During this period, employers have increasingly asserted that candidates' communications skills need serious improvement.

An Employer's Viewpoint

Here is a comment on the subject from John Levitt, a technical analyst for Johnson and Johnson:

> I have to communicate with all sorts of people, from manufacturing line workers to low-level managers to vice presidents and presidents. The communications I send out have to be designed to suit all audiences. My ability to effectively communicate to my co-worker can either help me get a

promotion or result in my demotion or even lay-off. At J&J we have yearly evaluations, and as the positions get higher the evaluations are modified to fit the position. The criteria for these evaluations are posted on our Intranet, and the major difference from senior analyst to technical lead, and from technical lead to manager is: "Does the person communicate effectively to the team or project members?"

Mr. Levitt's experience underscores the attention devoted to written communication in the workplace:

> People notice when an e-mail is poorly written; they might not point it out to you, but they will think it. And if an opportunity arises, you might get overlooked because of your communications skills (Levitt).

As this example demonstrates, communication within organizations occurs both laterally and vertically. While standards for quality are the same regardless of the direction of the message, different approaches are required for specific audiences. Employers are looking for job candidates who not only can communicate well with external customers, but can also get the job done with a variety of internal customers. Underlying your communications skills, then, must be an awareness of how well you communicate with all types of people in all types of situations. Knowing how to shift your style of communication when needed will separate you from the pack and provide greater opportunities.

To illustrate the point, let's see how 19-year-old Mark Staples, one of our profile students, reacts when an interview takes an unexpected turn:

Mark is doing well in a formal interview. He has prepared his accomplishment stories, practiced answering some difficult questions, and is feeling confident. The interviewer decides to test him to see what will happen if she changes the tone of the interview. She includes some funny comments and asks some down-to-earth questions to bring out more of his natural personality. Without thinking, Mark reverts to a more informal style of communication, becoming much more animated, casual, and direct. He throws in some slang expressions and tells a funny story about a really terrible boss for whom he once worked during high school. The interviewer realizes that although Mark can be calm and collected, in some cases he might also bad-mouth a former boss and show a less professional side. She is concerned about how well he would interact with a particular senior manager whose department would draw on this position. She passes him by.

You can see through this example that Mark needed to be much more aware of how he was coming across when he relaxed. He needed to maintain his composure, rather than shift communication styles within the interview. The key here is to know what is appropriate and inappropriate in a professional context and to use a communication style that reflects one's professional standards.

Assessing Current Skills

Personal assessment of written and oral proficiency is a good starting point in the process of improving communication skills. You can choose from several strategies, both subjective and objective, to determine your strengths and needed improvements. Jo Leonard, a college and career counselor in Lahaska PA, recommends first reaching out to your networking contacts for informal feedback:

> Contact former professors and/or mentors, asking them for their honest
> feedback on your written and oral presentation skills. Or assemble a short
> 360-degree evaluation and send it to your friends and family for comment.

Mock interviews, which can be videotaped and reviewed, provide another good way of assessing your present oral and interpersonal communications skills. You may wish to share the videotape with others, in order to get input on both your performance and on strategies for improvement.

For more objective assessment, experts recommend using one of the following tools or a similar in-depth diagnostic:

- The *Criterion* service is a Web-based application that evaluates a student's writing skills and provides immediate score reporting and diagnostic feedback to both writing instructors and students. Students draft and submit essays and receive a holistic score and diagnostic annotations within each essay. The Service is available at www.ets.org/portal/site/ets. (Click on "Criterion Online Writing Evaluation.")

- Myers-Briggs testing, discussed in the previous chapter, will also provide interesting insights into how you communicate, specifically in person, based on your personality type. The results from such a test offer you opportunities to take your communication skills to the next level by adjusting communications to certain aspects of personality – your own and others'.

Short-term Strategies for Improving Communication Skills

Whatever the results of your self-assessment of communication skills, take steps to shore up weaknesses and build on your current strengths. For sentence-level writing problems, begin by using the tutoring or academic support services on your campus to reduce or eliminate distracting grammatical or mechanical errors. At the same time, develop a plan to build on your existing communication strengths.

While you can take these steps with the near-term purpose of helping you land the job you want, keep in mind that improving communication skills is an ongoing challenge. Don't assume that you can make dramatic changes in the overall impact of your language immediately. You will need to keep making small and regular improvements to achieve noticeable results over time. Try some of the following strategies for jump-starting improvements in your vocabulary, diction, verbal poise, and overall confidence in writing and speaking.

- Use a dictionary when you read for pleasure or for business. By looking up words you do not recognize rather than skimming over them, you will expand your word-hoard permanently, because you will have learned the new words in a memorable context. Reinforce your learning by using the words in everyday conversation.

- Attend some local Toastmasters meetings. Toastmasters is a national organization designed to help people improve their public speaking abilities. Meetings are held in thousands of towns worldwide, are inexpensive, and provide great training for any life or career situation. Information and local chapters can be found at www.toastmasters.com.

- Because we are social beings, we tend to adopt the diction and speech habits of people with whom we associate. Make an effort to spend more time with friends, acquaintances, or mentors whose communications skills seem interesting and effective. Whether consciously or unconsciously, you will find yourself picking up some positive linguistic habits.

- Take advantage of low-pressure opportunities to share your ideas – either in writing or in public speaking, in small groups, perhaps – and invite feedback from your audience.

- Practice writing short, crisp thank-you notes to friends, co-workers, or family; this skill will be useful when you follow up on interviews during the job search. See Chapter 10 for guidelines and examples.

- Through family contacts, college staff, friends, or other social networks, set up a series of informational interviews. Use these interviews to explore different career fields and options, as well as to gain experience asking questions related to job qualifications, typical workdays, growth possibilities, etc. Remember that an informational interview is also an opportunity to present your positive attributes and professionalism. Many jobs are found through such networking, so make sure you are prepared. A simple informational interview might lead to a job opportunity.

- Practice articulating what you have learned in your college courses by putting together a professional portfolio. Reflect on the contents and purpose of each item, especially any connections you can draw between these achievements and job-related competencies.

Leveraging Your Academic Skills

As a college student, you have distinct advantages that you should leverage in the job search. The writing skills you develop in your courses – most notably, process writing and research skills – are directly relevant to the three major tasks of the job search: writing the application letter and resume, scripting accomplishment stories, and preparing for the job interview.

A good resume, like a good essay, emerges from a process, and includes the following stages, which may be repeated more than once in the course of writing:

- Drafting
- Getting feedback
- Revising
- Editing and proofreading

A good resume, or an effective accomplishment story told during an interview, also requires awareness of your audience. You will need to analyze the audience to create the resumes and tell the anecdotes that relate strongly to particular job descriptions. As you gain experience in the job search, you will also gain confidence in adjusting the contents and emphasis of your resume to maximize your chances of getting an interview.

For example, for a retail sales management position, you might emphasize leadership and interpersonal skills experiences that map with supervisory and customer service skills required for this position. However, for a business analyst position, you would likely choose to emphasize more quantitative and analytical skills and experiences.

Being selective about what you emphasize in a resume and organizing it to target a specific job are not the same as distorting your experiences or accomplishments. Rather, such selectivity is a legitimate way of bringing attention to the aspects of your background that are most relevant to a particular position or company.

In revising your resume, make sure you don't *underrate* your accomplishments as well. One strategy is to show your resume to someone who knows your academic or work experience well. Ask him, "Would a stranger get a positive impression of my skills from this document?" You should also get detailed feedback from your Career Services advisor, and revise your resume accordingly, before sending it to prospective employers.

Ongoing Communications

The stages of the writing process that you learned in composition classes can and should be applied not only to resume writing, but to less formal, but equally critical, correspondence with potential employers. These range from e-mails and voice messages to short demonstrations and thank you notes. While technical experience and skills are frequently in the forefront, many job candidates are surprised to learn the extent to which everyday writing and presentation skills influence their hiring and contribute to career success.

A good way to prepare for communicating in the nuanced manner of a professional is to practice using professional-level communication in your interactions with professors and staff at your college. For example, if you are going to be late or miss a class, alert your professor by one or more of the available channels – phone, e-mail, or hard copy message.

Consider this scenario, which involves another of our profiled students, Alphonse Barbaro:

With the assistance of his Career Services office, Al arranges to interview on campus with a prospective employer next Monday at 9:00 a.m. On the Saturday before the interview, Al's mother – whom he cares for on a regular basis – is hospitalized. What messages should Al leave for the various stakeholders in this situation, and what communication channels should he use? Why is Al's choice of message and channel important in this case? When Al finally meets face to face with the interviewer, how should he refer to his family circumstances in a way that communicates his professionalism?

Managing the First Impression

In preparing for interviews, it is useful to recall that a judgment about the first impression you create is usually arrived at within minutes of your initial meeting. Once this impression is formed and confirmed, it is usually difficult to alter. Much of that first impression stems from your handshake, body language, dress, tone of voice, and eye contact.

After the first impression, the ability to sustain a positive impression during an interview requires alertness and sensitivity to the situation. Jo Leonard recommends "reading the other person and altering your style to put them at ease and build rapport, a goal that is critical to effective communication." Paying close attention to the other person can provide simple clues to the personality of an interviewer. When meeting someone for the first time, take notice immediately of the following things:

- The tone and volume of his voice – is it shrill, loud, or gentle?
- Watch her physical communication style. Does she use her hands? Are they still and calm? Does she lean forward in her seat or is she sitting back and relaxed?
- Does he keep eye contact all the time or look away frequently? How is his general energy level? (Leonard)

It can be helpful to practice some "mirroring" or matching of an interviewer's characteristics for the first few minutes. (See Chapter 9 for more on this approach, including the suggestion that it should be used cautiously.)

Impressing someone in a first meeting, then, is not just about the words you use or the messages you convey by your appearance and tone of voice. It's also about "reading" the other person, putting her at ease, and using all your tools of persuasion, especially clarity of ideas and expression, to tell your story.

What is the first impression that others get of you in a professional setting? As suggested earlier, you can begin to answer this question by literally observing yourself in action. Many Career Services offices provide mock interview trials that include videotaping of the interview. If possible, you should use this service at least twice, so that you can gauge your progress between the interviews.

If you are diligent about networking, then a good resume, a professional-looking business card, and a well-rehearsed elevator speech will ultimately lead you to interview opportunities. To land the job you want, you will need a solid set of interview skills to convince the hiring managers to choose you. Whatever your sense of your abilities at this time, you will need to rely on your communication strengths and work to minimize any weaknesses.

Remember that as communicators, and as human beings, we are all works in progress. Using your professional portfolio, reflect on your classroom experience in writing or public speaking courses. You should be able to articulate some academic experience when your ability to communicate added value to a decision-making or problem-solving situation. By conveying to interviewers your awareness of the importance of communications skills – such as communicating effectively in a team – you are already moving in the right direction.

Nailing the Interview by Being Prepared

You can prepare for the interview itself by anticipating the need to discuss specialty and general education competencies gained through your coursework – as well as personal experiences and achievements outside the classroom. For the first need, practice telling a story that illustrates a behavior that all employers are looking for. These stories are known by their acronyms as PARs or SOARs, and they include three or four main parts.

In a PAR story, you tell of a Problem you faced, how you Approached it, and the positive Resolution you achieved. SOAR is an acronym for Situation, Obstacle, Action, Results. A SOAR story is an excellent way of articulating your accomplishments, and can be the most important part of the job search. SOARs provide the foundation for your resume, for your personal marketing plan, and for your interview. Without them you will feel ill-prepared and nervous at the prospect of answering *behavioral questions*, which are now commonplace (see Chapter 9).

Here's an example. In it, a successful teacher answers an interviewer's request to name one of his strengths:

> One of my strengths is listening. (Here is the *specific situation/problem*:) A student came in to my office to complain about a class and the workload. By listening carefully, I realized there was more to the problem than she was actually saying. I repeated back to her some of her own words and by doing so, drew out more information. Because I was listening carefully, she told me about personal issues she was facing that went well beyond problems in school. She hadn't really articulated to anyone else, including herself, the whole picture, which included health and financial problems. (Here's the *Action*:) I referred her to a counselor, who compelled the student to follow up with her doctor and a financial aid advisor. We both worked with her to develop a plan to complete the rest of the term while addressing her personal needs. Because I took the time to listen, the student had a workable plan that she followed through with. (Here are the *Results*:) She completed all her classes with a passing grade.

Whether you tell PAR or SOAR stories, you should follow similar guidelines for building and developing these proofs of your accomplishments:

- Script the stories carefully and well in advance of your networking or interviewing activities.
- Make sure the stories highlight your positive behaviors and skills.
- Rehearse the stories so that you do not stumble over transitions.
- Refine the stories based on using them in job search and job interview situations.

Most of your stories will relate to academic or career-related experiences relevant to the job you are applying for. You should also rehearse telling a genuine story of your own personal experience that adds dimension to your personality or character, such as finishing a half-marathon run, volunteering for community service, and other such activities.

Finally, if you want an interviewer to take you seriously, you must dress professionally too. This axiom applies to relationships with future co-workers and customers as well. Before you make an investment in your wardrobe for the purpose of the job interview, consult with your Career Services office about what you will need, and how you can acquire these items while staying within your budget.

Communication Skills for Building a Career

In the launching of your career, the stakes rise steadily for the importance of communication skills. Working productively with others becomes a more sophisticated and essential requirement as the complexity of your responsibilities multiplies.

Special attention must be given to the quality of your communications upward to your direct supervisor. According to David D'Alessandro, CEO of John Hancock, bosses want three things from their direct reports: "Loyalty, good advice, and to have their personal brands polished" (42). In other words, your boss wants your work to have a positive impact on his own career. Communicating upward effectively means being able to express your opinion clearly, honestly, yet tactfully. For example, when giving advice to your boss, do so before a decision has been made, not after; after the fact, your advice may be perceived as challenging the boss' authority. Good advice that is timely makes your boss look good. Your ability to move up within an organization will be largely based on whether you gain the trust of those who have power over your future.

For long-range career success, then, your actions and words need to engender the trust of others. It's also a good idea to develop productive relationships with peers in other departments, so that you develop a reputation as someone who is loyal to the larger organization. Finally, it is important to develop relationships with mentors both inside and outside your organization. These advisors may not have immediate influence over your current position, but they can provide insights and connections that can propel your career in the future. (See Chapter 11 for more detailed discussion of mentors.)

Playing Nicely in the Sandbox

As companies become less hierarchical, and more agile, and as they develop structures and processes to increase efficiency and productivity further, your ability to communicate effectively *laterally*, especially in teams, becomes paramount. Because of these structural trends, your ultimate career success will have a lot to do with your interpersonal communication skills. To get a sense of your current strengths in this area, reflect on how often you are able to do the following, whether in business or in personal matters:

- Be an effective leader of a team
- Be an effective follower within a team
- Persuade team members to your viewpoint
- See the value in another team member's viewpoint
- Negotiate and bring conflicting parties to a resolution of issues
- Create win-win solutions

If these skills are not prominent in your repertoire, work on improving your awareness of the motivations and perspectives of others. Take advantage of any in-house training, face-to-face or on-line, that your company provides in areas such as teamwork and communication in projects. If necessary, get buy-in from your supervisor for more extensive or formal training through workshops, conferences, or courses.

You should also do directed reading on teamwork, leadership, persuasion, and negotiation. Start with a classic, such as *The Leadership Challenge* (Kouzes and Posner) or *Artful Persuasion* (Mills), and read other items based on your own interests and the recommendations of others. Consider taking graduate coursework or continuing education that requires you to practice graduate-level communication skills.

Expanding the Limits of Your World

As your career progresses, gaining trust and establishing rapport with others depends not just on your ability to explain what you know; you also need to communicate effectively on matters that are outside your specific knowledge range. In such cases you will not be the sage but the seeker after truth. This calls for developing the communication skills associated with professional growth in your field, including asking good questions, demonstrating genuine curiosity, and applying good research techniques to emerging knowledge areas.

Another way to enhance your lifelong communication skills is to expand the range of your professional contacts to people outside your organization. Join professional organizations and become active in them, including participating in committee work. Connecting with colleagues in other organizations widens your network while deepening your knowledge in career-related topics.

Membership in professional organizations usually comes with a subscription to an organization or industry publication, which helps you stay abreast of new trends in products and services. Professional associations also provide continuing education as well as opportunities to attend conferences, make presentations, or even author papers. Conference attendance is an effective way to develop networking and interpersonal skills, which are transferable to other positions and companies. Presenting a talk or becoming published in your field is a milestone that enhances your value to current and future employers.

Enriching Your Language

Like any skill, communication effectiveness needs to be maintained and enhanced through life-long learning. One of the fundamental engines of such learning is reading. The connection between reading and communication skills is a powerful one. Your writing and speaking will improve over time if you expand the scope and depth of your reading. As your career progresses, you will be challenged to find efficient ways of keeping abreast of new ideas and trends in your profession, as well as larger societal trends. If you are not already a regular reader of business or technical books, or of non-fiction and literature, it is important that you try to expand the range of your reading interests. When you read something that you truly enjoy, ask yourself what made the writing so good. Identify the techniques the author used, and then practice using these elements in your own writing.

Expand the amount of time you devote to reading. Begin by reading as much as you can on topics or by authors that you enjoy most. Read everything that is available by your favorite authors. Before you have exhausted your favorite topics or authors, you are likely to have discovered an interest in related topics or new authors. Any approach that keeps you reading is valid. If your work schedule constrains the amount of time you can devote to longer readings, consider digital technologies such as audio books and pod casts. Ask colleagues or professional acquaintances to recommend their favorite new books.

Managerial-level communication skills may require that you explore genres unfamiliar to you. Some of the seemingly unrelated kinds of readings, including novels, poetry, and plays are the most effective for developing a tolerance of ambiguity and complexity that is essential for managers, business owners, and corporate leaders. For example, if during your career you become challenged by office politics, you may find that dramatic literature is as useful in suggesting coping strategies as a textbook on organizational behavior. You can gain deep knowledge of human motivations by attending dramatic performances. Beyond reading literature, then, your direct experience with other areas of the humanities, such as theater, visual arts, or music, is helpful in developing receptiveness to the ideas of others, your intellectual curiosity, and your appreciation for human diversity.

Experiencing literature and the arts is essential to ultimately developing the highest levels of communication skills, because stories, drama, poems and other arts provide opportunities to imagine the inner lives of other people. The greatest challenge in communicating is to know your audience. Art and literature introduce you in the greatest detail available to the widest range of human experience.

Language That Is Off-Limits
It should not need underlining that sexist or racially insensitive language is a sure disqualifier in the career, as in the job search. The limits of civility within the workplace are less forgiving than in society at large. Demonstrating sensitivity to physical and cultural differences – that is, respect for individuality and diversity in both verbal and non-verbal behavior – is essential to professional communication.

In the 21st century global economy, interpersonal communications skills will need to reflect even greater sensitivity to cultural as well as demographic diversity. Internet technology has enabled collaboration and expansion of business opportunities between more countries and more diverse populations. As a result, professional communication increasingly requires an understanding of the customs and perspectives of other cultures. Within the American workforce, the "graying" of the population also requires greater understanding of the communication styles of different generations of workers and customers. Strategies to prepare you for communicating in an increasingly diverse world include:

- Learning a foreign language
- Traveling to other countries
- Reading foreign newspapers, periodicals, or histories
- Joining professional or social organizations that include international and/or multigenerational memberships

See Chapter 11 for additional discussion of the cross-cultural elements of today's careers.

New Communication Technologies
To ensure that your communication skills remain up-to-date, you will need to adopt, if not master, some of the latest technological innovations. New technologies will provide you with insights into the values and customs of the generations of workers who are coming up behind you. As new productivity tools transform the workplace, you will need to keep pace by fine-tuning your use of developing communication forms such as e-mail, voice-mail, cell phones, blogs, Wikis, Intranets, virtual environments, and other as yet unavailable or unimagined devices.

Chapter Summary
Communicating professionally requires a level of attention to the details of your language and behavior that is similar to the demands of high-quality academic or social settings. Integrity and ethics rank with communications skills at the top of characteristics employers seek most in their new employees. All of your senses and sensibilities contribute to the effectiveness of your writing and speaking, and to your building relationships with others in the workplace.

Honest, factual, and flexible communication is fundamental to the job search process, because it helps you move toward your unique strengths and real aspirations. When everything on your resume accurately reflects your experience and knowledge, you do not have to worry about fielding questions outside your experience or knowledge. Instead, you can discuss the breadth and depth of your experience, and you can tell the stories of your accomplishments that are most relevant to the job at hand. You can also express genuine curiosity about the position and company for which you are interviewing.

Communication skills can be improved in a gradual but lasting way by taking steps to become more clear, efficient, and yet tactful with your language. Basic etiquette, common sense, respect for others, and a positive outlook can resolve many workplace communication issues before they occur. By developing a reputation for honest and effective communication on the job, you lay a solid foundation for promotion and career success. Your commitment to expanding the limits of your language, and the dimensions of your engagement with the wider community, will be a major factor in your eventual success.

Chapter Exercises:

1. Write a brief, handwritten, postcard-sized note of thanks to someone who provided a reference for you.

2. In preparation for a job interview, make an audio recording of yourself in a mock interview. Then, test the authenticity and tonal impact of your responses by playing the recording back while you are almost out of earshot of the speaker phone. Go to the next room, or around the corner. Instead of listening to the sense of your words, listen to the sound and tone of your answers instead. Do they sound confident? Authentic? Which words or phrases are either noticeably effective or ineffective as you used them? Does anything sound phony or out of place? Practice using the words and phrases that come across as genuinely reflective of your style, your tone, your self. And try replacing words and improving phrases that make you sound insincere or lacking in confidence.

3. Interview a family member, friend, or professor whose career path interests you. Prepare a set of questions ahead of time, and take notes during the interview. Among the questions you pose, be sure to ask: "If you were starting out (or changing careers) today, what trends, growth areas, or specific industries would you look to participate in? Why?" Based on your notes, write a one-page biographical sketch that summarizes the highlights of the person's career. What strategies for your own career can you derive from this biography?

4. Develop a two or three-sentence response to the following request: "Tell me a little about what you have been doing most recently."

   Example Response to 4: "I'm doing a paid internship at a medical devices company, and completing my last two semesters of a biomedical engineering technology program. I'm looking for a full-time position with a pharmaceutical, biotech, or healthcare delivery organization."

5. Practice articulating your strengths and weaknesses, as you would in an interview in response to the question "Describe one of your strengths." You can become accustomed to answering interviewers' questions about strengths by using the SAR or SOAR methods: Give a specific *S*ituation where you demonstrated this strength, include the *O*bstacles or problems you faced, describe the *A*ctions you took, and point to the positive *R*esults of that action.

Works Cited

D'Alessandro, David. *Career Warfare*. New York: McGraw-Hill, 2004.

Kouzes, James M., and Barry Z. Posner. *The Leadership Challenge,* 3rd ed. San Francisco: Jossey-Bass, 2003.

Leonard, Jo. President, Jo Leonard LLC. Personal Interview. 22 April 2007.

Levitt, John. Technical Analyst, Johnson and Johnson. Personal Interview. 14 December 2006.

Mills, Harry A.A. *Artful Persuasion: How to Command Attention, Change Minds, and Influence People*. New York: American Management Association, 2000.

CHAPTER FIVE
Researching Companies and Industries: Realizing Your Passion
Thomas Allen
Kim Brandt

The clearer your vision of what you seek, the closer you are to finding it.
— Richard N. Bolles

Chapter Goals:

- To evaluate a variety of research resources for suitability in the career planning process.
- To identify and evaluate companies hiring for a field of study.
- To assess industry trends and prospects.
- To apply specific research techniques and explore topics to maximize opportunities in the interview stage.
- To explore the career paths and job possibilities in fields related to a program of study.

Dedicating some of your precious time to researching prospective companies and industries is vital to your career launch and your long-term career success. If you are a traditional student, you will be entering the workforce after graduation with minimal experience. You will want to start identifying now the companies that hire in your field, learn where these companies are located, and get a sense of their company culture. If you are an experienced professional and returning student, you probably have a good grasp of your industry, but perhaps less awareness of other companies or options for enhancing your career. If you are a student who has been working in one field but is now transitioning to another field based on your degree studies, you will want to learn about your new industry, its companies, and its positions.

Company Research

Many people wait until they have a scheduled interview with a company before beginning company research. As a result, they put themselves into the position of evaluating available alternatives or concrete offers, rather than identifying the possibilities and searching for further information in preferred directions. In other words, they rely on job postings to determine where they will be working. If you are willing to put the time and effort into the research process, you can gain a chance to decide the type of company that fits your needs and desires best.

While the purpose and logic of research in the career planning process are self-evident, the variable that may make the greatest difference is motivation. As you learned in Chapter 2, the returns from your career-search activities are proportional to the amount and quality of your effort. If you are not willing to give your best effort to identify that "dream job" at a particular company, in all probability someone else will. The question to ask yourself is, "How hard am I willing to work to get the job I want?" If your answer is *not* "as hard as I have to," then it might not be the job for you. Your ideal job may go to someone else.

Company Research Variables

In researching companies you will encounter a wealth of information, not all of it relevant to your purposes. To sort through this deluge of information, here are some of the questions you should be pursuing through your research.

- Does the company offer positions related to my field of study?
- What is the company's reputation or image?
- How big is the company, in terms of both revenues and the number of employees?
- Would I be working for the parent company or a subsidiary?
- Is it a privately or publicly held company, and how would that status affect my work situation and long-term prospects?
- Does the company provide opportunities for advancement?
- Will this job be conducive to my professional growth?

The answers to these questions will focus your search and help you select the most useful variables from a wealth of information.

Company Research Sources

When students begin to research companies, they typically go to their favorite search engine and type in the name of the company. While this approach may yield a long list of hits, the information is not necessarily organized to meet your career-search needs, nor is it consistently reliable. The search engine is simply looking for the company's name, which may be linked to references and comments of all sorts, from all sorts of sources. A better approach would be to use some of the available resources organized to reflect the issues you are concerned with.

Forbes – www.forbes.com
The Forbes 500 offers a detailed list of the largest 500 American public corporations based on assets, profits, sales, and market value. Forbes Largest Private Companies shows a ranking of the top privately held U.S. companies and a brief description of the companies.

Fortune – www.money.cnn.com/magazines/fortune/
This is an assortment of lists including the largest public companies.

The Inc. 500 – www.inc.com/resources/inc500/2006/
Inc. Magazine creates this list including brief descriptions of the nation's fastest-growing private companies.

Working Mother – www.workingmother

A report of the 100 companies in America that are the "family-friendliest."

Hoovers - www.hoovers.com
A great source for company information and contact information for top executives. Check with your campus library or local public library to get this information for free.

www.vault.com Vault is well-known for its insider reports on thousands of companies.

The following chart diagrams the process for using company research in a job search:

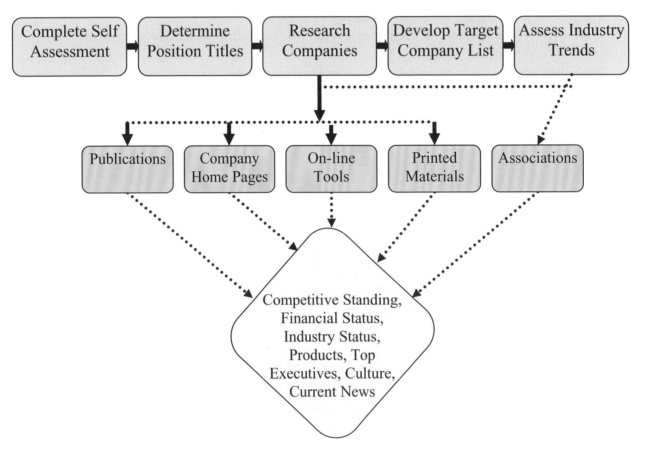

Process for Researching Companies

Complete Self Assessment → Determine Position Titles → Research Companies → Develop Target Company List → Assess Industry Trends

Publications, Company Home Pages, On-line Tools, Printed Materials, Associations

Competitive Standing, Financial Status, Industry Status, Products, Top Executives, Culture, Current News

Mark is eager to start his job search. He wants to build on his co-op position at the auto parts store and find a career position in business administration. Like many other students, he begins his search for an employer by going to the Internet. He brings up his favorite search engine and types in "business organizations." The search yields over a million items. Now Mark is overwhelmed and doesn't know what he should do for his next step. How can Mark narrow down his search for suitable companies? What other electronic resources could Mark use to find company information?

Now that Margaret is ready to start researching companies, she is concerned about finding a company that can fit with her family situation and needs. She is seeking a company within her area, because she can't afford to move and doesn't want her kids to change schools. She also wants to find a company offering positions that are in her field of study. Margaret begins her search by going to the local phone book and looking up companies. She finds several companies located within minutes of her home, but doesn't know which ones can provide the types of jobs she is searching for.

1. What can Margaret do to learn more about the types of positions available at the companies she has found?
2. Do you think Margaret is limiting her options by only using companies found in the phone book?

Industry Research

In addition to company research, you will want to examine the prospects for the industries in which companies do their business. The reasons for looking in this direction may be illustrated by the case of Al Barbaro, a dedicated and loyal employee for 25 years for a tool-and-die company that underwent a structural shift in an industry facing declining prospects and ended up laying off most of its best workers. It may not be possible to forecast the specific changes in store for particular industries 10 or 20 years ahead, but an awareness of current trends may help you to move in certain directions and avoid others.

Trends do not necessarily jump out at you. Jobs are created and eliminated all the time because of technology, as well as other factors. Over the next 20 years, more than 78 million Americans will reach their 60s and beyond. What will that mean for various industries? A likely consequence is that healthcare will grow in all categories even more than it has today. What other new industries could result from the graying of the population? Your industry research may at least suggest some tentative answers to such a question.

The field of computer simulation is another example, one in which remarkable growth is being driven by technology. While we may feel reasonably confident that the industry will expand, research may also suggest that the growth of jobs in the field may not be limited to game development alone, but may move into mainstream areas such as insurance and law.

Your understanding of the trends for an industry can help you recognize the potential of a company in terms of its future. Questions to ask about the industries you explore:

- Is the industry experiencing growth or decline?
- Are there new products or technologies affecting the industry?
- Which are the leading companies in the industry?
- What is my target company's competitive standing in its industry?

Consider that answers to the last question can be framed in a number of relevant ways:

- Is the company competitive in size and resources (revenues, employees)?
- Does it have a regional, national, or global reach?
- Is it competitive in quality?
- Is it innovative and forward-looking?

Sources for researching industries can be found at www.industrylink.com. Industry Link offers a huge collection of resources from 25 different industry Websites. Other sources for industry research include:

www.plunkettresearch.com
Plunkett Research offers business intelligence, industry trends, statistics, market research, sales leads, and corporate profiles in your choice of formats and access plans.

www.ibisworld.com
IBISWorld provides comprehensive and up-to-date research on over 700 industries; information includes statistics, industry analysis, and forecasts. (Membership fees could apply.)

Associations are one of the best sources to tap into for information on an industry. You can review the magazines and trade journals from the associations, visit their Websites, and become a member, which can also help you network at conferences and social events. Sources for associations are found through resources such as *The Encyclopedia of Associations,* along with numerous Websites.

There is also the U.S. government site www.usa.gov and the publication: *U.S. Industrial Outlook*, from the Bureau of Industrial Economics.

Developing your knowledge of an industry will help you forecast future trends, understand the competitive status of products, and find career opportunities.

Publications

While you may be familiar with a variety of Internet and Web-based resources, your career research can be considerably enhanced by making use of the print publications that have been dedicated to this purpose for years – and that still provide some of the most useful information. These print resources are available at bookstores or at your campus or public library.

Unlike some of the Websites dedicated to company or industry information, the print publications have large staffs and substantial funding, along with an established track record, to sustain them. By contrast, a Website may be unstable and impermanent. If you go to www.competia.com, for example, looking for information on the "more than 40 industries" this site has featured in the past, you will encounter a message from the site "owner" explaining that she has decided to end her service and will be doing only some limited teaching and consulting in the future.

Use the established print publications to help you determine a company's industry status, competitive level, and financial situation. Conduct your search also according to the ownership status of the company you are interested in. Publicly held companies, for example, provide more information based on their requirement to report finances to the Securities and Exchange Commission (SEC). You can review annual reports (10K), quarterly reports (10Q), 13Q ownership filings, and other reports at the SEC site http://www.sec.gov/edgar.shtml. Another source for establishing the financial status of a company is www.irin.com, which provides print copies of annual reports, as well as fact books and press releases.

Here are some of the leading publications on companies and industries.

- **Dun & Bradstreet's Million Dollar Directory** – Reports on the leading publicly and privately held companies in the U.S.

- **Mergent Moody's Manuals -** *Mergent Industrial Manual and News Reports* – comprehensive business and financial information on nearly 2,000 top industrial corporations listed on the New York Stock Exchange, the American Stock Exchange, and regional U.S. exchanges. (See also www.mergent.com/publish/news_reports.asp.)

- **Standard & Poor's Register of Corporations** – Indexes of companies by SIC code and geographical locations.

- **Thomas Register** – A guide to U.S. and Canadian manufacturers and service providers.

- **Ward's Business Directory of U.S. Private and Public Companies**

- **Encyclopedia of Business Information Sources** – A detailed listing of primary subjects of interest to managerial personnel, with a record of sourcebooks, periodicals, organizations, directories, handbooks, bibliographies, on-line data bases, and other sources of information on each topic.

You can use these kinds of resources to evaluate key issues, including the following.

Industry Status: Review the specialized publications above, along with industry journals, trade publications, and business magazines such as *Business Week, Wall Street Journal,* and *Financial Times.* Use the resources to prepare an outline of key facts about the companies you are interested in and review these facts before an interview. You may also find that former classmates or alumni of your institution work for some of these companies, enabling you to contact them (an excellent networking opportunity) to check some of your research findings.

Industry Competitors: Again, use the specialized resources and the industry journals, trade publications, and business magazines for this information. Many companies also release information at industry and trade fairs before making it available to the general public.

Company Financial Status: In addition to the above, detailed financial information will also be available in a company's annual report. Here you will find an audited set of financials, a five-year trend line of financial performance, and compensation and incentive packages for key executives and managers, along with other interesting information.

Let's check in with another of our familiar characters, as he begins to research the possibilities for his new career field.

> *Al is ready to start looking for companies that have positions for someone with his background and new degree in Electronics Engineering Technology. He decides to visit the Union College library to get industry information for electronics companies. He is overwhelmed by the number of publications available, and he isn't sure where he should be looking.*
>
> *1. How can Al organize the information he gathers at the library?*
> *2. Do you think his approach is the most efficient method for finding industry information?*

Company Home Pages

The home page of a company's Website offers key information for a job search. Most sites feature the company's products, top executives, history, mission statement, and locations; some sites also include press releases on current news and financial results.

A company's home page is one of the best sources for current news and initiatives. As a result, company recruiters love to greet potential new hires with the challenge: "What do you know about our company?" Recruiters know that one way to help identify a good future employee is to see if she is interested enough to learn something about their company and industry. If you are willing to do the research and check the information on a company's Website, you can set the stage for a positive experience.

Most company home pages are arranged to let you get to the critical information easily. You will find background information on the company's history, its mission and purposes, its locations, senior management, and available positions and typical career paths.

The Value of Product Information

A company Website will also outline its products and services, with descriptions, prices, and ordering information. By reviewing this information, a candidate could logically think about how he might help the company in promoting or selling its products or services. Because hiring managers are generally interested in the value a new employee might bring to an organization, your expression of interest in the company's wares could send a positive message.

Reading Sites for Tone and Culture

While you review the company's products and finances on its home page, notice also the style and tone of the Website. The non-verbal messages created by the design elements of the site can give you insight into the company's culture. For example, sites with flash graphics and current performance data may be concerned about projecting an image of competitiveness and high energy. Sites with cartoons from the 1980s and press releases from last year might be suffering financially and unable to spend time or money on their site.

The following examples of company home pages illustrate the kinds of information typically provided. Both companies are small, with 250 employees or less. As you can see, the first home page offers information on services, featured projects, news, career opportunities, and related links, plus contact information.

The second site features the company's mission and offers links to key features of the company.

Press Releases

Most company Websites also provide a section dedicated to press releases or news about the company. Such information is, of course, available in many other media, such as financial periodicals and the business sections of newspapers and of TV broadcasts. A company may release information about its products and services, especially when it introduces a new line. The company may also release information about organizational changes, new markets, financial results, and other significant changes. The enterprising candidate can use such information to her advantage.

Here is an example of a scenario based on actual events.

> Monica is preparing for a panel interview made up of the hiring manager, human resources director, several department heads who interact with the open position, and the regional vice president, who happens to be in town and has decided to sit in.

Over the last few years the position in question has turned over several times because of poor hiring decisions or poor performance. It is critical to the company to "get it right" this time. Monica has done well over two previous interviews and has prepared as well as she can for this session. Among the preparatory steps Monica has taken is to visit the company's Website and review its last three press releases.

The interview begins and, after a while, the regional VP comes in to meet the candidate. As the interview continues, Monica mentions that she saw this morning's press release about a new product line. She thinks this line may help the company fill a niche in the local marketplace. Several of the people in the group are unaware of the announcement, but the regional VP is both surprised and pleased by Monica's comment. He proceeds to inform the group that the department she is applying to will have a significant role in the launch of the new product line. Then he asks Monica some more questions about her views of the new offering. At the end of the interview, Monica thanks everyone and goes home to wait for a response from the company.

She does not have to wait long. Next day she gets a call and an offer from the hiring manager.

Monica's thorough preparation allowed her to learn the latest company news before the interview. Her additional research into the industry of her prospective company and into the local market trends allowed her to demonstrate that she was already thinking about how to bring value to the organization. She also showed her initiative and knowledge to the regional vice president, who was a key participant in the hiring decision.

Researching Company Leadership

Company Websites and annual reports, as well as the mainline print publications, also provide information about their senior management team. A brief biography may be offered, including title, education, and work history, along with a photograph.

Such information may be useful in several ways during the interview stage. Once you know the names you can also search through press releases and industry publications. Often senior managers will be interviewed in industry publications and give information about new products and services their companies are developing. While these senior managers may not be personally involved in your interviews, you can also convey to your interviewers that you know something about their company and its leadership.

Learning something about senior management may also give you some insight into the company's culture. Many companies hire mangers on the basis of common criteria, including a certain kind and level of work history and education. Your awareness of the company's leadership and a sense of its culture will again give you more topics to bring up during the interviews, which typically include the question, "Do you have any questions of us?" Here is another example of how learning about the senior management team helped a candidate do well during the interview process.

> Bashar has been with a large biomedical products firm for the majority of his career. He is contacted by a recruiter about moving to a start-up company's location in his area. The position is in middle management at a level on par with his current job. Bashar likes his job and is good at what he does, but promotions at the firm have been few and far between. He agrees to interview with the new company. His first interview is to be with the recruiter and the hiring manager.
>
> Bashar shows his good preparation at the interview by discussing industry trends and his experience with strategic projects at his current company. The recruiter calls Bashar the next day to arrange a flight to corporate headquarters to continue the interview process. Before departing, Bashar gathers the available material from the company Website, which includes biographies and photos of the senior management group.
>
> At company headquarters, Bashar meets the Senior VP of Human Resources. Knowing the background of this executive, Bashar is able to engage in a discussion of similarities in their work histories and educational backgrounds and to explore how these backgrounds might prepare them for positions in this company. Over the next several hours Bashar meets and interviews with most of the senior management team.
>
> Next day the recruiter calls and faxes Bashar an offer for a middle-management position at a salary higher than he had been expecting. He accepts the offer and launches a new stage of his career.

Contract Jobs and "Permanent" Positions

One of the questions you might face in the midst of a search for a permanent position is whether to accept a contract, or temporary, position offered through an agency or by a company to which you apply. The answer, of course, depends on your specific situation. The positive aspects of accepting a contract position include your becoming or staying employed in a desired field, and the fact that the opportunity could lead to a permanent position later. Companies sometimes "audition" new employees through a temp-to-permanent arrangement in which satisfactory performance leads to a regular, full-time position. The contract job also keeps a paycheck coming in and provides additional networking opportunities.

A drawback may be that you become less flexible in being able to conduct research and attend job interviews. As suggested in earlier chapters, looking for a job is a full-time job itself. The fact remains that you get out of a job search what you are willing to put into it.

In either case, very few positions in our free-market economy can be defined as "permanent." The *regular, full-time* positions on a company's roster are classified as "employment at will," meaning that either the employee or the employer can terminate the arrangement if they are unsatisfied with each other.

A source for learning more about contract services is Contract Employment Weekly at www.ceweekly.com.

Employment Agencies

If you decide to contact an employment agency, here are some guidelines to using this resource wisely.

- Find an agency through a referral, look through your local yellow pages, or check www.switchboard.com for a location.
- Determine if the agency specializes in careers related to your field of study; verify if they work with contract or regular, full-time positions; ask about their process for connecting you with a job lead.
- Send a resume and make an appointment to interview with a representative from the agency.
- Be prepared to take tests to prove your skill level.
- Follow up with the representative every week or two. This will keep you at a top-of-mind level among other clients.
- Avoid paying fees to the agency; the majority of fees are paid by the company.
- Because most agencies are paid by employers, they also tend to focus on helping companies fill positions and are not as concerned with your individual needs.
- Keep agencies as part of your job search process, not your primary option.

Mapping Your Degree to a Career Field

While college graduates with broad-based undergraduate degrees face the task of narrowing their career search to particular areas and industries, their broad-based education gives them an edge in being prepared for a wide spectrum of opportunities. Their lack of a specific focus also makes their career search more demanding and less certain in its prospects.

Graduates with undergraduate degrees in focused programs, on the other hand, start their search from a more planned and pre-defined position. Graduates with majors in engineering technology or Web graphic design or nursing, for example, have a pretty good idea of the general directions their careers will be taking. But they do not necessarily foresee the specific possibilities open to them. The engineering technologist must still decide on the subfields within engineering technology that she could pursue. She may also learn that with her background she could pursue a technical sales track, or one that leads to management and supervision instead of technical work.

The following information identifies *some* of the career possibilities associated with a series of focused degree programs at the undergraduate level. This information is meant to provide practical guidance, but it should not limit you in exploring other options that you are interested in.

Electronics Engineering Technology

Electronics engineering technology (EET) degree holders are prepared for careers in areas such as these:

- Product development and support
- Research and development
- Quality assurance
- Computer-integrated manufacturing
- Telecommunications and wireless systems development and support
- Biomedical instrumentation
- Test engineering
- Technical documentation
- Applications engineering
- Field engineering/service
- Technical sales/marketing

Here are some examples of the specific electronics engineering technology careers you could pursue with an EET degree:

Computer Systems Analyst: This is a consulting-oriented career track. You analyze a company's current computer systems and advise the firm on the types of systems that would better serve its needs. Through techniques such as data modeling, Computer Systems Analysts plan new and more efficient systems, specifying which hardware and software will deliver optimal results.

Integration Engineer: This position relies on teamwork to bring together various technologies to create more efficient, well-functioning systems. Integration Engineers work for a wide range of companies, from cell phone manufacturers to computer hardware and software firms, to consumer electronics companies.

Information Technology (IT) Business Consultant: By applying a range of specialized skills, including an understanding of current trends in information technology and a knowledge of business principles, IT Business Consultants can evaluate a company's IT systems and advise management on specific types of information technology to serve the company's needs.

Electronics and Computer Technology

Graduates with associate degrees in electronics and computer technology (ECT) are prepared for careers in areas such as the following:

- Electronic system equipment installation/maintenance
- Manufacturing equipment installation/maintenance
- Wide-area network (WAN) and local-area network (LAN) installation/maintenance
- Wireless communication systems installation/maintenance
- Telecommunications systems installation/maintenance
- Technical field service
- Technical sales/sales support

68

- Research and development support
- Quality control

Computer Information Systems

Computer information systems (CIS) careers are found in widely diverse industries, in positions such as the following:

- Game simulation programming
- Software engineering
- Systems analysis and design
- Applications support/maintenance
- Applications software consulting
- Web application development
- Database design
- Database programming

- Web programming
- Business applications programming
- Technical/application support
- Computer-related sales and marketing support
- Technical documentation
- Small business entrepreneurship and management

Some typical positions for CIS graduates include the following:

Web Developer: Works with the Internet and the hardware and software that continuously enhance its functionality. Duties include developing, launching, and maintaining Websites and Web-based applications. Uses programming and other technical skills to advance in a constantly growing field.

Computer Forensics: As one of the most rapidly evolving fields, computer forensics employs CIS professionals who work alongside law enforcement personnel to investigate and help solve crimes and corporate improprieties using computer and information technology.

Information Systems Security: With a goal of ensuring the security of an organization's Website and its computer systems, the cyber-security specialist evaluates vulnerabilities, installs protective systems, and troubleshoots critical system issues.

Computer Systems Analyst: Relies on analytical thinking, problem solving, and technical expertise in data modeling to advise management on the types of computer systems that optimize performance and best meet their firm's needs. Provides flexibility in structuring the position, including ability to work from home.

Database Administrator: From storing, managing, and extracting data to creating entirely new databases customized to the needs of a particular company, database administrators enjoy significant responsibility, growing challenges, and abundant job opportunities.

Network and Communications Management

Network and communications management (NCM) career opportunities are available in a variety of positions, including the following:

- Network administration

- Network analysis, planning, and management

- Network technical support
- Network troubleshooting and support
- Network security
- Network operations

- Voice or data communications analysis and administration
- Internet/Intranet administration

Some examples of current network and communications management careers for bachelor's degree holders include the following:

Data Communications Analyst: Analyzes problems with systems, including wide-area networks, local-area networks, Internet and Intranet connections; plans and implements solutions using methods such as information engineering, mathematical and data modeling, and cost accounting.

Database Administrator: Determines ways to organize and store data, ensure the performance of a system, add new users to a system, set up new databases, and effectively use the platform on which the database runs. Data integrity, backup systems, and database security are increasingly important aspects of the job for database administrators.

Network Security Specialist: Needs exist in both military and civilian occupations. In a military environment, the specialist creates methods for identifying and protecting information, sensitive operations, materials, and facilities from such threats as compromise, unauthorized disclosure, espionage, and sabotage. In a civilian context, he analyzes an organization's security risks and requirements and implements and maintains the security infrastructure to protect the business from security breaches.

Network Systems Administration

Graduates with an associate degree in network systems administration (NSA) will be prepared for career-entry positions in areas such as:

- Network administration
- Network operations
- Network security
- Network/IT technical support

- Local area network (LAN) administration
- Customer service
- End user service and support

Here are some examples of positions for NSA graduates:

Network Analysis, Planning, and Management: Network analysts use data modeling, structured analysis, or information engineering to design new systems or add new software applications to enhance network capabilities.

Network Troubleshooting and Support: Technical Support Specialists or Help-Desk Technicians provide technical assistance, support, and advice to customers and other network users. They work on monitors, keyboards, printers, mouse devices, and computer hardware to help install, modify, clean, and repair computers and train others in their use and care.

Health Information Technology

Health information technology (HIT) graduates hold associate degrees and work in a variety of healthcare industry settings, such as the following:

- Hospitals and diversified hospital systems
- Physician offices/medical group practices
- Pharmaceutical companies
- Clinics and ambulatory surgical centers
- Long-term care facilities
- Mental health centers
- Ambulatory care centers
- Rehabilitation facilities
- Insurance and managed care organizations
- Government agencies
- Educational institutions and vendor firms
- Surgical centers

HIT graduates may hold positions such as the following:

- Coder/Clinical Coding Specialist
- Data Quality Manager
- Health Records Technician
- Medical Records Specialist
- Insurance Claims Analyst
- Health Data Analyst
- Patient Information Coordinator
- Coder/Clinical Coding Specialist
- Applications System Analyst

Web Graphics Design

Graduates from a Web graphics design (WGD) associate-degree program design and develop effective Websites and other visual communication solutions. Agencies and companies that employ Web graphics designers include the following:

- Advertising agencies
- Marketing firms
- Website development companies
- eLearning providers
- Training and development firms
- Corporate communications departments
- On-line service organizations
- eCommerce providers

Examples of WGD positions include these:

Digital Graphics Editor: Modify and develop digital content, including drawings, renderings, and photographs.

Instructional Designer: Develop interactive Web-based materials for educational, training, and information purposes.

Media Communications Consultant: Work with public relations and corporate communications departments and advertising agencies to develop graphic communications materials.

<u>Web Page Designer</u>: Design Web pages and their graphic elements to improve communication with clients and users.

Game and Simulation Programming

Graduates with a bachelor's degree in Game and Simulation Programming (GSP) will be prepared for career-entry positions in areas such as these:

- Game Programmer
- Simulation Programmer
- Game Engine/Tools Programmer
- Game Tester
- Software Engineer

Examples of positions for GSP graduates include the following:

<u>Junior Programmer</u>: This is an entry-level game or simulation programming position, providing an opportunity to gain experience and learn skills related to an area of specialization.

<u>Engine/Tools Programmer</u>: This position deals with helping design and construct the engines on which games will run and the tools other programmers and artists will use to design game elements.

<u>Level Designer</u>: Responsible for creating mock-up playable game and simulation levels for game testing, based on design documents and concept maps.

Business Administration

Business administration careers are found in nearly every industry, including the following:

- Healthcare
- Insurance
- Finance
- Government
- Non-profit organizations
- Education
- Communications
- Retail
- Marketing

Combining a bachelor's in business administration degree (BSBA) with a specific concentration or major, a graduate is equipped for a specialized business career in one of the following areas:

<u>Accounting</u>: Accounting careers are found in nearly every industry, including public accounting corporations, multinational companies, small and large businesses, non-profit organizations, and government agencies. In addition to designing and implementing advanced accounting systems for specific needs, some traditional accounting careers take the following paths:

Public accountants handle accounting, auditing, tax reporting, and consulting for corporations, not-for-profit organizations, governments, and individuals.

Corporate accountants record and analyze companies' financial information.

Government accountants perform audits and investigations and provide general accounting services.

Business Information Systems: Bachelor's graduates in business administration with a concentration or major in business information systems are prepared for careers in areas such as the following:

- Database applications
- PC hardware and software assistance and training
- Internet coordination

- Business systems analysis
- E-commerce-based applications

Finance: With expertise in areas such as short-term financing, credit cards, factoring, mortgages, education loans, derivatives, commodities, international currency, interest rate exchanges, and international transactions, BSBA grads with a finance concentration may pursue career positions such as the following:

- Bank branch manager
- Budget analyst
- Credit manager
- Commercial banking officer
- Financial analyst

- Financial planning consultant
- Insurance representative
- Loan officer
- Security and commodities sales agent
- Broker

Health Services Management: BSBA graduates with a health services management concentration must remain current on healthcare systems, technological innovations, government regulations, and preventive care initiatives. They work in areas such as the following:

- Medical office supervision
- Patient accounting and billing systems
- Managed care coordination

- Medical computer sales
- Management of provider networks
- Facility direction and marketing

Hospitality Management: BSBA graduates with a hospitality management concentration are prepared for careers in areas such as management of tourism operations, casino operations, and hotel and restaurant operations; they may be employed in settings such as the following:

- Hotels and resorts
- Gaming and entertainment venues
- Restaurants and banquet facilities
- Cruise ships

- Schools
- Healthcare organizations
- Businesses

In a hospitality management career, professional responsibilities might include the following:

- Training, scheduling, and supervising staff
- Scheduling, planning, and purchasing supplies and equipment for daily use or specific events
- Managing reservation systems

- Resolving customer problems and handling emergencies

Human Resources Management: Bachelor's graduates in business administration with a concentration in human resources management may work in nearly every industry, including the following:

- Corporations
- Non-profit organizations
- Government offices

- Education
- Healthcare

HR management majors may find career opportunities in areas such as these:

- Benefits and compensation
- Employee relations

- Human resource information systems
- Training and development

Operations Management: BSBA/operations management careers can be found a variety of settings, including the following:

- Retail
- Manufacturing
- Aerospace
- Pharmaceuticals

- Electronics
- Healthcare
- Government

Bachelor's degree graduates in business administration with a concentration in operations management will be prepared for careers in areas such as these:

- Purchasing management
- Process re-engineering
- Quality assurance and control

- Logistics
- Facility management and supervision

Project Management: BSBA/project management careers can be found a variety of settings, including:

- Advertising
- Marketing
- Communications
- Applications engineering
- Product or service industries

- Computer software and hardware development
- Construction
- Finance
- Manufacturing

Project managers – also known as project directors, producers, creative directors, production managers, traffic managers, and team supervisors – are employed in ways such as these:

- Working with management to develop project parameters
- Selecting, hiring, and managing teams
- Monitoring results, documenting problems, and developing solutions
- Writing performance reviews

- Working on organizational change initiatives

Sales and Marketing: BSBA/sales and marketing careers can be found a variety of settings, including the following:

- Advertising
- Communications
- Insurance
- Real estate

- Education
- Retail
- Pharmaceuticals
- Finance

Bachelor's graduates in business administration with a concentration in sales and marketing will be prepared for careers in areas such as these:

- Sales management
- Advertising
- Promotion and public relations
- Marketing research
- Product management
- Internet marketing and sales
- Industrial buying

Related job titles include sales, advertising, marketing and promotion manager, and public relations/marketing research specialist. Specific professional responsibilities could include:

- Developing and managing marketing and advertising plans
- Monitoring and analyzing statistical data and market trends
- Preparing and conducting sales presentations, trade shows presentations, and meetings
- Directing product and corporate image publicity to target audiences

Security Management: Bachelor's degree graduates in business administration with a concentration in security management are prepared to enter career areas such as these:

- Federal, state, and local government investigation/intelligence
- Immigration and border patrol inspection/protection
- Criminal and compliance investigation/examination
- Air marshal service
- Hospital and healthcare security
- Private security management
- Lodging and entertainment security
- Corporate security/physical security management
- Executive protection
- Security consulting

As a security manager, security operations director, or on-site security specialist, the graduate could assume professional responsibilities such as these:

- Analyze company or industry security needs
- Evaluate physical or information security systems
- Set up, monitor, maintain, and upgrade security systems
- Train and educate staff and client

<u>Small Business Management and Entrepreneurship</u>: Bachelor's degree graduates in business administration with a concentration in small business management and entrepreneurship will be prepared for careers in areas such as the following:

- Website development
- E-commerce
- Retail
- Manufacturing
- Finance
- Real Estate
- Insurance

With a job title such as business owner, franchisee, or store manager, graduates could take on responsibilities that include:

- Creating and implementing new business plans
- Managing staff, payroll, and benefits
- Securing financial resources for initial funding or expansion activities
- Identifying and exploring new opportunities
- Small business financial accounting
- Internet marketing and sales
- Customer relations
- New business development

Career Track Research

As the examples in this section indicate, career research focused on companies and industries can be further enhanced by exploring the career tracks associated with particular programs and program concentrations. This additional information can lead you to the options that provide the best fit for your educational background. You will also be better prepared for the interview stage through your ability to link your background to potential job requirements.

Chapter Exercises:

1. Select a company that you may be interested in working for. Now, use at least two different methods for researching companies to answer the following questions:

   a. Is the company privately or publicly held?
   b. How big is the company both financially and in the number of employees?
   c. What are the company's products or services?
   d. Does the company have positions I am interested in pursuing?

2. Visit your campus library or the local public library and research a selected industry. You will need to provide the sources for your information and answer the following questions:

   a. Is the industry in a growth mode?
   b. What are the expected numbers of jobs for this industry in the next ten years?
   c. Name the three leading companies in this industry.
   d. What are the locations for the major companies?

3. Explore the career tracks associated with the program you are graduating from. Use print and electronic resources to determine the following:

   a. What are at least six kinds of companies or organizations in which you might work in jobs related to your major?
   b. Identify at least six kinds of positions for which you would be qualified at the career entry level as a graduate of your program.
   c. Provide the job descriptions for at least four specific entry-level positions in your field.

Works Cited

Graber, Steven. *The Everything Get-A-Job Book*. Holbrook, MA: Adams Media Corporation, 2000.

Krannich, Ron, and Caryl Krannich. *Campus Career Center's The Job Hunting Guide*. Manassas Park, VA: Impact Publishing, 2003.

Krannich, Ron, and Caryl Krannich. *Nail the Job Interview*. Manassas Park, VA: Impact Publishing, 2003.

Swanson, Richard W. *The Smart People's Guide to Job Hunting*. Denver: Buck Jones Books, 2001.

CHAPTER SIX
Job Search Documents
Corey Vigdor

"What have I gained?"
"Experience," said Holmes, laughing. "Indirectly it may be of value, you know; you have only to put it into words…"

— Arthur Conan Doyle (1859-1930)

Chapter Goal:

The purpose of this chapter is to help you create finely crafted job search documents such as resumes, cover letters, and reference sheets. This chapter recognizes that job search documents serve as the bridge between your educational and work experiences and the job you desire. It discusses both good and bad practices in document creation and suggests the latter might lock you out from gaining consideration. The goal of this chapter is to help you construct documents that you can use in your own job search with confidence that they will get you to the interview.

Introduction

Regardless of the career you want to enter, one of your goals should be to work in a position that you love, one that uses your skills and background and helps you grow as a professional. To obtain such a position you will undoubtedly have to do a great job in an interview showcasing your skills, talents, personality, and education. The key to getting that initial interview is the development of job search documents such as resumes and cover letters that promote interest in your candidacy.

As you become more knowledgeable about job search documents, you will see that they can be created in different formats and that differing opinions on styles and approaches can be equally valid. This chapter will give you solid advice about creating job search documents based on commonly accepted practices. It will also point out the common careless mistakes you need to avoid. These topics will be presented *in an applied workshop format* so you can quickly put the information and ideas to work in both analyzing job search documents and creating your own for use in your job search.

The following workshop components will be used to bring you closer to developing your own body of knowledge and documents:

- **Information**: You will read about the topic under discussion and develop a solid understanding and an information base.
- **Evaluation**: You will analyze previously submitted work from other Career Development students and use your expertise to suggest improvements. (The examples are real, but all the names, places, and times have been changed to protect identities.)

- **Application:** You will create your own job search documents for use in marketing yourself to potential employers.
- **FAQs**: Since you cannot ask questions directly, a series of frequently asked questions from students in prior Career Development classes will be provided.

Let's take a look at some common questions:

Q:	I already have a resume, cover letter, and reference sheet. Do I really need the information presented in this chapter?
A:	Job search documents cannot be too polished, well-organized, and effective. Remember that the goal is to get the job you want by way of an interview. How you get the interview is through your documentation. There is always room for improvement in this area and the more you know about good practices, the more you strengthen your candidacy. Do not let your documents stand between you and the job you desire.
Q:	Doesn't the Career Services office write job search documents for students?
A:	While Career Services advisors will help you fine-tune your resume if requested, it is up to you to create, maintain, and perfect your own documents. When you meet your Career Services advisor for the first time, you should already have a good resume in hand. Your interaction with Career Services will be more productive as a result.

Workshop 1: Resumes

Characteristics of a good resume include the following:

- It presents a clear picture of what you have been doing, what you know, what you can do, and what you have accomplished.
- It is properly structured, formatted, organized, and free of spelling and grammar mistakes.
- It shows employers your potential and how well you match up to their needs.
- It promotes your candidacy and moves you to the interview stage. A bad resume gets you immediately eliminated from consideration.

The Main Types of Resumes

Two widely used types are the chronological and the functional. Chronological resumes are organized into broad sections such as Objectives, Summary, Education, Experiences, Skills, and Relevant Coursework. Within certain sections, items are listed in reverse chronological order with most recent events first. The benefit of this type of resume is that it gives an employer a quick snapshot of how your career has developed over time.

Functional resumes present information similar to that found in chronological types. The distinction lies in the way each is organized. The functional resume is structured around qualities, skills, and qualifications. This type of resume works well for job seekers who wish to enter an industry where they have no relevant experience. It seeks to promote the notion of transferable assets – of skills that can be readily applied in any industry. The following pages provide examples of both the Chronological and Functional Resumes. The first example uses a Summary section, while the second features a Career Objective.

Chronological Resume Example

Name
Address
Telephone Number
e-mail Address

Summary:
Seasoned account executive seeking a challenging sales/marketing position in the automation field requiring proven skills in customer relations, lead generation, product marketing, closing, and add-on sales.

Experience:
Application Automation Consultants Inc., Chicago IL
Account Executive, March 1999 to present
- Increased district sales by more than 22% per year for last four years.
- Improved add-on sales by modifying client databases to more efficiently respond to customer inquiries.
- Experienced in resource development including operations, marketing, advertising, sales, and recruiting and hiring personnel.
- Managed membership with NACCB (National Association for Computer Consulting Business).

Personnel Network/Select Staffing, Bakersfield CA
Contractor, November 1998 to March 1999
- Managed and expanded IT clients in a variety of industries including Anderson Consulting, IBM, Allstate, and numerous other companies with local to global reach.
- Motivated and coordinated project teams to meet deadlines.
- Successfully recruited Information Technology professionals to fill time-sensitive contractual agreements.

Education:
Keller Graduate School of Management, Chicago IL
Master of Business Administration degree – anticipated May 20XX

University of Illinois, Champaign IL
Bachelor of Science, Psychology
Minor in Business Administration May 1994

Affiliations/Memberships:
Northwest Suburban Delta Zeta Alumni Association, 1997 to present

Functional Resume Example

Address   **Name**
                                                         Telephone Number
                                                         E-mail Address

Career Objective:
A challenging position as a Public Relations Specialist in an academic or civic
environment requiring skills in writing press releases, creating marketing materials,
and maintaining positive media relations.

Professional Experience:

PUBLIC RELATIONS

- As an Intern with the Detroit Department of Planning and Development,
  compiled press contact information through heavy phone contact with media.
- Gathered and organized press clippings on city planning and development issues
  to assist policy-makers.
- Attend City Council and zoning meetings, focusing on issues that impact
  tourism.
- As Marketing and Public Relations Coordinator for Wyandotte Tours, composed
  and edited copy, managed production time-lines, and coordinated development
  and distribution of marketing materials.
- Composed press releases, maintained media contact database, developed media
  kits, and prepared slide presentations for the sales force.

OPERATIONS

- Functioned as Project Leader for faculty management/relations, office and
  financial management, and campus operations for ABC Schools.
- Coordinated Standard Program Letters, tracked prospective student leads, and
  generated weekly lead reports for admissions staff, contributing to annual
  enrollment increases of more than 10% for last three years.
- Assisted students with registration, payment processing, and database
  management to positively affect retention efforts.

EMPLOYMENT HISTORY	**INTERNSHIPS**
ABC Schools, City of Detroit	Department of Planning and
Development School Coordinator	Public Relations Internship
May 2002 to Present	June to August 2000
Wyandotte Tours	WGN Television
Marketing and Public Relations Coordinator	Public Relations Internship
October 2000 to October 2001	September to December 1999

The remainder of Workshop One will focus on constructing chronological resumes. This type provides the most flexibility in usage and is more widely accepted for recent college graduates. Here are some of the key guidelines for constructing the chronological resume.

- Be positive. You are selling your skills and accomplishments. Don't exaggerate or misrepresent, but if you achieved something, say so. Don't try to be modest.
- Be brief. Include relevant and important accomplishments, but do so in as few words as possible. Concise is better since employers must read hundreds of these documents.
- Highlight dates and locations. Don't let them get lost in the surrounding information.
- Avoid personal pronouns, especially *I*. These convey a subjective quality, whereas you should strive for an objective, professional tone.
- Emphasize relevant experience. Highlight continued experience in a particular type of function and de-emphasize irrelevant positions.
- Stress your results. Elaborate on how you contributed to past employers: *increased sales, reduced costs, improved a product, implemented a new program,* etc.

Regardless of the type of resume you choose to develop, follow these format specifications:

- Develop the resume electronically in a word processing application and fit it to an 8½x11" sheet of paper.
- Use either Times New Roman or Arial font to project a professional appearance. Do not exceed 12-point font size, other than for your name, and do not go smaller than 10-point.
- Print the resume on light-colored quality paper (as opposed to pastel colors).
- Make sure there are *no* grammatical errors.

Q & A on the Basics

Q:	Can I use special paper with graphics on it to leave an impression?
A:	While you do want to stand out, you want to do so professionally. It is best to go with plain resume paper and stand out with proper formatting and appropriate and targeted information. The same goes for font choice. While there are many font choices, it is best to stick with Arial or Times New Roman and no smaller than 10-point.
Q:	Can a resume cover more than one page?
A:	A resume can be longer than one page, especially for experienced job seekers, provided that the information you present is relevant for the position you seek. Eliminate irrelevancies and work for a concise presentation. If you end up with two pages of solid and relevant material, use it at that length.

Workshop 1: Chronological Resumes

Information: Demographics

In a chronological resume, demographic information is provided at the top of the first page and contains your name, address, phone numbers, and e-mail address. Since this area is the first scanned by employers, it should convey a professional appearance. Distinguish phone numbers to indicate where the employer is calling – home, work, or perhaps your cell. You can list all three or just one, but make sure that when employers call you are able to have a conversation in a quiet environment. If they hear your phone message, make sure it reflects your professional side through an appropriate and brief message.

Evaluation: Demographics

What improvements can you suggest for the demographics section of the student sample shown below? Before looking at the list of already developed suggestions, come up with three improvements of your own.

Jonathan Fisher   Home: 678-555-5555
435 Water St
Decatur GA 30033
US

Resume Headline: Service Technician

Your suggestions:
1. _____
2. _____
3. _____

How closely do your suggestions match up with this (non-exhaustive) list?

1. Resumes do not need a "Headline." Remove this section.
2. Street should be spelled out completely
3. A single phone number can be assumed to be your home number. No "Home" designator is necessary.
4. Including "US" is not necessary when giving a state of residence. In Canada, citing the province is sufficient.
5. Section is unbalanced in that most of the items are on the left.
6. E-mail address is missing.

Application: Demographics

Utilizing what you have learned about demographic information in a resume through the information provided and your analysis of a poorly constructed section, create your own section in the area provided. Make sure it includes your name, address, phone number(s), and e-mail address.

Q & A: Demographics

Q:	Does it matter what e-mail utility I use?
A:	No. Many students have multiple accounts, and it is up to you to use the one that suits your needs. However, do make sure that the address is constructed in a professional manner and that you check it frequently.

Information: Career Objective, or Summary?

Directly following demographic information in a chronological resume is a career objective or a summary of experience. Objectives and summaries are written in the third person. Do not use personal pronouns here, and focus the attention of the reader on who you are and what you want.

The purpose of an objective is to communicate your desire to work in a particular industry and convey the assurance that you have the education and experience to do so successfully. A career objective is particularly useful if your experience and education are diverse, since it helps focus the reader on your qualifications for a particular position or career track. Avoid reference to a particular position, however. If the position you are seeking is filled and there is another opportunity that you would be happy to explore, you would not want to eliminate yourself from consideration. An example of a career objective might be: "A challenging position in the computer field focusing on database management and Web applications development."

People with significant work experience in an industry in which they seek to continue employment might use a summary statement instead of a career goal. The summary might begin as follows: "Over ten years of professional experience in the computer field..." A few concise statements elaborating this experience would then follow. (See the examples on pp 80-81.)

Evaluation: The Objective

What improvements can you suggest for this student's Objective section? Before checking the list of suggested enhancements below, can you come up with three improvements of your own?

OBJECTIVE:	To obtain a job in your company. With my educational background I believe I am an excellent candidate for this position. My Associates Degree in Electronics and Computer Technology has given me advanced knowledge, training, and skills to work in both the industrial and manufacturing fields.

Your suggestions:

1. _____
2. _____
3. _____

How closely do your suggestions match up with this list, which is not exhaustive:

1. The objective is not specific enough for an industry or a particular company.
2. It contains personal pronouns.
3. It's too long. Objectives should be short, focused statements.
4. The entire second sentence can be removed and utilized in a cover letter, where it would be more appropriate.
5. The fifth line could be added to the end of the fourth to tighten up the formatting.

Application: The Objective

Using what you have learned about Objectives in a resume through the information provided and your analysis of a poorly constructed section, create your objectives statement in the area provided.

Objective: _____

_____

_____

_____

_____

Q & A: Objectives

Q:	Is it even necessary to provide an Objective on a resume?
A:	If you have significant work experience in the same industry you are applying to, you might provide a summary instead of an objective. If you lack strong experience but have a good educational background suited for entry into that field, provide a career objective linked to your education.

Information: Education

As a soon-to-be or recent graduate, your primary qualification for a position is your education. It is therefore important to list the degrees you have earned, along with any associated special honors or awards – in reverse chronological order. If you have not yet graduated, state when you will do so. Don't include your high school diploma, since employers are interested in your college work and assume a high school prerequisite.

For the honors you include, a Dean's List award can be an indication of your aptitude for learning. At graduation, being recognized with Magna Cum Laude or Summa Cum Laude status should be prominently noted in this section. A *good* Grade Point Average is also worth citing. A GPA over 3.0 tells employers that you have worked hard and learned much in your academic career, qualities promising for the workplace as well. A GPA under 3.0 does not mean that you learned nothing. It does, however, suggest consideration for promoting other aspects of your education. The resume should feature your strengths and present you as an attractive candidate.

Here is a model you can use to create your own Education section.

Before You Graduate:
Education: Concordia Northern College, Columbus, OH
                    Candidate for a Bachelor of Science degree in Technical Management
                    Anticipated Graduation: March 20XX

After You Graduate:
Education: Concordia Northern College, Columbus, OH
                    Bachelor of Science degree in Technical Management, March 20XX

Evaluation: Education Section

What improvements can you suggest for this student's Education section? Before looking at the list of suggestions provided below, can you come up with three ideas of your own?

EDUCATION

- Smith Coll of Pennsylvania, 1986-1987
- Center for the Enterprising Youthe 1982
- Kennedy High School Barrington, Pennsylvania. March 1986
- Monroe University, Bachelors of Science Tech Mangmnt. Feb 2006, GPA=2.13

Your suggestions:

1. _____
2. _____
3. _____

How closely do your suggestions match up with this list?

1. There are spelling mistakes. *Youth*[e] and *Coll*[ege] are not spelled correctly.
2. February is not spelled out but March is. Keep these references consistent.
3. There is no need to list high school experience if you are a college graduate.
4. What is the "Center for *the* Enterprising Youth"? Where is it located? What credential was earned? Is it relevant to the career the applicant is seeking?
5. Don't list a GPA if it is below a 3.0.
6. Did the student graduate from Smith? If not, then leave it off.
7. The degree from Monroe University is not worded appropriately. It should be Bachelor of Science degree in Technical Management
8. The listings do not follow reverse chronological order.

Application: Education Section

Utilizing what you have learned about this section through the information provided and your analysis of a poorly constructed section, create your own Education section in the area provided.

Education: _____

_____

_____

_____

_____

Q & A: Education

Q: Which section comes first in a resume, Education or Experience?

A: If you have significant work experience in the industry you are trying to enter, put your experience first. If you do not have that significant experience but do have a strong educational background related to the field you are targeting, put your education first.

Information: Relevant Coursework or a Skills Section?

A Relevant Coursework section in a chronological resume is not a standard expectation. It is a possible addition, however, for students without significant experience for the career they are seeking to enter. As a replacement for the "Skills" section, it promotes details of the strength of your education. By noting the industry relevant courses you took, potential employers might conclude that they will not have to spend significant time training you, which makes you a more attractive candidate.

Alternatively, you might translate some of your key courses into skills-building experiences. Coursework with hands-on applications, project management, or teamwork activities, for example, could be highlighted in a Skills section as well.

Evaluation: Skills

What problems can you find in the Skills section below? Come up with three suggestions for improvement before checking the list provided afterward.

Your suggestions:

1. _____
2. _____
3. _____

SKILLS:

Technical Summary
> **HARDWARE**: Personal computer components, including hard drives, CD-ROM, memory, configuration NICs, video cards and printers
> **SOFTWARE**: Windows NT 4.0 Workstation, Novell NetWare 5.1, Windows 95/98, Microsoft Office 2000, TCP/IP, IPX/SPX, NETBEUI, Windows NT 4.0 Server, Windows 2000 Pro, Microsoft DOS 6.22.
> Related Experience:

> ·   Installation of operating systems and applications
> ·   Windows 95/98: Configuration of networking components, manage desktops, create and utilize shortcuts, configure modes of operation
> ·   Windows NT 4.0 Workstation: Installation and configuration; manage users and groups, administer both file and directory security, modify/manage registry, knowledge of roaming and local profiles, manage partitions through Disk Administrator; set up and maintain Remote Access Services
> ·   Novell NetWare 5.1: Manage NDS Objects using NW Admin and Console One, set up and maintain all levels of NetWare security including NFS and NDS security; manage Novell Distributed Print Services as well as queue-based printing, file server console management, server installation and configuration
> ·   Configure TCP/IP for multiple clients including Windows 95/98, Windows NT, Novell Client 32
> ·   Windows NT 4.0 Server: Installed and configured; manage network users and groups
> ·   Windows 2000 Pro: installed and configured
> ·   Utilization of MS Office Applications
> ·   Configure clients for Internet use
> ·   Personal computer repair and replace procedures
> ·   Troubleshooting of both hardware and software issues

How closely do your suggestions match up with this list?

1. Information is scattered and lacks a targeted approach. The applicant may actually know quite a bit, but the listing shows disorganization.
2. The section mentions a number of operating systems but does not fully communicate the depth of understanding or usage of them.
3. "Utilization of MS Office Applications." What does this mean exactly?
4. Some of the skills regarding Windows appear several times, thus creating the perception of duplication.
5. Format is not consistent. There are spacing and indenting issues.
6. Font types and sizes are not consistent.

Application: Relevant Coursework

Create your own Relevant Coursework section in the area provided.

Relevant Coursework:	More than _____ credits of coursework in the following areas:
	• _____ • _____
	• _____ • _____
	• _____ • _____
	• _____ • _____

Q & A: Relevant Coursework

Q: On my resume, I would like to use a section called Skills instead of Relevant Coursework. Would that be okay?

A: There is nothing wrong with a Skills section if you use it effectively (unlike the sample shown above). Students with degrees in technology areas are able to isolate lots of technical skills they have acquired and promote them through this category. Separate these technical skills from those best described in the cover letter, however. Teamwork and interpersonal and communication skills can be better supported with examples and instances in the narrative of the letter than in a resume.

Q: Should I consider all the courses that I took during my education as relevant? If so, wouldn't the list be too long?

A: While you should definitely consider all of your courses to be relevant to your growth and development, choose the ones you want to promote. The key to this section is determining what the employer would consider as relevant. You can find some answers to this question through company- and industry-related research.

Information: Experience Section

The Experience section of a chronological resume should always include the following:

- Previous employers
- Locations of employment
- When you worked there
- Your position's formal title
- Your responsibilities and accomplishments in that position.

As in the Education section, list your experiences in reverse chronological order with the most recent first. It is very important also to be factual and not to embellish or stretch the facts of your experience. Many of the points you are listing can be verified through phone calls or documents that you might be asked to provide later.

Make sure to stress not only responsibilities but also accomplishments. Use strong action words such as *spearheaded, created, performed, managed, led, supervised, accomplished,* etc., to introduce your statements.

Evaluation: Experience

What improvements can you suggest for this student's Experience section?

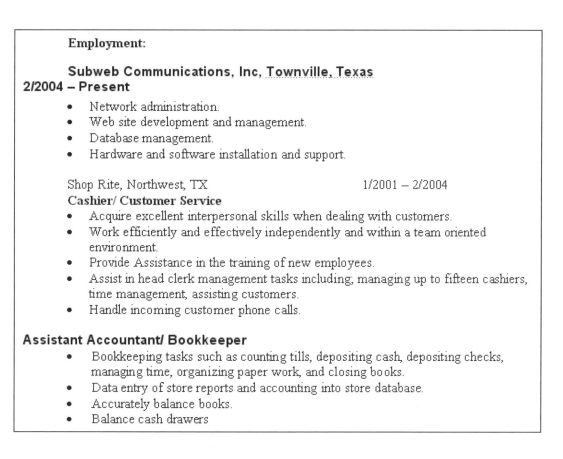

Your suggestions:

1. _____
2. _____
3. _____

How closely do your suggestions match up with this list?

1. The alignment of the items is not consistent throughout the section.
2. The font type and size are not consistent.
3. The last two jobs are not presented in the past tense

4. Several of the bulleted items are not presented via action words (e.g., "Network Administration"). This item could use *Performed,* or the bullet could be rewritten to state "*Served* as the primary network administrator."
5. The last job does not specify a place of employment, dates, or location.
6. Experience is a better word for this section than Employment.
7. Texas is spelled out fully in the first job, but the second uses the state abbreviation.
8. There is no mention of accomplishments.

Application: Experience Section

Create your own Experience section based on two jobs you have held, or on hypothetical positions.

Experience:

_____	_____	_____,_____
(Dates)	(Company)	(City, State)

_____
(Title)

Responsibilities/Accomplishments

- _____
- _____
- _____

_____	_____	_____,_____
(Dates)	(Company)	(City, State)

_____
(Title)

Responsibilities/Accomplishments:

- _____
- _____
- _____

Q & A :Experience Section

Q:	If I don't embellish my accomplishments, won't I be limiting the potential interest from employers and cutting down on my opportunities?
A:	When looking for a job, honesty is truly the best policy. Some studies do show that many job seekers take liberties with the truth when describing their experiences. Just as many widely publicized news stories feature high-profile people who have been caught. Such examples include a dean at a prominent university, the CEO of a large retail electronics chain, a candidate for a prestigious college football coaching job, and the head of a non-profit organization in competition for a large infusion of resources, who lost the bid as a result. Sooner or later, there is a good possibility of getting caught in a lie.
Q:	I don't have lot of relevant experience for the types of positions I am seeking. How should I proceed?
A:	Spend some time examining the details of your present and past positions. This may help you find the accomplishments, as well as acquired skills, that others would find valuable. Show pride in your prior work and promote what you have learned and achieved. No position is unworthy of being listed if you can show that you learned something important from it.
Q:	I have large gaps in my employment history. What should I do?
A;	Gaps in resumes are common, for many reasons. The best thing to do is to be honest about the reasons. Employment gaps can be "filled" with alternative legitimate activities: education, changes in career aims, moves to new locations, job searching after a downsizing, and others.
Q:	Should I list every position that I have held?
A:	Not necessarily, but do make sure that your recent past has been accounted for. To help you decide whether to include a position, consider several factors. First, if the position is directly relevant to your candidacy, include it, even if it was below the professional level you aspire to. Second, use the available space to gauge whether to include a position. If you are starting out in a career, try to keep your resume to one page and limit the number of positions listed accordingly. With additional experience in a previous or current field, feel free to use several pages, but keep the issue of relevancy in mind.

Information: References Section

Current thinking among experts in this field is that references and resumes do not belong together, and that listing references or stating that they are "Available Upon Request" should be avoided. Instead, the development of a formal Reference Sheet to accompany a resume and cover letter is advised. (See Workshop 3 of this chapter for more on this topic.)

Q & A: Miscellaneous

Q: Should I list my hobbies?

A: Generally, employers are not interested in your hobbies. You might mention them in an interview, given the opportunity, but leave them off the resume.

Q: I speak another language; should this be on the resume?

A: Absolutely. In our current global business environment, speaking another language is definitely an asset. You can list the additional language in a Skills section. If you are not using this section, mention the language in your cover letter.

Q: Wouldn't it be easier to have someone else write my resume for me?

A: It might be easier in the short run, but taking the time and making the effort to write your own resume will serve you well over a lifetime. As you move forward in your career, you should be making adjustments to your resume and allowing it to reflect your current status and future direction. Opportunities sometimes come unexpectedly and a good current resume will help you respond effectively.

Application: Your Completed Resume

As stated earlier in the chapter, there is no one way to create a resume. In fact, show the work you do on your resume to as many people as possible to make it as effective as possible. The version or versions that you ultimately settle on may then bear little resemblance to your starting version. The result will, however, be closer to the ideal if you build it on a solid foundation. In this exercise, you will have a chance to pull together the individual lessons for the resume sections and fashion a working document that you can continue to refine.

Using a word processor, create a resume from the information you have sketched out on paper. Make sure to include your demographic information, career objective, education, relevant coursework, and experience. While it is tempting to use a "Resume Wizard" found in most word processing programs, experts advise against using these tools for three reasons: (a) the results are difficult to alter when adjustments are necessary, (b) the step-by-step nature of them does not allow for personalization, and (c) the formatting does not hold when copying and pasting them into a Website.

The Uses of Portfolios

In addition to developing a resume that effectively presents your education, skills, achievements, and goals, consider the possibility of assembling your work and the evidence of your achievements in a portfolio. In most situations, the portfolio would offer supporting documentation for the summary and self-presentation of your resume and cover letter. In other cases – such as in certain specialized program areas related to emerging careers – a portfolio may be a *primary* mode of self-presentation to an employer, who is expecting to see samples of work and demonstrations of skills, rather than descriptions of completed work or projects.

The emerging field of game and simulation programming provides an example of a field that places primary emphasis on *electronic portfolios* as a vehicle for job seekers to demonstrate their skills and accomplishments. In this field, the portfolio allows job candidates to showcase their accomplishments, but more importantly to demonstrate abilities and skills that can be applied immediately to the positions they are applying for. The portfolio could serve a similar role in other design-oriented fields, including the field of Web Graphics Design, where employers are interested in seeing exactly what you can do for them if you are hired.

If you decide to create a portfolio, the artifacts to be included in the portfolio should be selected according to the specific skills the employer is seeking, and they should demonstrate your very best work. It is also important to research prospective employers to determine if they have a preferred format for receiving portfolios: Web-based, CD-DVD, or other. Creating a strong portfolio is an opportunity to set yourself apart from other applicants.

Workshop 2: Cover Letters

Information: The Basics

A cover letter is an often overlooked, yet extremely important, job search document whose task is to entice the employer to read your resume. The letter is your opportunity to show why you are an excellent match for the position you seek. To achieve this purpose, each cover letter should be personalized for a particular employer and position. To do this successfully, you need to analyze the advertisement or other job description to identify the skills and qualities being sought. The better your letter can show employers that you have the qualifications for the position, the more likely your resume will be read and you will be invited to interview.

A good cover letter, therefore, achieves the following:

- Tells an employer that you are a motivated person who knows what he is looking for.
- Gives a personalized, brief account of your qualifications and how they match the needs of the employer.
- Is visually effective – properly structured, formatted, organized, and free of spelling and grammar mistakes.
- Gets the employer to look at your resume.

A poorly constructed cover letter will get you immediately eliminated from consideration.

The following are the general cover letter specifications and principles:

- Three or four paragraphs on one 8½x11" sheet of white paper.
- Word processed using the same Times New Roman or Arial font as in the resume, and printed on a quality machine.
- In most cases, written in three paragraphs: (a) an opening paragraph that identifies the position you are applying for and suggests that you are a strong candidate for it; (b) a second paragraph showing how you match up with the needs of the employer and position; (c) a concluding paragraph that thanks the employer for considering you, reaffirms your strong interest in the position, and promotes further action such as a call or a visit.

- Structured in one of the common formats for business letters. (See the examples later in this chapter.)
- If possible, is addressed to the person doing the hiring, rather than "To Whom It May Concern" or "Dear Manager."
- Pays attention to whether qualifications are *required* or only *preferred*. If you lack a preferred degree or type of experience, you can stress other qualifications you bring to the position; if you lack a required element, your application is a non-starter in most cases.

Evaluation: Cover Letter

What improvements can you suggest for this student's cover letter?

Your suggestions:

1. _____
2. _____
3. _____

92334 Great Bear Road
North Umberton, CA 92456
Feb 3, 20XX

Attn: Hiring person

Hello:

I was really impressed by the salary range you are offering for this job, I do really appreciate

if you will consider me for the job by reviewing my resume. I hope that this will be the

starting of a good relationship and the beginning of a long and healthy career with your

company. I have a good background in dealing with people and I have been working in an IT

Department of Sheraton Hotels for the last two years. If you need more information about my

resume, I would be happy to facilitate that to you, Please consider me because I will not let

you down.

$$\text{Have a great day!}$$

$$\text{Bryan Wilkerson , Jr.}$$

Now check the following list of suggested improvements.

1. "Hello" is not a good opening. Do your best to identify the lead person in the hiring process for this position and address your letter to her. Some methods you might use include calling the company or checking its Website for information. If your best efforts are unproductive, use a generic phrase such as "Dear Hiring Manager" or "Dear IT Department Manager."
2. This cover letter does not have a focused opening paragraph. It does not clearly identify the position the writer is applying for and why he is a good candidate for that position.
3. Does not adequately market the skills of the applicant or recognize the needs of the position.
4. Lacks a concluding paragraph restating interest in the position and stimulating follow up.

Application: Sample Cover Letter

While there are many ways to construct a cover letter, the following style is suggested for its simplicity: all sections begin at the left margin, with no indentations. The blanks in this sample represent relevant information that you can provide as you construct your own letter.

Your Name
Your Street
Your Town, State Zip Code

Month Day, Year

Name of Person Hiring
Title
Company Name
Street
Company Town, State Zip Code

Dear _____ :

Please accept this letter and attached resume as an application for the _____ position advertised in last Sunday's Tribune. I believe I am well qualified for the position and would welcome a chance to explore it further with you.

Among my qualifications are the following:

- _____ degree in _____ from Arizona Northern University
- Over five years of experience in the _____ field
- Documented success in managing IT projects
- Strong teamwork and leadership skills

In my current position as _____ at _____ , I have earned recognition for successful management of _____ and _____ by applying my strong troubleshooting skills, solid leadership, and creativity.

I would appreciate the opportunity to show how my capabilities and talents could benefit (company name) . Thank you for reviewing my credentials. If I can provide any additional information, please contact me at (___)___-____. I am looking forward to hearing from you soon.

Sincerely,

(Your Name)

Q:	Is it really necessary to send a cover letter?
A:	Yes, always. If you just send a resume with no letter in response to an ad, how will the potential employer know what position you are applying for? Additionally, this is your opportunity to market yourself. If you do not include a cover letter, you will be reducing your chances of being selected for an interview.
Q:	Can I hand-write a cover letter to help me stand out?
A:	Nice try, but, no. A handwritten cover letter will help you stand out in a *negative* way. It is not an accepted practice and would be seen as unprofessional.

Workshop 3: Reference Sheets

Information: The Basics

A good reference sheet can supplement and support your application in the following ways:

- It provides the names and contact information of three to five people who can verify the claims you made in your resume and cover letter. These are people who not only know you and your accomplishments, but have attained positions of authority and respect themselves.
- References can be particularly effective in supporting your claims to leadership, creativity, or other intangibles. They can offer their judgments and cite examples they have observed.
- The reference sheet must be properly structured, well organized, and free of spelling and grammar errors.

A poorly constructed reference sheet providing names of people who cannot effectively support your candidacy will diminish your chances. Use the following specifications to assemble your reference sheet.

1. Use only professional references relating to your prior work experience or education. Friends and family will earn less credibility because of the assumption of personal bias.
2. Make sure that you include only people who agree to serve as references for you, and that they are aware you are looking for a new position.
3. Perform extra checks to ensure you have listed valid contact information. If a reference has moved from the location where you knew her, say "Former supervisor at …" or "Former professor at…" beneath her title.
4. Keep your references up to date on your job search activities so that they can weigh in appropriately when the time comes for them to vouch for you.
5. Design the reference sheet to have the same look and feel as your resume and cover letter. Keep font size and style consistent among all three of these documents. Print all three on the same type of professional paper.
6. List references in a preferred order for their being contacted. Employers may contact only the first few.

Evaluation: Reference Sheet

What improvements can you suggest for this student's reference sheet?

Your suggestions:

1. _____
2. _____
3. _____

Steven Jenkins
Present Address   **Permanent Address**
820 Jefferson Ave   P.O. Box 11110
Canton, Wa 93333   Canton, WA 98333
(233) 433-1250   (530) 824-9822

References:
1.   Professor Mary Cranewell
     Career Development Department
     Briartown College
     Riverton, WA 92351
     (325) 997-8823
     Professor Cranewell was my career development teacher in how to search for
     the ideal job.

2.   Professor William Bendix
     Senior Project Department
     Briartown University
     Riverton, WA 92351
     (325) 997-8823
      Professor Bendix is showing me how find problems and offer solutions.

3.   Anna Dupont
     Human Recourses Department
     14313 east
     Johnson, WA, 92432
     (2230 955-3100
     Emily has shown me the complications that are in the industry of management
     and how to resolve them

How closely do your suggestions match up with the following list?

1. It is not necessary to list addresses on a reference sheet (a phone number or e-mail address will do). If you *do* list addresses, make sure they are consistent in format and information. The addresses in this example show various format inconsistencies and spelling errors.
2. There is no need to number the references.
3. Where does Anna Dupont work? What is her title, phone number, and the rest of her address? (And what is a Human Recourses Department?)
4. It is not necessary to provide comments along with your references. If you do, they must be professionally oriented, coherent, and offer useful information.

Application: Reference Sheets

Create your own reference sheet in the area provided below.

References for _____ (insert your name**)**

_____ (insert reference's name)
_____ (insert title)
_____ (insert company or school name)
_____ (insert city, state)
_____ (insert phone number)
_____ (insert e-mail address)

_____ (insert reference's name)
_____ (insert title)
_____ (insert company or school name)
_____ (insert city, state)
_____ (insert phone number)
_____ (insert e-mail address)

_____ (insert reference's name)
_____ (insert title)
_____ (insert company or school name)
_____ (insert city, state)
_____ (insert phone number)
_____ (insert e-mail address)

Q & A: The Reference Sheet

Q: When should I give my reference sheet to a potential employer?

A: Be prepared to present your reference sheet whenever it is requested. Generally, it is good practice to include this document in your application along with the cover letter and resume. A strong list of references can add positive weight to your initial impression.

Q: Can I use personal references on a reference sheet? I have lots of cousins and many good friends who can vouch for my character.

A: While it is a positive indicator that people in your personal life are willing to tell others of your fine qualities, you should select references from only those who have seen you in an academic or work environment. Potential employers are expecting you to provide names of supervisors, mentors, co-workers, professors, or academic administrators who can attest to your abilities, knowledge base, and work habits directly. Their comments gain added credibility, because they have seen you in action.

Chapter Exercise: Pulling It All Together

At this point, you should be ready to develop a complete set of job search documents that are targeted for a particular position. This may be an actual position you are pursuing in a real job search at the end of a degree program, or in mid-career. If these circumstances do not apply, use the scenario sketched out below to guide your development activities.

Scenario: You have just learned that your spouse has received a promotion at his/her job. The only problem is that this promotion will force you to move to _____ *(Choose a state or province other than your current place of residence)*. Fortunately, you have just graduated from Evergreen State University with a _____ degree in _____*(Major)*. After you move to your new residence, you would like to put your education and other experience to work by entering the _____ career field in an entry-level position as _____ *(Job)*.

Using your actual circumstances or the parameters identified in the scenario:

1. Locate a specific job lead that interests you through searching career development and Internet resources.
2. Create a targeted cover letter that spells out your interest in the identified position.
3. Create a polished resume that effectively presents your qualifications for the job you have identified.
4. Create a professional looking reference sheet, listing people who can speak to your attributes and qualifications.

Submit these materials for review and commentary to instructors, classmates, co-workers, mentors, and other possible advisors. Use this feedback to enhance and improve your materials.

CHAPTER SEVEN
Executing a Personal Marketing Plan
Linda Dobbs Willis

Plan your work for today and every day; then work your plan.

–Norman Vincent Peale

If you have taken the advice in this book to heart, you have already accomplished quite a lot. You have considered the idea and the need for marketing yourself. You have incorporated habits and practices into your life that will promote personal and career success. You have formulated strategies for improving your communication skills. You have researched the career paths, industries, and companies available to you. You have produced a resume, cover letters, references, and perhaps a portfolio. Now, all these elements should come together as you plan your individual job search.

This chapter will help you conduct a personal self-marketing campaign. This will involve getting organized and keeping good records, developing a marketing strategy, networking, creating additional job search tools, and using the telephone effectively. The ability to successfully direct your own job search – in other words, to implement a personal marketing plan – will give you the confidence that you are in control of your own destiny as a professional.

Getting Organized

Start by setting up a designated area in your home or apartment from which to conduct your job search – this is probably your office or study area. If possible, use an area that you can close off so that you have absolute silence when speaking to prospective employers on the phone. Otherwise, just about any space where you can set up a working area will do, since you will probably be able to access your phone anywhere.

Tools you will need include:

- An electronic or hard-copy calendar
- Copies of your resume
- Self-presentation statements: an "elevator pitch" and 30-second and 60-second "commercials" for yourself
- Your portfolio
- An address book (electronic or hard copy)
- A computer with Internet access, if possible. (If this is not available in your home, use a computer at school or at the local public library.)

You will need a good calendar or planner for tracking interviews, networking events, career fairs, follow-up activities, and other events and appointments. It is very important that you set up a process that will help you keep up with each component of your plan. The last thing you would want to happen, for example, is to show up late for an interview, or worse, to miss one! It is just as important that you follow through on all promised activities.

Keep your address book handy for contacting potential references and for staying in touch with all your contacts as you advance through the job search. If at any time you encounter a lull in activities, check your address book to see whom else you might call. If you have not already done so, sit down and make a list of at least 100 people you know for use in your networking activities. Consult the list you use for sending out holiday cards. If you are young, you may want to get contact information for relatives and family friends from your parents. Whatever your age, consider who among your friends and family members is good at keeping track of people – such a person can be a valuable resource to you at this stage.

Once your contact information is set up, spend some time planning your activities. Decide how many hours a week you can devote to your job search and which specific hours you will be using. If you are working and/or going to school, plan to spend at least 20 hours a week in your job search. If you are not in school or working, make finding your next job *a full-time job*. Make this strategy explicit by spending at least 40 hours a week conducting your search.

Once your active job search is underway, you will be more than busy. Your activities will include the following, and more:

- Looking for job postings that fit your criteria
- Networking with your contacts
- Researching companies and salaries
- Setting up informational interviews and job interview appointments
- Preparing for interviews
- Following up after interviews
- Participating in user group and professional association meetings
- Staying in touch with the staffing agencies you have decided to work with.

If these activities do not lead to a successful outcome, you may want to revisit parts of this list, or repeat the entire cycle. In either case, you will have plenty of activities to keep you busy.

Developing a Marketing Strategy

Keep a list of your skills and your strengths and weaknesses handy, as suggested in Chapter Three. This will help you stay on track in looking for the kinds of jobs that provide a good fit for you. The list will also give you a pool of descriptors – key words or phrases to use in presenting yourself in various settings. These terms will also help you complete various documents, including job applications.

Revisit the priorities you established for yourself so that you stay focused on the kinds of jobs, companies, and industries you want to explore. Among such considerations, the following may help you chart the right path:

- Do I prefer a small or large company?
- An established company or a new venture?
- What kind of industry do I want to work in?
- What kind of work environment do I prefer?
- What kind of work do I want to do?

- Will the work be structured in a regular 8-hour day, or will I be on call or work overtime?
- What is the potential for growth in this position and at this company?
- What is the company culture like?
- What benefits are offered, and how do these meet my personal and family needs?

Based on a consideration of factors such as the above, develop a list of at least 20 companies that seem like good matches to your interests, preferences, and needs. If possible, include companies that have recently hired graduates of your institution. These companies may be favorably disposed to other such graduates. They may also be good matches for you, particularly in the kinds of work and work environments you prefer.

If you are interested in a particular kind of industry – music or education or hospitals or software consulting, for example – focus your search on companies in that field. Then look for a good fit according to other features and preferences. However, if you have no industry preference, you may want to look at a broader spectrum of companies and evaluate these according to the features that do matter to you. Use your research and networking skills to find the companies that match your preferences and needs.

You may want to dedicate certain days of the week for certain activities, or you may devote some time each day to a variety of tasks. Ultimately, you will probably find yourself doing a little of both. Just be sure that you are using every tool available to find the job that will be the perfect match for you!

Networking

While the next chapter – on launching an active job search – will give you a more in-depth perspective on networking, it is important to lay the groundwork here for use of this important job-search tool. Because networking is an activity that often bears fruit later, you need to plan for and begin to cast as many of these "nets" as possible now.

Now is the time to become active in user groups and professional associations. Such groups typically have at least a monthly function, and a specific part of these gatherings is often set aside for networking among the attendees. Get these meetings on your calendar and be prepared to take an active part in them.

A good way to become more active at professional meetings, trade shows, and industry conferences is to approach some of the speakers or presenters. You might see if you can meet with a particular speaker before or after her talk to ask questions or simply to visit with her informally. Such contacts help establish relationships and may lead to discovering the one person or piece of information that will yield the job you seek.

You should also go to the Happy Hours and other after-hours events, along with the more formal sessions and panel discussions. These informal contacts will broaden your knowledge base, and they can be a lot of fun. By the same token, going to some of the free vendor presentations and seminars will provide information and a chance to meet additional people and possibly form new relationships.

Apart from scheduled events, if you find that you have the time, call up someone you haven't seen in a while and invite him to breakfast or lunch, or just for a cup of coffee. This will be a gesture of friendship and an opportunity to renew ties. In the process, you may harvest a job lead or learn of another contact you might approach.

If you are a graduate, or perhaps only nearing graduation, get involved with your local alumni association. Fellow alums are people who share an important challenge and a major set of accomplishments with you. As graduates of the same institution, they are often eager to recommend their peers since they know something about the quality of your education. Many alumni groups also maintain active job boards or other career-related services.

You can also follow up with the Career Services office of your institution and take advantage of the career and job-prospecting services they offer. Though these offices work primarily with current and soon-to-be graduates, some also provide information, contacts, and services that can help alumni enhance their careers. If you are a graduate-to-be, the Career Services office should be your primary point of assistance for planning and managing your job search. Visit this office often and stay in contact.

Creating Job Search Tools

As suggested in prior chapters, your job search will require development and use of an effective resume, likely in a number of versions appropriate to the situation. You may also want to assemble a portfolio, in both hard copy and electronic formats. In some of the current fields, such as the game and simulation industry, several demos of design projects are commonly expected to be included in a portfolio.

Additional tools that can increase your chances during a job search include thoughtfully designed and readily available versions of the following:

- A business card
- An "elevator pitch" – that is, a short self-presentation suitable for a very limited time frame
- 30- and 60-second "commercials" presenting your strengths and skills in slightly longer time periods.

These are tools of opportunity. They are meant to take advantage of a limited opportunity to make a strong enough impression that can lead to more extensive follow-up. Because employers and other contacts in the working world lead busy, crowded lives, these brief encounters can lead to significant opportunities for those who make a good initial impression.

Your Business Card

In some ways, this is the most effective networking tool you can have. If you are already employed and have a company business card that effectively represents the skill set you wish to market, you can, of course, use that. If you are seeking a career entry position or a career change, you will do well to create your own personal business card. Use it when you make new contacts as a tangible reminder of yourself. It will also help the other person reach you later should she hear of something that might interest you. Employers may also be favorably impressed by your well-designed personal business card.

Business Card Design

There are many appropriate designs and formats for a business card – just be sure to keep your design professional and conservative. Any artwork you use should reflect the industry you are in. A great source of templates and an economical source for cards is www.vistaprint.com. You may want to visit this site to see what they offer. Microsoft also has business card templates available at www.microsoft.com.

You can also design your card using a Word template and have your cards printed at a local office supply outlet. Alternatively, you can design your cards and print them yourself on card stock from an office supply store; however, cards made this way will not be as sturdy as those you get professionally printed.

To use a Word template for business cards, follow these simple links: Tools » Letters and Mailings » Envelopes and Labels » Options. Scroll through the options until you find a Business Card. Click OK. Enter your text and then click New Document, and you will see a full page version of your business card.

Put your name and contact information on the card. Be sure the print is large enough to be read easily (usually no smaller than 12-point type), and use a font that is easy to read (such as the Times New Roman font used in this text). For security reasons, fewer people are giving their address on cards now. You will need to be the judge of that.

In addition to contact information, indicate your skill set and/or relevant experience. You may also want to list your degree if you are a recent college graduate. Just be careful not to use the logo of your college or university without proper authorization. In fact, the best policy is just to avoid school logos since they do not really "belong" to you. They may also create the impression that you worked for the institution rather than studied there.

Sample Business Cards

After reviewing the template and examples below, *create your own business card.* Place an initial order (or have yours printed locally) and test your cards in the marketplace. As you hand out your card, observe the reactions of your contacts. You may decide revisions are needed – or that the card is working very well for you.

Here is a simple business card template:

Name
Phone number
Email address

Concise skill list
Relevant experience
Degree name (optional)

Here are some examples to consider:

Randall Wachtelinger
277-461-8820
rwachtel@hotmail.com

7 years experience in Public Switching Telephone Networks
5 years experience in Audio and PC Networks
Skilled in CCNA 1-4, WAN/LAN
Home audio installation
PC installation and upgrade

Nate Morgan
B.S. Biomedical Engineering Technology
B.A. Biology

8068 Riverside Parkway
Statetown, New York 20649
976-888-6070
nmorgan@hotmail.com

> **Wanda Garcia-Chan**
> 888-766-9999
> wgarciachan@yahoo.com
>
>
> 5 years customer service experience
> 8 years project management
> C++, Java programming

Your Elevator Pitch

The term "elevator pitch" relates to the need for a brief but significant comment about yourself that you might use in the time it takes to travel a couple of floors in an elevator. This is your professional self-introduction in the typically rushed environment of the present-day working world. Use it when you meet someone in passing in a business setting. Have it ready also for networking events, career expos, job fairs, and similar occasions. Remember that the elevator is moving, so make your pitch in a sentence or two – no more.

Consider the following examples, and then write your own statement. To make your pitch comfortable for you, start using it when you meet someone new. Use it also when you introduce yourself at job fairs, career expos, professional society meetings, and networking events.

> Hello, I am ……………… I have 20 years of customer service experience and a degree in business administration, with a major in accounting. I am also proficient with the Microsoft Office suite.

> Hi, there. My name is……………..…..and I specialize in servicing and maintaining AT&T wireless equipment.

> Hello, I'm ……………I'm a customer service specialist supporting various credit card portfolios. I'm passionate about quality customer service.

> I'm …………… and I am a senior reporting analyst at a network operations center specializing in developing a trending database and troubleshooting network-based problems.

> Hello, I'm…………....., a senior at Whitewater State University pursuing my bachelor's degree in Business Administration and majoring in business information systems.
>
> Hello, I'm……………I am a senior at Kennesaw College studying Network and Communications Management. I specialize in configuring and maintaining Ethernet networks.
>
> Hello, my name is……….…..I will earn my bachelor's degree in Computer Engineering from Talleyrand Technical University in May. I specialize in hardware interfacing and software troubleshooting.

Try practicing your elevator pitch with friends or colleagues, and do it while shaking hands. You can use their comments and suggestions to improve the content and delivery of your presentation.

Your Commercials: 30- and 60-Second Spots

If you are in a job-seeking mode at a networking event or job fair, or in a job interview, you will want to roll out a "commercial" for yourself, one that goes beyond the elevator pitch but still observes the principles of concise delivery of important information in a limited time. Just as TV commercials are aimed at capturing and holding the viewer's attention in a concentrated time frame, you should be able to tell your story in a convincing way in 30 to 60 seconds.

You may find that you use the 60-second version more often because it best tells your story of skills, experience, and qualifications for a job. The shorter version is useful when you are on the phone with a prospective employer and you want to tell him something about your qualifications but are still pressing for a personal interview. In any setting, the elevator pitch is an introduction followed, as the conversation develops, by your commercial.

At this point, you may be wondering how to go about inserting a commercial into a conversation. Part of the answer is to be a careful listener, because the commercial is actually your effective answer to the familiar request: "Tell me a little about yourself."

This is a question that makes job-seekers of any age squirm. Studies show that 70% of the people asked this question in job interviews fail to give a satisfactory answer. Because of the pressure of the job interview, many applicants get sidetracked by the issues of "What do I say?" "What should I not say?" and "What do they want to hear?" The *worst* answer to this question – one that interviewers hear all too often – is, "Well, what would you like to hear?"

The *best* answer, especially in an interview, is your well-planned and well-delivered commercial. Given the opportunity, use the 60-second version to present a fuller picture of yourself. The 30-second spot will need to focus more on the specific skills sought by a particular employer. Meanwhile, the 60-second commercial can actually be anywhere from 60 to 75 seconds. A shorter version probably doesn't tell enough. A longer statement may make the interviewer wonder when you are going to stop!

Your 60-Second Commercial

A good approach to creating your 60-second commercial is to revisit a list of what employers are looking for in employees (see page 9, for example). Match these qualities to ones that you possess.

Here's a pretty representative list. Employers look for people who are:

- Good communicators
- Trustworthy
- Energetic
- Positive in their attitude
- Flexible
- Good team players
- Dependable
- Confident
- Competent
- Competitive
- Open-minded
- Goal-oriented
- Leaders
- Customer oriented.

Among the top characteristics sought by employers you will usually find the first three above, but any of these, if presented convincingly, will gain an employer's interest. Notice also that employers' leading preferences are for both team players and leaders. This is not a contradiction, since all of us might need to fill both roles at different times.

To fashion your commercial, select your three greatest strengths to focus on. Then add brief examples to illustrate or "prove" your strengths. For instance, if you say you have strong leadership skills, offer an example of when you successfully led a group. After you present your leading strengths and "prove" them, describe your skills and abilities. Emphasize skills that meet the needs of the job you are interviewing for.

Your answer to the invitation, "Tell me a little about yourself" in an interview is really a sales message. You are now your own agent selling your services to an employer. Spend a little time thinking about what to say in that commercial. The right words – that also truthfully reflect who you are – can really make you sparkle! The wrong words – those that evoke negative emotions – can detract from the impression you are making. These are words to banish from your commercial.

Once you have created your 60-second commercial, it will need little revision. Who you are doesn't change much through the years. The part that you will want to tailor to a specific job is your list of skills. Make sure to emphasize the skills that match the job. You may also want to rearrange the order in which you present your skills, to bring up those most valued in a particular job first.

Here are some words that can add energy and credibility to your presentation.

"Success" Words and Phrases
Dedicated
Positive; positive attitude
Make things happen
People person; work well with people
Organized
Leader
Team player
Enjoy challenges
Communicate effectively
Organized
Self-confident
Responsible; take responsibility
Initiative
High energy level
Goal oriented; goal setter
Flexible, adaptable

Here are words that can suck the credibility from an otherwise effective response in an interview or other conversation with a prospective employer.

Negative Words and Phrases
Just: "I just helped out on the project."
A little: "I have a little experience in that."
Only: "I only worked there three months."
Try: "I'll try to get it done by next week."
Haven't yet: "I haven't screwed up yet."
Probably: "We'll probably finish on time."
Maybe: "Maybe I can do it."
I guess: "I guess that's causing the problem."
I think: "I think I can."
Whatever: "Whatever the reason, that approach didn't work." "Oh, whatever!"
Hardly: "I was hardly ever reprimanded."
"I achieved *almost* every goal set by my supervisor."
"*No*, that's *not* the point!"
"I *can't* understand why he wants to do that."
"We *didn't* get enough time/support/money to complete the project on time, and we *didn't* think it mattered anyway, so we *didn't* tell the boss the project would be delayed, but she *didn't* have to fire us just for that!"

One other point to keep in mind when creating a commercial: don't include any information an employer can't legally ask you about. This means that you will not mention your age or marital status or whether you have a family or a disability. These conditions are required by statute to be excluded from consideration for employment in the interest of fairness to all applicants.

Here is an example of a 60-second commercial by a person who has gained professional experience in the military and technical skills through education. Would you agree that this person seems believable as someone who values hard work and demonstrates a willingness to take on challenges? Note the highlighted words in this presentation.

> I am a *hard-working, dedicated professional*, and in the past my supervisors and peers have recognized these qualities in my work. While I was in the service, my commanding officer recognized my *hard work* and *dedication* to *duty*, my *leadership*, and my *contributions to our unit* by awarding me the Army Commendation Medal. Also, pursuing my degree in computer information systems at Fisk University has required a great deal of *sacrifice* and *hard work* to complete in three years while maintaining a GPA of 3.75.

> I am *supportive* of my peers and supervisors. I *thrive* in dynamic environments that require *flexibility* and *teamwork* to *accomplish* the tasks assigned to me. I pride myself in being able to find *creative solutions* to difficult problems. My *technical strengths* include coding in C/C++ and Visual Basic, and I have *good written communication skills*. I believe I can apply these abilities to make an *immediate contribution* to this company.

Here is another effective commercial. Notice how this person makes the most of his management and leadership experience.

> I have *successfully led* purchasing department *professionals* for over ten years in upper *management* positions. In addition to setting *goals* for my departments, I *oversaw* inventory control and *contributed* to the company's *profitability* in these areas. I am very *organized, detail-oriented,* and effective as a *multi-tasker*. In addition, I have developed strong *problem solving* skills and good *communication skills*.

> My knowledge of *managing* inventories and purchasing should help in *building* a strong *team* to provide great *customer relations*. I believe that my *organizational* and *people skills* would help support sales and profitability *goals* and provide *strong leadership* to this department.

Here is a good example for a candidate with a strong work background who wants to explore a career shift from software design and project management into an upper-management position.

> I have 15 years experience in software design and deployment and 10 years experience in software project management and customer support integration. I have maintained hardware and software through technically

advanced implementations for 52 company locations across six states in the Southeast. My duties included reporting on call center operations to senior management through a variety of structured reports. I also developed and maintained diagnostic utilities for automating application support. All of these tasks included management of high-visibility customer relationships.

My recent completion of a bachelor's degree in business administration, coupled with my years of problem-solving and supervisory experience, make me a strong candidate for your regional manager position.

Here is a commercial from someone who has worked in office support and is now seeking advancement into a supervisory position.

I have worked for four years in progressively responsible positions in large office environments for both government and private employers. My background is focused on office support functions including record keeping and customer service. I am very accurate, highly detail-oriented, and have excellent computer skills including proficiency in Microsoft Word, Excel, and several relational databases.

I'm very organized and able to set and beat deadlines for myself and others. During the completion of my recent bachelor's degree in human resources administration, I also gained valuable experience in team projects and project management techniques. These experiences, along with my strong communication and people skills, will make me an effective leader of the Engineering Support department.

Now take a look at several examples that need more detail and more specific skills description. Notice also how these candidates have weakened their responses by including inappropriate information and negative language. These weak areas are highlighted for emphasis.

I have been employed at *various* companies for the past *few years* working in *different positions* with diverse groups. I have gained valuable experience in teamwork, communications, multitasking, and conflict resolution between external and internal customers. This experience has taught me the value of working under rigid quality guidelines; however, I believe that since I am *49 years old*, my maturity should allow me more opportunity to work on my own and make my own decisions. I think I'm capable of handling *most* situations and don't need a boss *hanging over me* all the time. For example, I set up a local area network for one of my previous employers while I was *recovering from an auto accident that was really the other driver's fault.* I think my *fairly* stable work history, combined with my management and technical skills, can make me an asset to your company with *very little* additional training and orientation.

Here is the second flawed example. Notice the negative language and the inappropriate personal information this candidate includes. Knocking a past or current employer is also likely to raise a red flag.

> During my tenure with my current employer, I worked over 80 hours a week for 5 weeks in order to complete a contract job on time. I accomplished these duties while still assisting *my wife with our three kids' home schooling and music lessons.* I was promoted to team lead within two months. My real passion is *to become a successful small business owner.* I am intrigued by the idea that I could work for you and develop skills that will help me *open my own business* in the near future. I look forward to helping you strengthen your operating procedures. I just hope you will work with me in turn, since math and accounting *have never been* my strong points. I am a fast learner though, especially when I have a *decent teacher.* I certainly hope my next boss can do a *better job of teaching me* the ropes than my current one.

Consider a final example. Here the applicant designs a fairly positive message, but then undercuts it with negative or inappropriate information and language.

> I have a bachelor's degree in business with a specialization in project management and network administration. I am a very reliable worker with a solid record of completing projects with high quality and on time. Being single gives me the opportunity to help out beyond regular hours. For example, in my last job we faced a project deadline when a few key people didn't show up. I was able to stay and work all night. Another strength I have is my energy, which comes naturally to someone who is only 25 years old. I am also dedicated. I can almost always get the job done right the first time. I will be counting on you to teach me anything else I need to know.

How would you rewrite these less-than-ideal commercials?

Your instructor may now ask you to write your own 60-second commercial and then practice delivering it to other students in the class. Their suggestions can help you strengthen the contents and delivery, as can hearing their examples.

Your 30-Second Commercial
This shorter self-presentation will suit your needs during a telephone interview, particularly when you are really trying to land an in-person interview. The 30-second spot will also suit your needs as an initial introduction at a networking event, a career expo, or a job fair. In this briefer version, as suggested earlier, you should focus mainly on the skills that fit the employer's needs.

Here are two good examples:

> I am a senior at Marcuse University, and I will graduate in May with my bachelor's degree in Biomedical Engineering Technology. I also have an

associate degree in biology, and I believe my skills in medical imaging, bioinformatics, and programming, along with my understanding of the human body, can be real assets to your company.

I recently obtained my degree in business administration from Rochelle Business College. Prior to that, I held management positions for over ten years. During this time, I managed inventories and dealt with vendors; set and met sales and profitability goals; and managed inventory, purchasing, and profit analysis. In addition, I have strong problem solving abilities and excellent communication skills that will add to the effectiveness of your department.

Once you have written your commercials, make them into conversational statements. Practice your response in front of a mirror or with someone who knows you well, to get her reaction and advice. Just be sure that you can deliver your commercials with energy and conviction – and without notes!

Let's take a look at some sample 30-second commercials from our three job-market candidates – Mark, Margaret, and Al. How would you advise each of them to improve their spots?

Mark Staples:
I will earn a Bachelor of Science degree in Business Administration in two months. In pursuing this degree, I improved my understanding of business processes and methods, and polished my skills in accounting, finance, and marketing. I'm also good at working with people. In addition, I am skilled at using spreadsheets and managing databases. I can make effective professional presentations, and I function well in groups.

Margaret Engler:
I will gain my Bachelor of Science degree in Technical Management in September. In addition to my new degree, I have four years experience as a legal assistant, with strong skills in office management and legal documentation and research. I have used MS Office extensively and developed strong project management abilities as part of my education. I am especially good with work requiring attention to detail. I believe I would prove an efficient addition to your company.

Al Barbaro:
I will obtain my Bachelor of Science degree in electronics engineering technology in September. As part of this degree program, I spent many hours in hands-on applications involving current technologies including analog and digital systems, hardware and software interface, and use of appropriate test equipment. In addition, I will bring to your company a 25-year track record as an effective supervisor and reliable employee in the manufacturing sector.

Using the Telephone Effectively

Of course, you can also deliver your elevator pitch, 30-second spot, and even your 60-secomd commercial *on the telephone*. The phone will be one of the most useful tools in your job search. It offers an effective means of communication and saves you time. Remember that time is one of the most precious resources you have, especially because it's in limited supply.

When you are on the phone with a prospective employer, pay attention to your wording, vocal inflection, and volume. Because you do not have the added dimensions of gestures or facial expression, your choice of words and the way you deliver them are your only means of communication. To make your points, you need to be clear and concise and to identify yourself and your purpose to the listener.

Most of the time, your purpose is to get an interview. Keep pressing, gently, for that goal. It will help also not to give out too much information. While you should effectively answer any questions, keep your answers brief. Add an offer to meet with the employer: "I would welcome an opportunity to sit down and talk to you. Would you have 30 minutes sometime next week?" "I'm glad to know you are interested in my skills and experience. I would be happy to come in for a visit to give you a better idea of who I am and how I could contribute to your company."

Making Calls

Before you place a call to a prospective employer, make sure your environment is completely quiet. In receiving calls, the same thing is important: you want to be able to shut off all devices and quiet anyone else in the room quickly. A better approach may simply be to go to a room where you can shut the door and talk in private. Plan for this ahead of time.

Before placing a call, think about what you will say if you get someone else, or someone's voice mail. Will you leave a message? If so, what will you say? It's a good idea to have some kind of "script" prepared for a voice mail message, for speaking to someone else, or actually getting the person you call (an increasingly rare event these days). Your script, or approximate plan for what you'll say, should include an opening phrase that helps the person receiving your call to at least categorize you.

Here are some practical suggestions for using the telephone in a job search campaign.

- Set up an environment that will give you absolute quiet when you call or receive a call from a prospective employer.
- Be careful to enunciate words fully and to pronounce them properly. Avoid words or expressions that are difficult for you. Never have anything in your mouth.
- Consider using a script or having key words or phrases posted in your phone area. These might include your list of skills, the name of your degree, and relevant experience.
- Use the name of the person you are speaking to.
- Be courteous and professional. Say "yes" and "no," not "yep," "uh-huh," or "nope."
- Smile while you talk – you will sound more pleasant.
- Try standing up – you will have more vocal energy.

Consider the following examples for various parts of the process.

Opening Examples

> "Hello, I'm Alicia Hendrick, and I'm a recent graduate of Markham University with a degree in marketing."

> "Hello, I'm Jackson Mafalda, a recent graduate of Talladega University, and I'm calling about your opening for an information technology specialist."

The very next thing you should do is to ask the respondent if this is a good time to talk, and let him know about how long the call would take. If he is busy or expecting to leave for a meeting shortly, he will only be thinking about how to get rid of you – instead of listening to what you say. Try the following segues:

> "Hello, I'm Julian Lasker, a recent graduate of Manhasset University in computer information systems. Do you have a moment to discuss the IT opening?"

> Or, alternately, "Is this a good time for you to discuss the IT opening?"

Scripting a Call

To help you develop a "script" for navigating through the various stages of a job-prospecting call, consider the following outline. This approach would be suitable for calls you make to the hiring manager, rather than to someone in a Human Resources department.

Opening:

Be sure you are speaking to the right person.

"Is this Mr./Ms. _____?"

"Are you the manager/head of the _____ department?"

Then: "I'm Rebecca Fullbright. I'll be graduating from Compton College in May with a bachelor's degree in business administration, concentrating in project management."

Be sure to enunciate your first and last name clearly. This is not as obvious, or easy, as it sounds – many people have trouble pronouncing their name so that others can catch it the first time. You may need to spell your name out.

Purpose:

Immediately state why you are calling – don't make the respondent guess.

"I am interested in a position as_____."

Avoid saying that you are calling in response to a job posting or ad, which is likely to get you transferred to the Human Resources department.

Instead, try to get the name of a hiring manager to whom you can send your resume. If you are, in fact, responding to a specific job posting, use the wording in the ad to guide your own choice of words:

"I am calling to see if you have any openings for people with the ability to configure and install LAN networks, along with good communication skills, customer service experience, and teamwork skills."

Sell Yourself:

Make a brief statement of your qualifications that speaks directly to what you know they are looking for and makes the recipient of your call want to talk to you further. Focus on how you can benefit her department or company. This could easily be your 30-second commercial, as long as you have tailored it for this specific position.

Express your skills in terms of action as much as possible, focusing on what you have done and what you have to offer. Be sure you can deliver your entire pitch in 30 seconds at a natural pace and without pausing; a pause can allow your listener to object. Because you are on the phone, you can refer to a script or a written version of your commercial. Do not *read* either of these, however; practice delivering them until you sound natural and fluent.

Remember Your Goal:

Your goal is to arrange a *meeting*, not an *interview*. A meeting is a more flexible concept that offers a chance for an introduction in a less structured format, with fewer specific demands on either the applicant or the employer. A good sales technique is to offer more than one meeting time: "Would next Tuesday be good for you, or would Thursday be better?"

Close:

In closing, if you have been successful, confirm names, dates, and places with an enthusiastic recap.

"Thank you for your time, Ms. Morrison, and I look forward to meeting with you next Tuesday morning at nine."

See Appendix A for a suggested worksheet you can use to create a call script for yourself.

Handling Objections

The more you work at using the phone effectively, the better your success rate will be. To increase your chances of success, be prepared to respond to objections or other barriers. The objections presented here are among the most frequently heard by recent graduates with little or no experience in their new discipline.

Objection: "S/he is not in."

> ***Possible Responses:***
>
> "Thank you. Do you know when Mr./Ms. Employer will be back in the office?"
>
> "Thank you. When might be a good time for me to reach Mr./Ms. Employer?"

Objection: "Why don't you just come to our HR office and fill out an application?"

> ***Possible Response:*** "I'd be happy to do that. If you have 20 minutes available on _____, I would be happy to come in, complete an application, and discuss it with you to answer any specific questions and show you how I might be an asset to your company."
>
> ***If the employer still declines a meeting:*** "I will be in to fill out the application on _____. I will also give you a call on _____ to answer any questions and see what you think."

Objection: "Just send in a resume."

> ***Possible Response:*** "I would be happy to do that. However, if you have 20 minutes available on _____, I would be happy to bring in my resume, discuss it with you, and explain why I believe I can be an asset to your company."
>
> ***If the employer still refuses a meeting:*** "I will put my resume in the mail (or attached to an e-mail) to you today. I will also give you a call on _____ to answer any questions and see what you think."

Objection: "We don't have any openings."

> ***Possible Response:*** "I would still appreciate a visit with you. If you expect to be hiring at any time in the near future, it would still be worthwhile for us to get together."

Objection: "I don't do the hiring."

> ***Possible Response:*** "Can you tell me who is responsible for hiring? Do you mind if I use your name when I contact him or her?"

Objection: "You'll have to talk to personnel."

Possible Response: "Since you work with/oversee (name the applications area), I'm sure you would be a better judge of my skills and experience."

If the respondent still refuses a meeting: "Can you tell me who is in charge of personnel? Do you mind if I use your name when I talk to him or her?"

Objection: "We only hire people with experience."

Possible Responses (new graduate with no work experience): "Yes, I have _____ credit hours/years of classroom experience with (name relevant skills)."

"I have classroom and team project experience with (name skills)."

"I have a great deal of hands-on lab experience from my education at _____"

Objection: "You must have on-the-job experience."

Possible Response: "As a part of my educational experience, I had to work independently, just as I would on a job. My college experience also required that I perform many of the same kinds of tasks and solve the same kinds of problems that I would in a paid position."

Also, if appropriate to the position, mention team projects you worked on or led.

Objection: "I'm really too busy to see you."

Possible Response: "I promise not to take more than 20 minutes of your time to show you how I can benefit your company."

Barrier: The employer still does not agree to a meeting.

Possible Response: "Thanks for taking the time to discuss your company's plans and priorities, Ms. _____. I learned some things that will be helpful in my search."

Using the Internet Effectively

As Chapter Five points out, the Internet can be a valuable resource for job search advice and for researching companies.

As a job seeker, you should be frequenting at least six job-posting Internet sites on a regular basis. You can visit a dozen or so of the many sites available, decide which ones fit your discipline and objectives best, and maintain an active presence in those. Also, you will notice that in addition to posting job openings, many of these Websites offer excellent career and job search advice. One of the best is Career Builder at www.careerbuilder.com. Clicking on the Advice Resources toolbar will give you these drop-down box options:

- Career Resources
- Career Fairs
- Job Seeker Toolkit
- Career Advice
- CB Bookstore
- Salary Calculator

Each of these Web pages will yield a wealth of information and advice from experts in the field, and you will find their guidance helpful and up-to-date.

Another excellent source of on-line job seeking and career advice is the Riley Guide at www.rileyguide.com. Topics here include:

- Resumes and Cover Letters
- Network, Interview and Negotiate
- Salary Guides and Guidance

Another great on-line resource is www.fortune.com, where you will find some of the most highly regarded business and financial news as well as links to the following:

- The Fortune 500
- The Global 500
- The Best Companies to Work for

Fortune.com is also an invaluable Website for advice on continued professional growth and development. It should certainly be in your career "toolbox."

In addition, check with your college or local public library for password-accessible databases that can provide additional information on companies. A particularly useful database of this kind is Hoovers North America (www.hoovers.com), where you can research industries, specific companies, their competitors, and even top company personnel.

Developing a Relationship with a Hiring Agency

In addition to the work you do with your college's Career Services department, you will definitely want to consider working with a hiring agency as well. (See Chapter Five on evaluating agencies and determining whether to use this additional resource.)

Keep in mind that many companies today only hire through agencies. Some of these agencies specialize in placing temporary workers, an option you should not overlook as well. Many temporary positions lead to full-time work at a company. Hiring you as a temp gives the company a chance to evaluate you with no risk, just as it gives you a chance to evaluate the company. If you are undecided about what you want to do, working several temporary positions at different companies will give you an opportunity to see what such jobs and companies would really be like. You will also be meeting new people and expanding your network. As a big plus, you will be drawing a paycheck while you make up your mind!

Another benefit of working with an agency is that many of them will keep you in their database. You may hear from them again about job possibilities months, even years, later. Though you may be happily employed by then, it's always nice to have additional options.

Staying Positive

Use every avenue available to you to obtain your first career position or to make a career change. Maintain a positive attitude toward this process. Believe in yourself. Be prepared to talk to anyone at any time. Stay with the process until you find the right position, where you have a chance to flourish and become the person you have been working so hard to become!

These are the strategies that can maximize your job search chances:

- Be organized.
- Manage your time effectively and meet deadlines.
- Stay in tune with changes in your career. You may need to add a skill or think about pursuing a new path.
- Keep your job search tools updated. You may want to use them for an unexpected opportunity.
- Network in the job search and beyond. Networking, like life, is all about creating relationships.
- Build a self-directed career – one that you control.

Chapter Exercises:

Assume the role of a Career Services advisor who is meeting, in turn, with Mark, Margaret, and Al to review their 60-second commercials. How would you advise each of them to improve their presentations?

Mark Staples:

As a recent high school graduate, I have a variety of work experience as a youth softball coach, camp counselor, and retail employee. I realized quickly that I needed a degree to advance in a career, so I began college and will soon have my Bachelor of Science degree in Business Administration. In addition to the skills developed as part of my degree program, I was able to work several months in a co-op position in the business office of a local auto parts store. I look forward to bringing my newly acquired skills and business experience with spreadsheets, databases, and office management tools to your company.

Margaret Engler:

I am a dedicated employee committed to developing a professional career. I'm very ethical and reliable. I have served for several years with the public school district and in community governance. I obtained a certificate in legal assisting to begin my career in a law office, where I established a strong record as a conscientious employee who can be counted on to get the job done with minimal supervision. I am eager to apply my bachelor's degree in technical management to working with a company such as yours that will benefit from my organizational and office management abilities. I am also skilled with MS Office and especially valuable when attention to detail is important.

Al Barbaro:

You will find me a very dependable employee. I have a 25-year track record in manufacturing, where I was involved in activities including reading blueprints, inspecting parts, and supervising other employees. I used this background as a stimulus to return to college for additional formal education to obtain a Bachelor of Science degree in electronics engineering technology, which I will complete in September. My highly practical education has given me new skills in working with analog and digital electronics, interfacing of hardware and software, and use of appropriate test equipment. I look forward to applying these skills to make a positive contribution to your company.

Follow-Up Activities

1. Set up an appointment for a practice interview with your career advisor or someone on your campus who has experience hiring people. If you are already employed, you may want to make this appointment with someone at your company. In advance, send a copy of your resume to this person and specify a position you want to "apply for."

2. Dress and prepare for this practice interview as you would for a real job interview. Use your elevator pitch to introduce yourself at the beginning of the interview and incorporate a version of your commercial into the interview. As part of your close, ask the interviewer for a business card, and offer her your card in turn.

3. Attend at least one on-campus and one off-campus job fair. Use your elevator pitch and commercials as you visit with various company representatives. Collect business cards and use them to follow up on the contact. Give them your card.

4. Attend a networking event. Practice your networking skills and using your elevator pitch and commercial. Exchange business cards.

5. Repeat these kinds of activities until you are comfortable with the techniques involved.

Appendix A
Worksheet for Developing a Call Script

1. Introduction: Identify yourself, and state what you do (your current job) or have recently done (your expected graduation or degree).

   _____
   _____
   _____

2. "I am interested in a position as...."

   _____
   _____
   _____

3. Describe your qualifications. Use your 30-second commercial targeted to this position and focusing on how you can benefit the company.

   _____
   _____
   _____
   _____

4. Your clincher: the key point about you (e.g., "I'm experienced in this area and also have a recent degree in .." "I'm technically strong and good with co-workers and customers."

   _____
   _____
   _____

5. Goal: "When could I come in for a meeting? Would _____ or _____ be better for you?"

   _____
   _____
   _____

If the call does not lead to an appointment, ask for referrals.

- "Do you know anyone else who might be looking for someone with my abilities?"

- "Do you know anyone else who might be looking for someone like me?"

- "Do you know anyone else who might benefit from my skills?"

CHAPTER EIGHT
Launching the Job Search
Kirsten Nicholas

Loving your job and career will go a long way to loving your life – so, take the time to find your career passion.

– Randall S. Hansen, Ph.D.

Chapter Goals:

This chapter is dedicated to helping you gather and apply the knowledge and tools needed to begin your successful job search. Searching for a job is more than a necessary evil you have to endure; it is a process that requires planning, dedication, and effort, but can also yield great rewards. So, where do you start? The first step is to accept the fact that searching for a full-time job … *is* a full-time job!

Investigation

Let's start at the beginning. Where do you go to look for jobs and job possibilities? Most people today would answer, "Start with the Internet." While the Internet is a great tool for job searching, it is not the place to start. To be successful in your job search, you might apply one of Steven Covey's Habits (see Chapter 2): "Start with the end in mind." In this case, consider the goal of your search. In the job search process, the goal can be visualized and detailed in your mind as *your dream job*.

Many students have a difficult time identifying that dream job. Those who do must also reckon with the reality that they will likely not move into that position at the beginning of their career. They will need to work their way up to reach it. Knowing how to find the right path to the ultimate position becomes part of their current challenge.

Knowing What You Want to Do

Deciding what you want to do for the rest of your life may seem like a daunting task. The rest of your life is a long time, we hope, and the question gains added weight from that perception. In fact, most people do not enter the job market and simultaneously launch a lifelong career. In the current economy, the norm is that people end up making several industry changes and many employer changes over the span of their careers.

Make use of this likelihood by shortening your perspective and thus easing some of the pressure. Ask yourself what you want to do for the next five years – in both your life and your career. Do you want to buy a house, get married, have kids, travel, move to Montana, and work in the biomedical engineering technology field? Knowing what you personally want to do can help lead you to an appropriate career path. Similarly, knowing what you are passionate about can help determine what job, field, or industry is appropriate for you.

Discovering Your Career Passions

Do you have a philanthropic interest, a passion you cannot avoid? If so, why not use that passion as a stimulus for your career? If not, what do you enjoy doing or what might make you feel satisfaction at the end of the day? Still too difficult? Try the opposite question: What do you hate doing? Often people know exactly what they don't want in a job but have a difficult time describing what they do want.

There are questions you can ask yourself to help you determine where your passions and interests lie. A helpful hint to knowing what types of questions to ask is to be as specific as possible. Below is a short list of questions that may help trigger some pointed responses to assist in the process of discovery.

- What do you enjoy doing?
- What do you love doing?
- What do you hate to do?
- What are your strongest skills?
- What skills come naturally to you?
- What have been your favorite classes and subjects?
- What occupations seem interesting?
- What subject areas do you enjoy reading about?
- What size company do you want to work for?
- What kind of a working environment would you prefer – formal or informal, relaxed or hard-charging?
- What city do you want to live in?
- What region of the country would you like to work in?
- Is there a specific state or region you would not like to work in?
- What issues are you personally passionate about?

In answering these questions look for common themes throughout your responses. These common elements can help you to identify your passions and strong interests – either directly or by contrast with your choice of "undesirables." Once you have identified the things you feel strongly about in terms of both life and career, you can begin to link them with available job opportunities, industries, and regions.

Checking in With Your Self-Assessment Results

A personalized approach based on soul searching may yield valuable answers to the important questions about your future. This approach does require some self-interpretation and some leaps from one kind of evidence to another kind of conclusion.

In Mark Staples's case, he gets some help in reaching a conclusion based on his self-analysis, as the following example shows.

Mark is thinking about his future one night and tells his girl friend Ginger that what he really enjoys about his job at the supermarket is talking to one of the assistant store managers about product packaging and product placement on the shelves, and the ways that optimum placement can stimulate sales. Ginger tells him, "Maybe you should take some courses on retail marketing at the university, along with your regular program. You might be able to put some focus in your resume and also discover your real interests in the business world." "That's good advice, dear," says Mark. "It reminds me of why I want to marry you."

If your self-searching does not lead to these kinds of useful inferences, you can also make use of the many self-assessment instruments designed for this purpose. As you learned in Chapter 3, excellent vocational self-assessment instruments are available that have been widely used and steadily improved over the years. Among the leading instruments are the Myers-Briggs Type Indicator (MBTI) and the Strong Interest Inventory (SII). These are available on the Web in many varieties that are *like* the originals. For the official assessment instruments themselves, which have been tested for validity and reliability and refined over the years, check with your Career Services office. By going through Career Services, you will likely also get help with evaluation of the results.

Informational Interviewing

Perhaps you feel that self-assessment, both formal and informal, provides only part of the picture by clarifying your interests and preferences. Another source of information for your career search is to talk to people who are already in the careers you are exploring. For this purpose, consider setting up some informational interviews. These are a means of asking questions about jobs while not asking for a job. The University of Minnesota defines the process in the following way: "An informational interview is a meeting with a professional used to obtain first-hand impressions of work in a specific field and to gain career advice (St. Paul campus Career Center)."

The basic concept of informational interviewing is to find people working in the job, company, or industry that you are interested in, and ask them questions about that job, company, or industry. You can also use informational interviews as a way of building relationships for the purpose of networking. These interviews can also lead to job opportunities, but the focus needs to be on information gathering. Because this format is meant to be a low-pressure, non-intrusive way of gaining information and building contacts, requests for jobs or job leads are out of place.

Informational interviews can be job related, company related, or industry related. The job related interview focuses on the skills, attributes, and qualifications necessary for a specific job or type of job. Company related interviews may explore what it's like to work for a certain company or seek a perspective on the various departments and divisions of a company. Finally, the industry related informational interview focuses on the companies in a given industry, the major trends, and some of the leading challenges in the industry.

Preparing for the Interview

Setting up an informational interview with someone you know can be a simple process. Gaining an appointment with a stranger may be more challenging. One way to help you bridge the gap to someone you don't know would be to create a script to help you through the approach.

Begin with an introduction of yourself and your affiliation. Next, explain what you are seeking – including the fact that you are *not* seeking a job interview – and state why you want to speak to this person (e.g., her experience, expertise, reputation). If you are in the same geographic area, ask to meet in-person. Stay flexible in your availability. You might also sweeten the deal by offering to buy him lunch or coffee. Assure the person your meeting will not take long – perhaps 20 minutes during a workday.

If you are not in the prospective contact's area, try to set up a telephone interview of 20 minutes or so. Finally, if the person you have contacted is unavailable or uninterested, you may want to ask for a referral you could contact.

In preparation for the interview, make sure you are appropriately dressed. Use the guidelines for a job interview (see Chapter 9 for some details). Making a good first impression is important, as is showing professionalism in your approach. Make sure you have an appointment with the person you want to meet, unless you are going to conduct an informational interview at a networking event through casual conversation. Prepare the questions you want to ask in advance. Finally, send a thank you note to your contact after the interview.

Here is a set of possible questions for an informational interview.

Informational Interview Questions

Job Related:
- What do you like best about your position as _____?
- What kind of impact has this position had on your lifestyle?
- What advice would you give to someone just entering this career track?
- What kinds of tasks do you complete during a typical day or week?
- What types of advancement opportunities are available for entry-level candidates in this career track?

Company Related:
- What is the corporate culture of this company?
- Does the company promote or encourage continuing education?
- What types of training programs does the company offer?
- What are some of the goals of the company for the next few years?

Industry Related:
- What kinds of challenges is the industry currently facing?
- Who are some of the major and minor competitors in the industry?
- Are there any likely changes that may affect the industry in the next few years?

Organizing

Knowing what you want to do is only part of the battle. Being prepared to conduct your search in the most efficient and effective way is just as important. If your search is disorganized and hit-or-miss, you may never encounter the best opportunities. Do yourself a favor by carrying your systematic self-assessment approach into setting up a search process that can maximize your opportunities.

Establish Your Job Search Headquarters

Use some of your available tools for this purpose. Essential provisions include a computer with Internet access, a printer, a fax machine, and a telephone. If you don't have these items at home, arrange to use them at school through the Career Services office. You will also need office supplies of the kind you have used in your studies – notebooks, binders, pens, highlighters, notepads, Post-it notes.

Take advantage of technology also to eliminate paper clutter and to help you track progress. For example, instead of keeping a paper list of companies you want to call, make an electronic list you can save, update, and manipulate on an ongoing basis. Keep the physical space organized as well. Set up your search headquarters like a school or work desk environment that is conducive to efficient and effective work habits.

Gather Your Search Documents

Before you can properly launch your career search, you will need to prepare your portfolio and assemble its major job documents. As you learned in Chapter 6, the key documents include resumes, cover letters, references, and other supporting items. Have these documents ready to go prior to beginning the actual search, or you will end up spending too much of your search time composing them in a rush. The result may be poor document quality and poor self-presentation.

Target Your Job Search

The next step in launching a successful job search is to narrow your search field by targeting the job categories you have identified as relevant and applicable to you. For example, if you do a Google search for "engineering jobs," you will get about 62 million hits; if you then search for "electronic engineering jobs," you can reduce the hits to "only" about 10 million. Clearly, by adding other qualifiers to your search term (location, industry, company size, etc.), you can narrow the search to a manageable size.

Even in the broader search mode, you can select from the hits produced by using the first several pages of responses first, since these usually include the most pertinent information available to the search engine. In this broad-gauge format you will also find a mixture of both companies and search engines related to opportunities in your specified area.

In addition to qualifiers such as location or industry versus job title or job type, you can also focus the search by selecting sites that post jobs in your targeted areas. The right choice of sites will help you find relevant and appropriate opportunities more quickly. For example, the job board Monster.com is relevant to a huge population of people and companies, basically anyone who is looking for a job or an applicant. On the other hand, Dice.com focuses mostly on technically related jobs.

You can further limit your search by setting criteria for jobs based on your interests and passions. Use the results of your self-assessments to discover what you feel passionate about. The more specific and targeted you can be in your search, the more relevant and promising will be the results you receive from your sources.

The targeting strategy has important caveats, however. One is to limit your search to jobs you are qualified for. Another is to avoid imposing overly restrictive limits on your job possibilities. For example, if you decide you want to work in San Francisco only, you will bypass a rich set of opportunities in the surrounding area, including those in Silicon Valley, just south of the city. As another example, if you want to work in the sports industry, you will find opportunities in college athletics, high school athletics, private athletics, and in the minor leagues of professional sports. But if you search only for jobs in professional sports or at the major league level, you will bypass many possibilities that share important aspects of your interest in sports. Make your target large enough to provide maximum opportunities in a carefully defined career area.

Get Registered and Use Technology to Your Advantage

A step that will save time later in your search is to register with the appropriate on-line job banks (such as Dice.com and others). Set these resources as favorites on your Internet browser. Before you begin the actual job search process, sign up for any accounts you will need, upload the appropriate documents, and complete the on-line profiles.

You may also choose to organize your Internet favorites into categories or folders. For example, you may have one folder labeled "daily," which contains the sites you want to visit every day. Other folders may hold the sites you visit on a weekly or monthly basis. You may also want to set reminders in your calendar to identify items you need to complete, in a fashion similar to tasks in Microsoft Outlook or appointment reminders on your cell phone.

Be Systematic

You do not maximize opportunities by simply sending out your resume to numerous recipients and then waiting to see what happens next. A better approach is to follow up on the resumes you have sent, and be prepared to receive phone calls that should not come as a surprise. Developing a system to track (a) where you have applied, (b) the jobs you have applied for, and (c) the timing of your applications will serve your needs best. The system does not have to be complicated. Take advantage of basic tools available in Microsoft Excel or Word, or another system. These tools offer useful features, such as allowing you to sort information and group it into columns that you can quickly scan.

Here is a basic example of a job search tracking system.

Date Sent	Follow-up Date	Company Name	Job Title	Sent	Contact Person	Contact Information	Notes
8/14/XX	8/30/XX	Devine and Gough	Office Manager	E-mail		hr@devinegough.com	E-mail response stating receipt of my resume
8/15/XX	9/01/XX	Trader Jones	Human Resources Assistant	Fax	Ms. (Amy) Mullane	551-660-1234	

Give Yourself the Gift of Time

Many job seekers forget one important detail about the job search: It takes time to be successful. As suggested earlier, searching for a job can be a full-time job, so give yourself time to do it properly. Successful job seekers often block out time on their calendar for the search process. Setting this time aside represents a commitment for them, similar to the scheduled time on their calendar for classes, for work, or for dinner with a friend. Holding true to this commitment is a recognition of its special importance.

Al Barbaro wants to be systematic about his job search. He sets up a tracking system that provides regular feedback on the resumes he has sent out. Al also sets aside an hour each evening for his search of new opportunities and job postings. He lets his friend Marty know that he will be busy each evening from 6 – 7, since Marty likes to drop over unannounced. Marty kids him about how important he's gotten since he went back to college, but sees that Al is serious about his "busy" time, and learns to accept it.

Getting organized will help you begin your job search, but you also need to organize your time to complete the search successfully. Focus on organizing your time in terms of computer-based searches, networking opportunities, and hidden job market opportunities. Although the Internet is an invaluable resource, you may want to limit this aspect of your search to no more than a third to a quarter of your time. The remainder of your time will be well spent on getting in front of people, building your network, and exploring the hidden job market. (More on these activities later in the chapter.)

Control your time also by setting up some internal cycles that capture the natural rhythms of the search process. Perhaps on Mondays, Wednesdays, and Fridays you search for and apply for openings. Then on Tuesdays, Thursdays, and Saturdays you follow up on the resumes you sent out. You might go further still and detail which search tools you will use on certain search days. For example, on Mondays you might scan nationally based sites for jobs, while on Wednesdays you navigate through the local or regional sites.

In thinking about the time your search will require, prepare yourself for a prolonged campaign and don't become discouraged by the lack of immediate results. For the kind of focused search you are launching – for a position meant to lead to a career and your "dream job" – quick results would be surprising. Typically, it may take as many as 100 resumes sent out before you receive a phone call or e-mail asking for an interview. Be prepared to give the process time to prove itself, and don't leap to the conclusion that your techniques are not working.

Tap the Hidden Job Market

According to www.job-hunt.org (a Web-based guide to job sites), only 15-25% of the jobs currently available are posted on the Internet or advertised in any formal manner. This proportion is consistent with the number of positions that many experts consider to be in the open job market. In other words, you need to tap into the hidden job market if you want to reach the other 75-85% of available jobs. A basic definition of this larger market is that it includes jobs that are available but not advertised.

The hidden job market has emerged for several reasons. First, advertising job openings is expensive. Companies can save a lot of money by using word-of-mouth methods and internal postings. In addition, results from newspaper ads, on-line postings, and radio announcements are often slow in coming when the need is immediate. Finally, these public methods lack quality control. Many of the respondents do not meet minimum qualifications (but respond anyway).

The "hidden" job market may emerge through use of in-house publications and internal recommendations that quickly create a pool of better-qualified applicants. The method of personal recommendations does seem to produce better candidates, because the referrals come from people who know the organization well and who are willing to stake their reputations on the quality of the candidates they recommend.

To understand how people outside the company might uncover this hidden job market, let's consider the role of networking in the job search process.

Network Patterns

In a networking process, you interact with people who are interested in sharing information and services with others and have an interest in common with them. In the context of a job search, networking is a way to meet people for mutual gain and reward. For you the reward may be a lead to a job; for someone else, it may be a chance to sell a product or service – including the job he wants to fill. Networks based on professional affiliations – engineers, accountants, nurses, and other professionals – have a related purpose of fostering the well-being of their profession by attracting new people with energy and ideas.

The larger your network the more potential it holds for helping you and providing help to others in your common interest group.

You can think of the networking process in terms of the idea of Six Degrees of Separation. This concept is based on a reckoning of the number of contacts each of our contacts may have. If you are one "step" away from each person you know, and two "steps" away from each of the persons your acquaintances know, then, like everyone else, you are no more than six "steps" (or degrees) away from each person on Earth. (An assumption that each of the world's 6 billion people knows, on average, about 42 people results in the six degrees expressed in the concept.)

To grasp this startling idea, consider the following example. Assume that you only know three people in the entire world. For you, these people make up your entire network, and they are your line of direct contact. Assume that each of your direct contacts also knows three other people, and that each of these people also knows three others. Based on the three people you know, then, the actual size of your network – at only three degrees of separation – is 40 people (including yourself). See the chart below for an illustration.

In other words, your real network is much larger than just your direct contacts. The people at several levels of separation from you are also part of your network and can be helpful in your job search. These contacts of your contacts may be able to channel information back to you, or to pass your resume along to yet other contacts within a much wider network of associations.

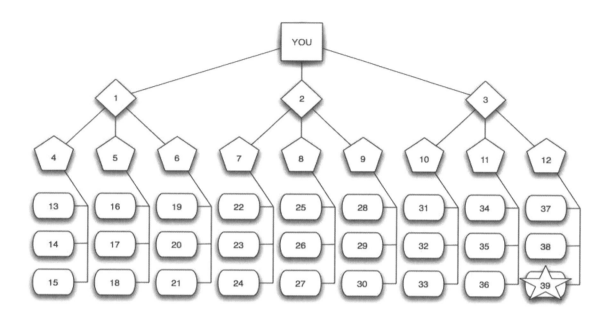

Growing Your Direct Contact Pool

People are often hesitant or shy about whom they include in their line of direct contacts. Many think only of their closest friends and family. To elevate your job search, challenge yourself to go beyond these comfortable associates and increase the number of people in your direct contact line. Include anyone you interact with on a regular basis, such as co-workers, faculty members, and administrators. To grow the pool, participate in activities where meeting other people is possible. The table at right lists places where networking may occur. Can you think of others?

Places to Network
• Job Fairs
• Organizations
o School related
o Professional
o Religious
o Civic
o Personal interest
• Career Centers
• Companies
• Volunteer Groups
• Conferences and Trade Shows
• Member Directories
• Internet Discussion Groups

Job Fairs

Job fairs provide another excellent opportunity for building your network and tapping the hidden job market. Job fairs may be sponsored by a variety of organizations, and they differ in significant ways depending on that sponsorship.

A college, university, or a consortium of colleges and universities typically hosts university fairs that students can attend prior to graduation. The focus is on getting recognition on campus for the employers and on getting employer names out to the students. You may have opportunities to interview right at the job fair, but the primary purpose is to provide a chance for students and employers to meet and greet each other and to facilitate networking.

University fairs generally focus on the types of students the institution is trying to promote. If the institution has a great many undergraduates seeking jobs, for example, the companies attending will be prepared to discuss entry-level positions and be willing to help recent graduates transition into their organizations.

Privately sponsored job fairs are typically organized by companies seeking to earn revenue from these events. The sponsoring company may charge companies or job seekers (or both) for the chance to participate. Because these fairs are open to the public, they may attract a large number of candidates with a vast array of backgrounds, skills, and abilities. Competition is strong as a result, and the focus of job seekers and companies is varied. Some privately sponsored fairs do focus on certain groups of candidates or companies. The Women for Hire job fair, for example, focuses primarily on women looking for opportunities (men can attend also).

Corporate fairs are sponsored and hosted by private companies. Typically these are held when a company has a very specific set of needs or a large number of open job requisitions. Such fairs are usually bounded by the requirements of the openings. For example, if Lockheed Martin were hosting a job fair, they might require that all attendees have active security clearances. At the other end of the spectrum, a fair hosted by United Airlines might be open to anyone seeking employment, because United's positions are not constrained by many specialized requirements.

Professional Organizations

Organizations and associations provide excellent opportunities for networking that unlock doors to the hidden job market. Depending on their purposes, such organizations provide focused opportunities to learn, build contacts, or serve their profession. It is not enough to simply join, however. To realize any of these benefits, active participation is required.

Many professional societies have student chapters at universities, with memberships offered at reduced cost. If a student chapter is not available at your institution, you may still be able to join through the national group. The national organization may sponsor local chapters that hold events and regularly scheduled meetings. These meetings are the ideal venue for networking and building contacts that could lead to job opportunities.

Some prominent examples of professional associations:

- Society of Human Resource Managers (SHRM)
- Institute of Electrical and Electronics Engineers (IEEE)
- Association of IT Professionals (AITP)
- Hospitality Finance Technology Professionals (HFTP)
- Society of Women Engineers (SWE)

Other Networking Opportunities

Your college or university is itself a major source of networking activity. Your courses put you in contact with peers in similar areas and give you a chance to demonstrate skills such as leadership, good communication, and teamwork. Remember that after several degrees of separation, your classmates may be able to link you to opportunities in the job market. Your college also offers you a chance to participate in student organizations and clubs. Student government, interest groups, professional societies, student newspapers, and alumni organizations are examples, each of which offers networking opportunities.

Religious, civic, and social service groups offer opportunities as well. Through regular attendance at services, meetings, and functions, you are likely to encounter a stable core of other members. You can establish ties and open channels of communication with them about your career planning needs.

Another form of networking opportunity, one that has grown considerably in the last ten years, is the Internet discussion group, which focuses on an area of shared interest. To gain the benefits such a group can bestow on your job search campaign, make sure you present yourself in a highly professional manner. Avoid hasty or overly emotional postings that are based on incomplete information, and check your messages for appropriate language and grammar. Just as people form hard-to-change first impressions upon meeting you, your on-line colleagues will be forming judgments based on your initial postings.

Be cautious also in using popular social networking sites such as MySpace and Facebook. While these sites offer definite networking opportunities, they can also create images of you that may not jibe with your search efforts in the professional community. A larger number of potential employers are reviewing such sites to gain an additional perspective on job candidates. The types of pictures and information you post on these sites can have an impact on how you may be viewed in both the formal and hidden job markets. Even the people who are linked to you as friends and the pictures they have posted are a representation of you and your associations.

Perhaps this sounds a bit hypocritical. If you feel like saying, "I'm who I am, and that includes being loyal to my friends as well," remember that employers are thinking not only about how you will fit into their company culture, but also how you will impress customers and clients. As a simple rule of thumb, consider this: Do not post anything on the Internet that you would not be proud to show your parents or grandparents.

Chapter Summary

A great deal of planning and forethought goes into a successful job search. To maximize the possibilities of the search process for yourself, do some soul searching as well as some formal self-assessments, if need be. Use these to help identify where you want to go and what you want to do. Then, get organized. Set up a place, establish some regular times, and assemble the tools you will need to conduct your search. Remember that more time spent in preparation will likely produce more and higher-quality results.

Once you are set up and organized, begin your search by using a broad array of methods, sources, and approaches. Don't rely solely on the Internet. Explore both the advertised and the hidden job markets through networking, job fairs, professional organizations, and on-line discussion boards. Accept the fact that quick solutions to your long-term career needs will not be forthcoming. Trust, however, that careful planning and solid execution will maximize your opportunities.

Questions for Discussion:

1. What role does passion play in your self-assessment for a job search?
2. What steps are included in the plan for organizing your job search?
3. What is the hidden job market, and how can you tap into that market?
4. Why is networking important in the job search? How can you build and expand your network?
5. What role should the Internet play in the job search process?

Chapter Assignments:

1. Write a one-page paper on how to use your interests in focusing your job search.
2. Create a tracking method for the jobs you apply for and the resumes you send. Include the following categories of information:

   - Job Title
   - Company Name
   - Resume Used
   - How you learned of the job
   - Application Date
   - Employer Contact Name
   - Employer Telephone/e-mail Information.

3. Who is in your network? Develop a chart that shows your direct contact line.
4. Create a list of organizations and associations that could be of value in your job search. Explain why each organization is a good fit for your targeted job search or choice of industry. Identify the organizations in which you will become an active participant.
5. Write an informational interview script that you could use when calling on a stranger for an appointment.

Works Cited

Hansen, Randall S. "The Complete Idiot's Guide to Choosing a College Major."
Oct. 2007. "Quintessential Careers: Finding your Career Passion." Accessed 12 April
2007 www.quintcareers.com/printable/finding_career_passion.html.

"The Hidden Job Market." St. Paul Campus Career Center. University of Minnesota. Accessed
4 April 2007
http://www.stpaulcareers.umn.edu/jobsearch/find_positions/hidden_market.html.

CHAPTER NINE
Navigating the Interview
Kirsten Nicholas

An interview is no different than an exam; preparation is the key to success.
— Adam Vergne, Micron Technologies

Interviewing is a skill that must be learned. The key to a good interview is to communicate to the employer that you have the necessary skills to succeed.
— David Ho, Sandia National Laboratories

For many people, interviewing is the most intimidating part of the job search process. With a little analysis and preparation, however, you can tame the interview and turn it to your advantage. This chapter will help you do that. You will learn key strategies and techniques, and learn how to compose your knowledge, skills, and abilities into talking points for the interview. Talking points are your opportunity to go beyond just answering questions to making a distinct statement about yourself.

The Importance of the Interview

How important is the interview in the hiring process? If you give it a 10 on a 1-10 scale, you would not be overrating this vital component of the job search.

Why is interviewing so vital? For companies, recruiting and hiring new employees is an expensive endeavor. Hiring managers need to know more about you than simply what you listed on your resume. They try to gauge your personality to ensure it fits the company's culture. They check to see if your long-term goals align with the company's goals for the position. They look for a match between your aspirations and what the company can or is willing to provide.

David Woodhead, field recruiter for the Transportation Security Administration, provides the following view of the subject:

> I want to know several things about candidates before hiring them. Among these are how well the person will fit into the organizational culture. If the workplace is a relaxed, informal environment, a person's degree of informality and ability to relate on a personal level is as important as their ability to relate on a professional level. A person more comfortable with a high degree of formality may not fit well in a smaller organization that values the ability to share information informally, without going through different hierarchical levels. The same can be true for a person who interacts best by dealing with their informal network within the organization, but who eschews putting every thought

in memo form before it can be communicated. This personality type probably wouldn't fit best in a more formal organization big on procedures and processes. (Personal Interview, 29 November 2006. Used with permission)

The Skills Employers Value

Because employers use the interview to assess candidates in a broader way, it is helpful to know what kinds of broader skills and qualities employers value. Let's say that the employer knows from your resume that you can do cost accounting. You've listed your prior cost accounting experience, the accounting degree you've earned, and your CPA certification. The employer might then use the interview to get a better sense of your other qualities – how you relate to others, to your work, and to your goals.

Review the table showing the ratings of desired skills in the National Association of Colleges and Employers (NACE) poll on page 9 in Chapter 1. NACE's 2007 Job Outlook provides insight into the qualities and skills employers seek in candidates.

Types of Interviews

Knowing the purposes of the many types of employment interviews will help you prepare for each of these types. Since many interviews are part of a series, handling the earlier ones will increase your chances of being called back for the later ones.

Prescreening Interviews

No doubt you've heard the saying, "You never get a second chance to make a good first impression." Keep this point in mind as you prepare for the prescreening interview. Companies use the prescreen to gauge your interest in them and their position and to determine if your basic skills and general personality fit with their organization.

Prescreen interviews are usually conducted by recruiters who ask general questions about your qualifications based on your resume. Recruiters may also seek to verify the accuracy of your claimed job responsibilities and work history, although this function is also performed by the HR office at the time of hiring. Typical prescreen questions include:

- Why are you interested in working for our company?
- Why are you interested in this position?
- Why are you looking to leave your current job?
- What are your salary expectations?
- When would you be available to start?

Being thoroughly prepared for a prescreen interview is as important as being fully prepared for an in-person interview. To ensure you are responding the right way, keep your resume handy for reference. Bring also a list of the companies you have applied to, the jobs you applied for, the dates of application, and any contact information you have used. This information will give you the reference tools during the prescreen session to answer questions appropriately and confidently.

The In-Person Interview

Interviewing experts have said that interviewing is mostly mental. While they have a point, it is also true that physical and verbal aspects play an important role. Mastering the mental, physical, and verbal components of the interview should be your goal in seeking to maximize your chances of success.

Composure is the key to all three of these! Being able to master your nervousness and command the proper body language will help you create a positive impression. Preparation for the interview should include practice in providing good eye contact, maintaining an upright posture when sitting or standing, and speaking in a firm, clear voice. At the same time, being yourself is vital. Practice should help you achieve these goals without straining the bounds of what is natural to you and coming across as artificial.

In-person interviews can last from several minutes to several hours. They can also be conducted by a single interviewer or a group of interviewers, as you will learn from later sections of this chapter.

The Scheduled Telephone Interview

Scheduled telephone interviews typically take the place of in-person interviews when a candidate does not reside in the hiring company's area. The telephone interview may also be a "screening interview" that leads to a decision by the company to bring the candidate to its location for an in-person interview.

Unlike the prescreen interview, however, the telephone interview is typically conducted by the hiring manager. Otherwise, telephone interviews are similar to in-person interviews in length and in the types of questions asked. It is imperative therefore that you treat a telephone interview as seriously as an in-person interview. Preparation should include a set of questions for the company that you have thought out carefully and can deliver in a professional manner.

Individual and Serial Interviews

While individual interviews occur between you and one other person, such as the hiring manager, a serial interview is set up to bring you into contact with several different individuals at different times. All of the serial meetings are nonetheless between you and one other person.

In these serial interviews you will likely be answering some of the same questions from different interviewers. Your answers should therefore be consistent, since the interviewers usually check with each other to compare impressions. Sometimes even the *emphasis* you put on certain topics can create an impression of inconsistency. Let's say you left a former job for another because you wanted to do more work in test engineering *and* to enjoy life in a big city. If you stress one reason over the other with different interviewers, you may create the impression that you are giving different answers to the question of why you changed jobs.

Group Interviews

In this situation, you may be meeting with a group of 3-4 people, or as many as a dozen. Interviewing in this format is efficient for the employer, but can be stressful for the applicant. If you are facing a group interview, practice with friends or colleagues will likely pay dividends.

Group interviews typically start with an introduction of the interviewers. Jot down these names and their functions so you can use them in your replies:

> *Well, Ralph, customer service was a critical part of that operation. As I mentioned in the question Sharon asked, I successfully managed the...*

Make sure you are addressing all the people in the room when you answer a question. Direct your attention beyond the person who asked the question, and shift your eyes between all the interviewers. In some interviews, a person may take part without asking any questions, maybe just quietly observing. This person may, in fact, be a senior decision maker whose approval is necessary for the hiring decision. Make sure you include this person in the scope of your eye contact as well.

Finally, some companies use a group format on both sides of the process. Thus, you may be responding to questions from a group of interviewers – along with your fellow applicants Jennifer, George, Jack, and Jill. To make the best impression for yourself, answer questions independently. Do not just chime in: "I agree with Jennifer. I would take the same approach in that case." Answering a question this way can make Jennifer, who mentioned the idea first, look like the better candidate.

As part of a group being interviewed, try to convey your individuality. Make your answer the best you can, without referencing another candidate, even if you agree with her position. On the other hand, don't take positions like a political candidate running for office. And don't take opportunities to make competitors look bad. Even if one of them flubs an answer, don't point out the error, but wait to be asked the question yourself and then give it a proper answer.

Interviews for a Promotion

Sometimes promotion interviews are a casual conversation with your manager or a higher-level executive. They may also be part of an actual competitive interview process including other internal or external candidates. Regardless of the circumstances, there is only one way to handle these encounters – professionally.

You would likely convey the wrong impression by assuming that you have the inside track for a promotion over other internal or external candidates. You may have earned consideration over other internal candidates, but the company is still interested in how you would work with these others if you were promoted. You may have an advantage in your knowledge of the company over external candidates, but companies also look to outsiders for their fresh perspective and new ideas. Assume nothing, but use the promotion interview to reinforce a positive view of your dedication, leadership, and skills.

Types of Interview Questions

The types of questions you face may vary depending on the type of the interview and the style of the interviewer. The type of the interview may be defined by the background of the interviewer. Sometimes the questions are dictated by the company. Sometimes you may encounter several interview styles combined in one interview.

Skilled vs. Unskilled Interviewers

Some interviews are conducted by an interviewer who has mastered the art of interviewing through experience, aptitude, and perhaps training. Typically, the skilled interviewer will ask questions highly relevant to the job and to your skills. These questions provide the interviewer with the maximum amount of job-to-person relevance for choosing the best candidate.

You may also encounter an unskilled interviewer. This could be a hiring manager who is close to the work but not very good at assessing people's suitability for it. It could also be someone with little interviewing experience. Such an interviewer may unintentionally ask irrelevant or even illegal questions (more on these later in the chapter).

Regardless of which type of interviewer you encounter, your approach to the interview should be to answer all questions to the best of your ability and work to show the interviewer your knowledge, experience, and abilities.

Behavioral Questions

Some interviewers emphasize behaviorally based questions. Examples might be: "What would you do if you saw a co-worker taking company supplies home for personal use?" or, "How would you handle an irate customer who bursts into a busy production environment?" You might answer such questions by giving a preferred answer. Better yet, try telling a story of your past experience that illustrates the preferred response.

When you respond to behavior-based questions, make sure you clearly demonstrate the point you want to make. For example, if an employer asks you to "describe a time when you were disappointed in your performance," you need to tell a complete story. Explain what happened, how it happened, and what the outcome was. When the question is negatively based, end your story with a positive outcome: "What I learned from this situation was…" or, "This mistake has made me more careful in …."

Role Plays

An interviewer may also ask you to assume a role related to the position, and show her how you would handle a problem situation. For example: "I am an angry vendor and you are the store manager. You have been called to the shoe department by a sales associate to respond to a dispute over shelf placement of the vendor's product. Show me how you would handle this situation." Your response would be judged not only on what you say, but on the way you deal with the emotions generated in the situation.

Typically, a role-play request would be inserted within a more traditional question-answer type of interview. This can create some pressure on the applicant, who may be caught off guard or feel embarrassed at the "playacting" requested. It is best to be prepared for this possibility and to include it in your practice for the interview. Keep in mind also that the purpose of a role play is to evaluate your judgment, not your acting ability.

Testing

Like colleges and universities that use an ACT or a SAT exam as a predictor of success, many companies use tests to measure competencies related to their positions. The competencies then become predictors of success in the positions.

To the company, testing is a way to eliminate discrepancies between the skills you say you have and the skills you actually have.

This means some interviews are more than just question and answer sessions. You may still deal with questions-answers. But then the interviewer may put you in a little room with a computer and ask you to complete on-line testing for MS Word and Excel programs, or a paper and pencil test on your knowledge of electronics and mathematical equations.

The testing required should be directly related to the job for which you are applying. In the simplest sense, this means you should not be required to complete a test on electronic circuits if you are applying for a job as an administrative assistant, for instance. Nor should you be asked to take a keyboarding speed test if you are applying for a job as a design engineer.

A less obvious problem with competency tests is that these are often home-made and not always designed in a way that fairly measures your knowledge and aptitude for a particular job. Such tests may be focusing on specific aspects of the job, which would not be familiar to anyone who hadn't already held that job. A fair and valid test would measure general knowledge and skills in an area, along with potential for long-term success.

Testing may also vary by the organization's external requirements. If you are applying for a job with the government or a government contractor for whom a security clearance is required, the types of testing used will be much more intensive.

Additional testing and checks are more general in nature. Every employer is likely to use, as a baseline, a standard battery of tests and checks. These are typically a drug test, a background check, and a reference check. Psychological test batteries are also common.

Handling Difficult or Illegal Questions

Interviews are fluid processes, and this makes them unpredictable. You might anticipate many of the questions in the process, but it's difficult to know the curve balls that might be thrown at you. Suppose in the middle of your interview you encounter this question:

> *What would your current manager say you need to improve most in your performance?*

Perhaps you have always received above-average performance reviews, and your manager has never cited areas for improvement. What would be an appropriate answer?

It is fairly common for an interview to include a question that stumps you. If so, make sure the question does not throw you off balance for the rest of the interview. Dodging the question is not appropriate, nor is telling the interviewer you don't know or can't answer the question.

However, delaying your answer may be a good option. You can tell the interviewer you are not sure and would like to think about it while you continue the interview:

> *That's a tough one. Would you mind if I come back to that question a little later? I would like to think about it a little more while we continue the interview.*

If this is your response, make sure you come back to the question at the end of the interview, even if the interviewer forgets about it.

> *Earlier you asked me what my manager would say I need to improve upon. I want to make sure I answer this question for you. He would say...*

Here is a list of questions that might make you hesitate in an interview. They will be less "difficult" if you think about them beforehand and plan for a suitable response.

Sample Difficult Questions

Tell me a little about yourself. (Answer: your 60-second commercial.)
What do you know about our company?
What are two of your strengths and two weaknesses?
What makes you a better candidate than our other applicants?
What salary are you looking for?
Why should we hire your?
What are you looking for in a position and in a company?
You seem to be overqualified for this position. Why do you want to take a step down?
What are your short-term and long-term goals?
What do you look for in a manager?

For a list of common interview questions, see Appendix A.

Illegal questions create a different scenario. Illegal questions are typically those that violate Title VII of the Civil Rights Act of 1964. The Act was passed because such information can lead to discriminatory personnel decisions. For a complete version of Title VII of the Civil Rights Act, see http://www.eeoc.gov/policy/vii.html.

In an employment context, questions are illegal that seek to identify gender, religion, ethnicity, sexual orientation, race, disability, family status, and other similar categories. Such questions should not be asked during an interview or any other part of the employment process. Nevertheless, some interviewers ask questions about these matters, perhaps out of ignorance; others may ask them knowing they are illegal, perhaps hoping the applicant will answer them anyway. Your response to these kinds of questions will determine if you are still a candidate at the end of the interview process.

> ### Sample Illegal Questions
>
> How old are you?
> Do you have kids?
> Are you planning to have kids?
> Are you married?
> Do you have a significant other?
> Where do you live?
> Where were you born?
> What is your family background?
> Does your religion prohibit you from working holidays and weekends?
> Berteau … is that a French name?
> Are you considered part of a minority group?
> Do you have any long-standing health conditions?

Flying off the handle at these questions may reflect your indignation and relieve your anger, but it will not help your chances for the position. Losing control of your emotions may also come back to haunt you later. People within similar industries talk to each other, and you might earn a label as having a quick trigger and a poor attitude. A better response to an illegal question would be to tell the interviewer that you are not sure how the question relates to the position for which you are applying: "How does my religion pertain to the qualifications for this position?"

On the other hand, if you are highly interested in a position and a company, you may want to take a completely different approach. You might try turning an illegal or inappropriate question in a positive direction by refocusing the answer to suit your needs. For example, if an interviewer asks about commitment conflicts because of your children, you might reply, "Actually, my children are a key motivator for my success, and they have never had any negative bearing on my previous work commitments. May I tell you a little about how my children have inspired new ideas I was able to use in my current position?"

At this point, let's put the ideas and suggestions of the previous pages into a strategy and plan for managing the interview process.

Interview Planning and Execution

To this point, you have been focusing on the theories and general categories of interviews and interviewing. To put these ideas to productive use, you will need to prepare and practice. The more preparation and practice you engage in, the more comfortable and successful you will be during the interview process.

In the remaining pages of this chapter you will learn some of the strategies you can apply before the interview, during the interview, and after the interview to maximize your chances of success.

Before the Interview

Here are the things you should do to prepare for the interview. Plan for and execute *all* of these activities.

Research the Company:

Show the interviewer you know something about the company by checking recent news articles and looking up some basic operating and financial information about the company. (See Chapter 5 for more on this.) Work in these references during the interview. They will help you show your resourcefulness and help you stand out above candidates who did not prepare.

Verify Basics:

Check the time, location, and any special directions, such as driving routes, parking instructions, or the floor of the interview room. Make a trial run to the location to ensure you don't get lost or delayed on the interview day.

Ensure Proper Attire:

Make sure your suit is clean, your shirt or blouse pressed, your stockings matching your outfit, and your shoes polished. If you are wondering whether you really have to wear a suit, the answer largely depends on the place where you are interviewing. For any corporate environment the answer is always yes. For an interview outside the company or organization, ask the interviewer or the person scheduling the interview, "Would a suit be appropriate attire for this interview?"

It is better to be overdressed than underdressed. First impressions are important, and your clothing will contribute to that impression, which will also be compared to that of other candidates. In addition to a suit, you will do well to choose a conservative look. You want the interviewer to remember your attitude, skills, and experience, not your bright orange shirt and polka dot head band.

Items to avoid, for both genders, include cologne or perfume. Some people are highly allergic to these substances. You will want to avoid a choking interviewer. On the other hand, showering and (for men) shaving prior to the interview are vital.

For women, make-up should be subtle; blue eye shadow outlined in charcoal is not a good choice, for example. Women wearing a suit with a skirt should make sure the skirt is at least knee length when they are sitting down. Pantyhose are a necessity. Earrings should be studs, rather than large dangles or loops. Jewelry in facial piercings should be removed for a professional interview. Tie or comb back long hair to avoid unconscious fidgeting or playing with your lovely locks during the interview. Nails should be neatly trimmed and nail polish colors neutralized.

For men, beards and mustaches should be neat and closely groomed. Long hair should be pulled back from the face or cut into a shorter, more conservative style. Piercings and tattoos are generally not included in the range of conservative approaches to male grooming. If you have tattoos on your forearms, wear a long-sleeved shirt.

Review and Practice:

Be sure to review your resume and talking points for the interview. Talking points would be the qualities, skills, and qualifications you want to feature. Think about ways to get them into the discussion as well, through examples and brief stories that illustrate your claims, for example. Review the likely questions you will face (see Appendix A for common questions and page 145 for difficult questions).

In addition to your review and preparation, remember to practice. Working through an expected interview with a friend or colleague will be a most helpful way to identify weaknesses, strengths, and opportunities. The feedback from this "friendly interviewer" can help you make the necessary adjustments before the real interview.

Prepare End-of-Interview Questions:

While your own questions for the company can be asked at various times during the interview, the early stages are typically devoted to answering the interviewer's questions. Your own questions may therefore come near the end of the interview, which means some of the basic information would already have been covered. In any case, plan your questions to demonstrate a depth of character and a desirable work ethic.

Start by reviewing the company's Website to gather the basic information presented there. How long has the company been in business? What are its main products and services? Who are the main competitors? Asking questions about these basics during the interview would suggest lack of preparation or interest in the company. Avoid questions as well about the perks and benefits and times off that the company offers. These would indicate an interest in what the company can do for you, rather than in the work that it offers through this position.

Instead, ask questions that demonstrate your interest in the work, your knowledge of the company, and your excitement about the position. For example:

> *I read in the paper that your company recently merged with Verizon. Can you tell me what kind of impact the merger will have on this position? Will there be an expansion of the cell phone services you provide?*

Good interview questions are ones in which you gain information you cannot learn on-line or in the news archives, and which reflect your work-related values.

See the box on the following page, as well as Appendix B, for a list of the types of questions you might ask during the interview or at the end of the session.

Arrive Early:

Arrive at the interview location approximately ten minutes prior to your scheduled interview time. This will allow you to complete any necessary paperwork prior to the interview or complete any mandatory testing.

Be courteous:

Make sure you are polite and friendly to everyone you meet at the location. This is not only a good idea generally, but may reflect well on the impression you create here. The security guard could be a cousin of the person you are interviewing with, and the receptionist may be asked for his opinion based on your initial encounter.

First Impressions

The following will help build a good first impression that may also be lasting.

Appearance: The key concepts are to be conservative, clean-cut, and professional.

Punctuality: Arrive a little early to give them a chance to prepare and to clear up preliminaries in the process.

A firm handshake and a direct gaze suggest you are forthcoming and forthright.

A smile will show your personality. It will also help relieve your nervousness and that of your interviewers.

Portfolio and resumes: Bring several copies of your resume in a portfolio. You could also put any relevant work samples in your portfolio for reference during your interview. Also, bring a copy of your employment history for easy completion of any employment applications.

During the Interview

Wait until you are asked to be seated.

Maintain steady eye contact with all the interviewers in the room. If you have a problem with direct eye contact, look at an imaginary dot on the interviewer's forehead.

<u>Listen</u>: Do not interrupt the interviewer during her questions. You may not be anticipating exactly what she is asking.

<u>Clarify</u>: If you are not completely sure of what the interviewer is asking, seek clarification. Similarly, if the discussion gets side-tracked and you forget the original question, ask for a reminder to help you get back to the point.

<u>Convey confidence, not arrogance.</u>

<u>Body language</u> can help you project confidence during an interview and help form an impression in the interviewer's mind about what kind of person you are. A common impression related to body language is that a person who slouches is not a good worker and is not presentable to customers. A good rule of thumb for maintaining the appropriate posture is to sit with both feet flat on the floor. This will also help with nervous foot tapping or leg shaking. If you are not comfortable in this position, try simply crossing your ankles. Leaning slightly forward instead of sitting back in the chair can also help demonstrate your interest and attentiveness.

Some people display symptoms known as nervous ticks when they are under pressure. Stuttering is an example, as are leg shaking, hand massaging, hair fiddling, and similar movements. If you are subject to any of these, learn to control them. In practicing for the interview, establish the posture that leaves you most comfortable. Find the posture also that limits involuntary movements. For example, if you tend to wring your hands, try putting one hand on each knee or clasping your hands together in your lap. If your foot wants to tap, plant both feet flat on the floor with your knees bent at a 90-degree angle. If you play with your hair when you are nervous, make sure your hair is brushed back out of your face, and clasp your hands in your lap.

<u>Mirroring</u>: Psychologists tell us that people tend to gravitate toward those they see as similar to themselves. Mirroring is a technique used by interviewees to make interviewers feel more comfortable with them. Here's how it works: As the interviewee, tune into the interviewer's body language and mannerisms and try to mirror these postures and actions. Mirroring is also different from mimicking, in which you would copy movements as they occur. Mirroring actions are used throughout the interview and not necessarily at the same time as the interviewer's actions.

Note how the interviewer is sitting. Is he leaning forward or back in the chair? Does he use his hands when he speaks? Does he use certain words consistently – for example, *teamwork, collaboration* or, conversely, *leadership, initiative, stepping up*? Is he soft-spoken or loud, talking in a hurried manner or at a relaxed pace? Identifying some of these tendencies and trying to mirror them during the interview can help you create a subconscious connection with the interviewer. Avoid overusing this technique, however, or it may turn into mimicking that can trigger a negative response.

Remember also that your primary focus should be on projecting an open, straightforward impression through your body language. You may also want to focus on controlling involuntary movements. Only when you have a firm grasp on these basic needs should you consider techniques such as mirroring.

Give complete information: If the interviewer comes back to you for clarification of *who, why, where, when,* or *how*, you probably did not provide enough information when responding to her questions. Make sure to tell the full story and provide the necessary details. Some interviewers will not follow up on their questions and instead will simply discount your abilities.

Concluding the Interview

Even if you have been asking questions during the interview itself, most interviewers will ask at the end if you have any questions. The answer to this question is always, "Yes"! Make sure you have at least one good question prepared for the final phase of the interview (see page 148). You may also want to write down any questions that come to mind during the interview in your portfolio. But remember, this is still not the time to ask about salary and benefits. Let the interviewer raise the salary question with you.

Say, "Thank you": Like your grandmother always told you, "Mind your P's and Q's." Thanking the interviewer for his time is basic courtesy and is always appreciated.

Next steps: At the end of the interview, confirm what the next steps in the process will be. You can do this by simply asking, "What are the next steps in the hiring process?" This question can tell you several things, including what you need to do and what the timeline for follow-up is. If the interviewer's response does not indicate the time frame for the hiring decision, you may want to follow with another question: "How soon do you plan on making a decision or moving to the next step of the process?"

Collect a business card: If you are not presented with a card by each of the persons you interview with, ask for one. This provides you with the contact information necessary for the appropriate thank yous and follow-ups.

Close the interview with a firm, confident handshake. Let it be a symbol of your interest, appreciation, and good will.

After the Interview:

Within twenty-four hours after the interview, make sure that your thank you note has arrived in the e-mail inbox or mailbox of the interviewer. Send a thank you note to each interviewer you met with. Today, an e-mail message would likely be appropriate for most locations and companies. However, a handwritten thank you note may still gain a favorable reception. The handwritten note conveys a personal touch and indicates your willingness to go to the extra effort to prepare and deliver it.

Follow-up: If you have not heard back in the time frame indicated in the interview, send an e-mail or make a phone call. Sometimes the hiring process is lengthy, so be prepared to wait. Beyond that, following up tells the interviewer you are still interested in the position. Be careful not to call or e-mail too often, however.

Make notes: After the interview is over go to your car or the company cafeteria and write down the points that seemed to come across well and those that left some margin for improvement. Note also any questions that tripped you up during the process or answers you gave that you would now want to amend. These notes can help you prepare for the next interview, either at the same company or elsewhere.

Telephone Interviews

As suggested earlier in the chapter, success in a prescreen interview or a scheduled telephone interview can be enhanced if you prepare for them as you would for the in-person interview. If the telephone call is scheduled, be sure you are ready about five minutes prior to the call. If the call is a surprise, the caller will usually ask if this is a good time to talk. Make a considered decision in that case. Taking the call is obviously the best response, but if you are in your car driving, in a noisy location, or in a situation where you cannot devote full attention to the interview, ask the caller if you can reschedule.

For a scheduled interview, make sure you have a copy of your resume for easy reference. Use it to point out key qualifications to the interviewer. You will also want to have a tablet for notes during the interview, and a working pen or pencil. These will be assumed to be tools in your possession. However, if the phone call is a surprise, it's appropriate to ask the interviewer for a few moments to gather a notepad and pen.

A quiet place for the interview will make a positive difference. For a scheduled call, turn off your favorite radio station, arrange for a baby sitter for your young kids, and take the call in your prepared location. If the call is a surprise that catches you in the midst of changing diapers or watching "Sesame Street," ask the caller to reschedule.

Make sure your cordless phone is fully charged before the interview. You don't want the phone to die during the call or to send the annoying beep that signals a low-battery warning. You will also want to turn off the call-waiting feature during the interview.

Clarify whom you are speaking with and what her job title is. Since you cannot obtain a business card at the end of the process, gathering contact information is important. Make sure you get the correct spelling of the interviewer's name.

Think about your phone message beforehand. The employment-related call may come at a time you are not available, and your recorded message is then part of the initial impression of you the company receives. Your playful message, backed by a heavy rap beat or a set of barnyard sounds, will not help you create a positive first impression with the prospective employer. At a minimum, make sure the outgoing greeting indicates your name.

Many cell phone companies now provide a service that plays music on the line while you are being located. Make sure the music chosen for this time supports your professional image.

Voice quality: Telephone interviews place additional demands on the respondent to make the meaning clear, since there is no body language, gestures, or facial expressions to gauge. You need to rely on voice quality – loud and clear works fine – and tone. For the tone, try the simple method of smiling when you speak. This will convey something of your interest and enthusiasm to the interviewer.

<u>Closing</u>: Just as in the face-to-face interview, prepare some appropriate questions for the end, inquire about the next steps, and thank the interviewer.

Chapter Summary

Interviewing is a vitally important part of the job-search process, and your success in the interview can determine your possible employment with a company. Interviewing is also a skill that you can improve with planning and practice. By using the techniques, strategies, and guidelines discussed in this chapter, you should be prepared to do well in any interview scenario. Here are some of the keys to mastering the interview opportunity.

- Interviewing is mostly mental, but physical aspects can be important. Maintain your composure, and remember that first impressions are lasting.

- Practice will maximize your chances. Practice answering interview questions in a mirror or with assistance from friends and associates. The time spent preparing can strengthen your presentation and lessen your nervousness.

- Confidence speaks volumes, while arrogance is an opportunity killer. Don't let confidence turn into arrogance. Present your skills confidently, but don't undercut or criticize competitors or possible co-workers in the process.

- Always be positive. Refocus illegal or inappropriate questions to provide positive answers that showcase your abilities. Answer all questions with clarity and in detail.

- Good communication skills are the leading quality employers look for in a candidate. Honesty and integrity are just as important. Convey these qualities by (a) planning and practicing what you will say; (b) ensuring that your responses are honest and forthright; (c) avoiding slang, slander, or street jargon; and (d) enunciating your words and speaking up to ensure the interviewer can hear you.

- Emphasize your knowledge, skills, and experience. Show the interviewer what you can do and how you think by using stories of previous experiences or examples of how you would handle certain situations. Give details to present a full story of your abilities.

Chapter Assignments:

1. Create a tracking method for the positions you apply for and the resume versions you use. Include at least the following: Job Title, Company Name, Resume Used, How I Learned of the Position, Application Date, Employer Contact Name, Employer Telephone and E-mail.
2. Complete the following chart to help you compose a good set of possible answers to the question "Tell me a little about yourself."

"Tell Me a Little About Yourself"

1. My current situation is....

2. My technical project experience includes......

3. My previous work experience, volunteer experience, or relevant skills include.....

4. I want to get this position or work for this company because.....

5. Putting it all together.......

Questions for Reflection:

1. An interviewer poses the following challenge: "For your first project with the company, I ask you to move Mt. Fuji. Tell me how you would accomplish this task." Why is the interviewer asking such a question, and how would you respond?

2. Why is it important to show you are both a team player and a leader?

3. What is the purpose of a prescreen interview?

4. List three differences between a prescreen interview and a telephone interview.

5. What are the top five things employers look for in an interview, and why are they important?

6. What is appropriate attire for an interview?

7. How does your personality relate to the interview process? Should you try to project a certain personality, even if it's not yours?

Appendix A
Common Interview Questions

1. Tell me a little about yourself.
2. How did you learn about us/this opening?
3. What is your current GPA, and how do you think this reflects your abilities?
4. What was your least favorite or worst subject in college? Why?
5. What motivates you or drives you to do your best?
6. Tell me about your previous work experience.
7. Why are you looking to change jobs/career tracks?
8. In your working life, what has been your greatest achievement?
9. What would you say was your biggest contribution to that company?
10. Please describe two of your strengths and one of your weaknesses. Now, tell me how this position might bring out your strengths and minimize your weaknesses.
11. Identify one of your short-term goals and one long-term goal, and tell me how these are related to each other.
12. Describe the best and worst jobs you've had. What would your ideal job be like?
13. Describe the worst manager you ever had.
14. How would others describe you?
15. Tell me about a time when you were working under pressure. How did you handle it?
16. Tell me about a time when you had to work with difficult or uncooperative group members. How did you handle the relationships?
17. Tell me about a time when you had a complex project to complete or a situation to resolve. What steps did you take to accomplish the task? Did you complete the project or resolve the situation?
18. Given that your work history is not technical or that you do not have much work experience, why should we hire you? (What do you think you could contribute to our company?)
19. Is there any other relevant information I should know about you?
20. What range of salary are you looking for?

Appendix B
Questions You Should Ask in an Interview

Before going into an interview, do your homework. Check the company Website, read current reports, press releases, and corporate literature, and learn as much as you can about the company.

This initial research will show the employer that you are interested in the company, are thorough, and are knowledgeable about research. In the interview itself, you will be prepared to ask insightful and intelligent questions about the company and the position you are applying for.

1. Why is the position open? Is it a newly created position? If not, why did the last person leave?
2. What is a typical workday like in this position? What are its primary challenges?
3. How are evaluations done? How do I get feedback about my performance?
4. What are some short-term and long-term goals you'd like to see achieved through this position?
5. What would you consider to be a successful performance in this position?
6. What leeway would I have in establishing my own goals and deadlines?
7. How much employee turnover is there?
8. How does the company contribute to the employees' professional development?
9. What are the company's plans for future growth?
10. How has the company done through the recent economic downturn?
11. What makes this company different from its competitors? (Use research to identify the competitors.)
12. What is the company's niche in its industry?
13. What is the corporate culture at this company?
14. How would you describe your management style?
15. What are the goals of the department?
16. Does the company promote from within?
17. What is a typical career path for this position?
18. What kinds of assignments might I expect in the first six months on the job?
19. What are the major responsibilities of this job?
20. Do you have a training program for this job? Who would be training me?
21. How is performance evaluated, and how often are performance reviews done?
22. What do you like best about your own job and about this company?
23. How soon do you plan on filling this position?
24. Would it be prudent for me to call you in a few days and ask how things are shaping up? (This question opens the door to call them back and check in.)
25. May I please have your business card?

CHAPTER TEN
Making Follow-Up Count
Barbara Yetman

Pleasure in the job puts perfection in the work.

−Aristotle (384-322 BC)

This chapter will present the finishing touches to the interview process, including thank you letters, appropriate follow-up activities, and effective use of references. Assuming a positive outcome in the job search, you will be able to explore the job offer in light of prior self-assessments, career goals, and current market demand, ultimately determining if the job is both a personal and professional fit. To increase the likelihood of a successful match for you, this chapter will introduce strategies for examining organizational culture, the work environment, growth potential, and work/life balance. Finally, practical ways of evaluating compensation packages will be offered as contributions to a thoughtful and informed decision-making process.

After the Interview

By now you may have realized that the interview process is a lot like dating. You don't want to appear too anxious about the next encounter, and yet you may need to make the first follow-up move.

At the conclusion of the interview stage, it is quite acceptable to ask when the next step in the process might come. The question also signals to a prospective employer that you are interested in pursuing the position further. Assuming that you are one of several candidates interviewed, ask the employer when he might make a decision and if he has a preferred method for follow-up (e.g., e-mail vs. phone). As you're leaving the office, if you have not collected business cards, be sure to ask the receptionist for the names and titles of the individuals with whom you have interviewed. You'll also want to secure the correct spelling of names for your follow-up thank you letters. To make the best impression possible, include the receptionist in this list. It's wise to never underestimate the influence of "family" members!

Reflections and Impressions

As you replay the interview in your mind, make a point of jotting down notes about your impressions, questions, and perhaps even points you wish you had made, but didn't. Do this as quickly as possible while the interview is still fresh in your mind. When you're finished, you may draw on these reflections to develop a note of thanks that serves to restate your interest and qualifications, or provides additional relevant information. Should you be called back for a subsequent meeting, these notes will serve equally well as a refresher in preparation for further discussion.

Spreading the Word

The interviews are done, you think. The toughest part is over. Now it's time to sit back and play the waiting game until an offer is made? Absolutely not! You have quite a few items to attend to immediately following the interview, not least of which is making some important phone calls.

No doubt you were asked to provide a list of references as part of the application process. Assuming that you received approval from these individuals before listing them as references (as you should have), recognize that you should also maintain contact with them throughout the interview process. Drop a note or leave a message notifying them of your interview schedule. Once the interview has occurred, anticipate the positive and assume that you are a contender for the position. Alert your references that a phone contact may be coming. Here, too, your notes may be of value.

Let your contacts know the name of the company, the names and positions of people with whom you've interviewed, and some of the particular points these folks may be interested in hearing about. Remind your references of the experience, skills, projects completed, or personal traits that you feel are relevant to your candidacy. Your references will be better prepared, and you'll be better off.

Also be aware that prospective employers may also conduct an extended background check with former managers that have *not* been listed by you as references. Keeping these individuals informed of potential calls may prove equally important, particularly if you have any concerns about past experiences or difficult work relationships. If necessary, you may want to appeal to these contacts to consider aspects of your employment that went well as opposed to the trials and tribulations that linger in people's recollections. And remember, everyone makes mistakes as part of a learning process. If you grew as a result of these experiences, share that fact with your former employer and express your appreciation for any assistance she can provide with these new employment prospects. Be equally prepared, however, to communicate these same "lessons learned" during a follow-up interview for the new position, should the question arise in response to a reference check.

Finally, if you have any inside contacts in the new organization, or know people who do, be sure to let them know of your interviews. Share with them all the positive aspects of the experience and confirm your interest in the company. (Stay away from the negatives, as these may come back to haunt you if you are hired.) Chances are this information will make its way back to the employer, serving as further support of your candidacy.

Thank You, Thank You, Thank You

At the very least, thank you letters are simply good etiquette and, for this reason alone, will often distinguish you from some of the competition. At the most, they are a strategic weapon in the search for a job and a career.

Consider the impact of the following pair of messages:

1. Thanks for dinner, Aunt Edith. It was really good.

2. Aunt Edith, that was one of the best dinners I've had in a long time! It's obvious that you worked a long time on this meal to achieve such perfection. I had no idea that mashed potatoes could be so creamy and tasty. And the gravy made such a difference. I would love to learn how to make gravy like yours. In fact, I would be happy to stop by next Wednesday for dinner, if that would work for you. I'll bring the groceries and my appetite.

If you were on the receiving end of either of these expressions of thanks, what would be your reaction? In response to the first, you might be impressed with the simple display of good manners, but the second expression communicates much more than etiquette. "Clearly this boy knows good food and appreciates the details! You bet I'll invite him back; after all, he not only appreciates fine cooking, he's bringing something to the table."

The second message contains all the components of a strategic thank you note:

- Expression of appreciation for the opportunity
- Attention to detail
- Reminder of what you "bring to the table"

If you were to translate this approach to an interview, your letter might begin something like the following:

> Dear Ms. Gonzalez:
>
> Thank you for taking the time to speak with me about the sales position at Glendale Pharmaceuticals. I particularly enjoyed learning about the company's philosophy and commitment to customer satisfaction. I can now better understand how Glendale has achieved its outstanding reputation. As mentioned in our discussion, I share this philosophy and take pride in making the extra effort to ensure that my customers receive the best advice, the best service, and the best products for their needs...."

Also included in this letter might be a particular example of how you "made the extra effort." The strategy is to make the employer remember you and your potential value to the organization. Keep the message concise and close it with a confirmation of your interest in the position.

Other Considerations

There are two schools of thought about thank you letter formats. One holds that it should be hand-written, the other that it should be word processed. Perhaps the middle ground is the best approach. As long has your handwriting is neat and legible, opt for the hand-written note. It conveys a personal touch and is less likely to be inadvertently tossed out before being read. If your handwriting had your mother telling the neighbors that you were destined to be a doctor, consider it a liability and keyboard your note.

Of course, all this debate is moot if the employer prefers follow-up by e-mail. Regardless of format, make sure the thank you letter is free of grammatical and spelling errors, and is sent within a few days of the interview. A delayed response creates an impression that you do not value the position or the importance of timeliness. Worse yet, you risk losing the position to a competitor who beats you to the punch. Finally, if sending your letter by regular mail, be sure to use appropriate stationery that follows the same rules as those for proper attire in the interview: conservative and professional.

And Remember, People Talk

As best you can, when sending multiple thank you notes to individuals within a particular organization, tailor the message by referring to something specific you discussed with each interviewer. Sending identical thank you notes to everyone may create perceptions of laziness or insincerity.

Taking the time to develop a well-constructed and thoughtful follow-up letter may very well bring you from "Thanks for the memories" to "Thanks, I'm looking forward to seeing you on Monday."

The Waiting Game

Once the thank you letters have been sent and references notified, there may be a waiting period that tests your patience and your nerves. Just how long should you wait before following up on the follow-up? If you had the luxury of securing a definite timeline when closing the interview, then you have the answer to this question. Unfortunately, candidates often hear something like this:

> *We're wrapping up the first round of interviews next week and then we'll evaluate where to go from there.*

In these cases, you can apply a few rules of thumb.

Wait long enough to avoid being a pest, but don't wait so long that you appear uninterested in the position. Translation: follow-up by phone within a week to ten days of the interview unless advised to do otherwise at the close of the interview. An exception to this rule might be a competing offer. If you have the good fortune to receive another job offer while waiting to hear about your preferred position, make a call. Let the employer of choice know that you are very interested in the position but have received another offer and are being pressed for a decision. It is perfectly acceptable then to ask if you are being considered as one of the top candidates for the position, as well as to ask when a decision might be made.

Final Tips on Effective Follow-up

Effective follow-up is a wonderful opportunity to provide further proof to an employer of your personal attributes and work ethic. Timeliness, attention to detail, understanding of basic etiquette, strategic thinking, and effective communication are skills valued by all employers. But follow-up activities such as thank you notes and phone calls can also serve another purpose – that of damage control.

Perhaps you fumbled an answer to a critical question, or forgot to mention a key point that might have made a strong impression. Your follow-up activities can counter the negative effects of the omission. Taking the time to acknowledge these points in your thank you notes or in the follow-up phone call may very well lead you to a second round of interviews. And, once again, you've shown the employer another side of you…self-reflection.

Evaluating the Offer

To return to the dating analogy, you may be familiar with this piece of folk wisdom: "You need to kiss a lot of frogs before you find a prince." The same can be said about work experiences. Some jobs are merely stepping stones in the career journey, others are simply mistakes. To minimize the odds of making a bad choice, you will need to consider some key questions before you choose. After all, you will spend approximately half of your waking hours on the job. Taking the time to evaluate the offer thoroughly may save you time, aggravation, and money. Begin this process as soon as you complete the interview.

The Position

It's easy to get caught up in the excitement of "landing the job" and, as a result, overlook critical details of the position.

- First and foremost, does the job feel like a good fit? Is it interesting, challenging, and related to your field of study? Review the self-assessment and self-discovery exercises you completed in Chapter 3 and apply them here.

- Consider the position in relation to your short and long term goals. Will it build on your strengths, develop your weaknesses? Prepare you for advancement?

- Have you evaluated the requirements and stipulations of the position (for example: work hours, travel requirements, the need for relocation)? How will the position impact your personal or family life? If sacrifices are required, are you prepared to make them?

By asking yourself these questions, you will be in a better position to evaluate the offer and ultimately make a knowledgeable decision. People who enjoy their work generally put more effort into it and are ultimately more successful than those who don't. Realize, however, that the *position* itself will need to be viewed in an even broader context.

Marrying the Company

So you love the position and the work you'll do, but have you met "the family" – your co-workers, supervisors, and perhaps even clients? In many cases, the interview process will provide a natural avenue for some of this assessment, but to get a comprehensive view of your future, you will need to do additional work.

If you didn't do your homework *prior to the interview*, be sure to research the company thoroughly before accepting an offer. Characteristics such as size, scope of operation, and organizational structure may provide additional insight into the stability of the organization and into its culture.

A review of the company's history, recent performance, and industry outlook can provide a good indication of stability. Financial reviews, stock analyses, and annual reports may prove great resources for this purpose. Company culture, on the other hand, is not so easily researched. Somewhat like the challenges employers face in trying to assess a candidate's soft skills during the interview process, the culture of an organization may manifest itself in different ways at different times, requiring a candidate to be particularly and deliberately observant.

What is company culture? Generally speaking, it is the sum total of an organization's values, beliefs, and ways of doing business. It is exhibited in a company's processes, policies, products, and services. Most importantly, it is expressed in its relationships with and concern for people, whether employees, clients, or the general public.

One way to size up the culture of the organization is to arrive a little early to the interview and observe the general atmosphere including the nature of the working relationships among employees. For instance:

- Do people treat each other with respect?
- Are guests greeted with a smile and an offer of assistance?
- Is the physical environment welcoming, well-maintained, and suitable for accomplishing the type of work that will be expected of you?

During and after the interview, through observation and questioning, you may want to assess the following:

- Is there a clearly articulated mission statement? (This may well provide insight into aspects of a company's culture, not to mention its future. A poorly constructed mission may be indicative of a lack of vision and direction.)
- Are employees aware of the mission?
- What are the values of the organization, and how are they communicated to employees?
- Is there a company code of ethics?
- Is there evidence of a collaborative work environment in which open and honest communication is valued?
- Is there a balance between work and home life?
- How is performance evaluated? How often?
- What type of training and development opportunities are provided?
- What is a typical career path for someone in the prospective position?
- Was the interview process organized and professional?

Again, throughout this evaluation process, keep both short- and long-term goals in mind. Both pros and cons apply to any work environment, so identify those aspects that appeal to you and that contribute to your larger plan. For instance, there is a certain prestige in working for a company with a household name or a prominent place in its industry. In many large organizations, specific functional areas may have well-defined training programs and career paths to further your advancement. On the other hand, these defined channels may also limit your ability to transfer across departments to gain a broader range of knowledge and skills. Advancement opportunities in larger organizations are typically more plentiful, but so is the competition.

Conversely, smaller organizations, by their very nature, may provide several avenues for rapid growth. Smaller companies tend to draw on the multiple talents of their employees, providing exposure to various aspects of the business operation. Yet, training and development programs may be limited or even non-existent. People who are self-starters and problem-solvers may find these less structured environments exhilarating. The relatively intimate working conditions tend to facilitate more immediate recognition of outstanding work ... although the same may be true of mediocre performance. In smaller organizations, opportunities for advancement may come quickly, but they may also be restricted to a few select positions.

As you reflect on these considerations and other observations made during the interview process, share your thoughts and concerns with trusted colleagues, friends, and family. Try to learn from their experiences and insights, but realize that the final determination on personal fit is a decision only you can make.

Bringing Home the Bacon

At last, the long awaited call comes. You are the top candidate and the company is pleased to extend you an offer to join the family. Your heart leaps with joy at the prospect! And now, also, the ball is in your court. To accept or not to accept, that is the question ... or, as the game show had it, "Deal or no deal?"

By this stage of the process, you should have a fairly definite idea of whether you are truly interested in the position. During the interviews, you have come to understand the demands of the job and the nature of the work week, including the amount of travel that would be required, if any. You have established whether or not your position will be compensated for overtime; and if overtime is required, you have a sense of how extensive that might be. Similarly, flex time, training opportunities, and performance evaluations have been discussed. Your evaluation of the company and the position should be nearly complete, pending the final offer. If not, these are questions you should pose when discussing or negotiating the offer.

Too often, candidates hinge their acceptance largely on the base salary. And while there is a reality in having to meet one's living expenses, it is important to look at the full compensation package. It is just as important to look at compensation in light of personal and family considerations, life and career goals, and ultimate value.

The compensation package typically includes benefits such as medical and dental insurance, vacation and personal time, paid holidays, pension/401K plans, tuition reimbursement plans, wellness programs, etc. Additional compensation in the form of bonuses, commissions, company car, and stock options may also be available. As you weigh the offer against your daily living expenses and your personal goals, be sure to factor in the impact of these items.

A number of resources, particularly the Bureau of Labor Statistics (www.bls.gov), the National Association of Colleges and Employers (NACE) (www.naceweb.org), and your college Career Services office, can assist you in establishing the market rate for jobs in your field. They can do so both with regard to average starting salary and long term earning potential. And while benefits packages may require a little more research to determine their competitive standing, one convenient resource is right at your fingertips: Ask friends and family about their benefits.

Certain components of a compensation package often cause concern for the novice job hunter. Of particular note are bonuses and commissions. By their very nature, these perquisites are not guaranteed, but there are ways to estimate their potential value *and* your prospects of attaining them. If an employer indicates that your position will include either or both of these elements, ask the following questions. (Most companies are fully prepared to respond.)

- What performance goals or targets must I meet to earn a bonus and/or commission?
- For someone at my level of experience, what is the average bonus and/or commission during the first year of employment? The second year? For a seasoned professional?
- What is the average annual base wage increase for employees in this section of the company?

Similarly, you should clarify the status of other perks, such as a company car. Will you be issued a car or given a monthly allowance towards purchase or lease of a car of your choosing? Is the car restricted for company business or is it available for personal use as well? (Be aware that you may be taxed on the personal use of a company car as part of your larger compensation package.)

With regard to tuition reimbursement plans and participation in 401K/pension plans, ask when you will become eligible to participate. Many organizations require a one-year waiting period. Ask about other conditions of participation. Are there restrictions and/or limits on tuition reimbursement? Does the company match contributions to the 401K, and if so, at what rate?

Finally, review the details of the medical benefits plan. You will want to establish the cost of the employee contribution, extent of coverage, and other conditions of the plan. Depending on your personal situation, these could be significant factors in estimating the overall value of your compensation package.

Accepting or Rejecting the Offer

In a perfect world, the offer is extended, and it meets or exceeds all of your expectations! You say yes, the employer is pleased, and all's right with the world. In the real world, however, the offer is likely to be somewhat less than the ideal, and you may find yourself contemplating "deal or no deal?" How can you make the best decision in these cases?

There is no single answer to this question, but consider the following scenarios involving Mark, Margaret, Al, and, finally, *you*.

SCENARIO	LEVEL OF RISK
1. The offer is for less than Mark wanted, but rather than research the offer, he decides that negotiating additional compensation is not worth the risk of losing the job. He accepts the offer.	Mark has not evaluated the situation. Were his expectations *reasonable*? Was the offer *unreasonable*? Without evaluation, Mark has no idea whether the offer might, in fact, be a fair one. As a result, he may enter the position with a level of discontent that could manifest itself on the job over time.

2. Margaret analyzes the situation and recognizes that the offer – while less generous than expected – meets average market rates for comparable positions and still satisfies all of her financial, professional, and personal goals. She accepts the offer.	Margaret has conducted a thorough assessment of the situation and has made an educated decision to accept the offer. Her satisfaction with the position is likely to be greater.
3. Al analyzes the situation and recognizes that the compensation – as proposed – will not meet his basic cost of living expenses. He decides to negotiate because all other aspects of the position meet his professional and personal goals. The position, overall, is a good fit.	Al has recognized the practical need for a certain salary. What is not known is whether the salary offer meets fair market value, and what type of offer he intends to negotiate. If the salary offer meets fair market value and Al's desired amount is greater, he may risk losing the offer. What other options might he consider?
4. *You* analyze the situation and conclude that the company is offering less than the market rate for the position. The position meets your short-term needs financially, personally, and professionally, but you feel a need to negotiate at least a market rate for the position to avoid feeling short-changed over time.	You have recognized that, over time, an offer below the market rate could adversely affect your desire to stay with the company. Your decision to negotiate is based on a solid assessment of the market and the situation.

Regardless of the situation, recognize that most employers do not expect you to give them a decision on the spot. In fact, most employers would prefer that you take time to review the offer since this assures them that you have carefully considered all aspects of the position and are comfortable with your decision. As discussed in previous chapters, it's all in the communication. If you are truly interested in the position, be sure to convey your enthusiasm, but ask if you may have a day or two to review the details before accepting the offer.

The Fine Art of Negotiation

Let's face it, asking for more money from an employer you barely know is tantamount to asking Aunt Edith for a cost of living increase in your next birthday card. Awkward. But fear not! Where asking Aunt Edith for an increase is just plain tacky, negotiating a starting salary does not need to be.

If on reviewing the offer you feel a need to negotiate, keep in mind that the majority of employers are well aware of the going market rate for their positions. After all, they are competing with other employers for the best and brightest talent. Their human resources are their greatest investment, and in order to remain competitive in the industry, they must also be competitive in compensation.

Still, employers work within defined budgets and established salary ranges, so there are limits to the negotiation possibilities. More than likely, if you are an entry-level candidate in the field, the offer extended to you is on the low end of the range, with some limited room to increase the package if warranted.

For the mid-career applicant, there may be greater negotiating room based on the experience she brings to the position. If you are making a career change and entering a new field, highlight those experiences (and transferable skills) that set you apart from the typical entry-level candidate. For instance, managerial expertise, ability to meet goals and deadlines, and customer relations experience are skills of value to nearly all employers, no matter the business. If you are currently employed in the same field, be sure to highlight key accomplishments and/or technical expertise relevant to the company you are pursuing. Use such experiences to your advantage by demonstrating to an employer how these past experiences will enable you to become productive, faster.

Regardless of your status (entry level, career changer, career enhancer), be prepared to clearly articulate your rationale for higher compensation, being careful not to insult the employer while communicating your perceived worth. Focus on transferable skills from other jobs, the scope of your education, hands-on laboratory or other applications experience, and other work-related talents that warrant reconsideration of the offer. These types of arguments suggest value-added potential to the employer, whereas your financial needs are only as relevant as the average market conditions. Just because the salary offer doesn't allow you to maintain a high-priced sports car and a second house at the beach, don't expect the employer to re-evaluate!

Taking It to the Limit
So, you take a deep breath, review the results of your research, and ask the employer to bump the starting salary from \$38,000 to \$42,000. It wasn't too painful, you were professional and respectful, and you feel good about having had the nerve to ask.

And he says no.

What went wrong? The reality of the situation, as noted earlier, is that employers have established budgets and salary guidelines. Depending on market conditions, they may have more or less wiggle room at any given moment. Your specific request to bump the salary may have painted you into a corner. A better strategy would be to follow Margaret's example and frame a more general question like the following:

> I'm very excited about the position, but based on the general market rates
> for similar positions, combined with my (XYZ) experience, the offer is
> lower than I had anticipated. Is there any room for discussion?

Without specifying a salary level, Margaret has now given the employer an opportunity to sweeten the pot in a variety of ways. If the salary part is firm, perhaps other factors are open to negotiation – an accelerated period for review or an extra vacation, say.

And so, the employer tells Margaret he will discuss the possibility with his own supervisor and get back to her. The following day she receives a call.

And he still says no.

Basically, Margaret now has two options: (1) reject the offer, and thank him for the opportunity to interview, or (2) accept the original offer and confirm her enthusiasm for the position. Either way, she needs to be prepared to know what she will do *and say*, should the situation arise.

Small Worlds Getting Smaller

Sometimes – no matter how tempted you are – you know in your heart that the relationship is not meant to be, the position is not a fit for you, and you simply have to say no to an offer.

Keep in mind that even the largest of industries can also be a small world. Employers often know their competitors personally through professional and civic organizations, social networks, and mutual business contacts. Likewise, people regularly move from organization to organization. The employer from Alpha Electronics who extended you an offer today might be interviewing you next week for a position in his own start-up firm. Or perhaps the Beta corporation suddenly has an opening for a more advanced position than the one you initially pursued. And the Beta technical manager remembers that your portfolio demonstrated many of the skills now being sought.

By now you know where this is going: Never burn bridges. Always extend the courtesy of a reply to an offer of employment, even if that reply is, "No, thank you." Do so with appreciation for the opportunity and openness to future discussions. You never know where the job search will lead.

But enough about *not* accepting offers; let's end on a high note! Whether or not you choose to negotiate, accept an offer with enthusiasm!

> I'm very excited about the opportunity to join your organization, and I look forward to becoming a contributing member of your team. I accept!

OR

> I completely understand the budget constraints at Delta Company. I want to confirm my interest in the position and my appreciation for the offer. I accept!

And so you've accepted the offer, the position is just what you've been looking for, and you're on your way to a successful and fulfilling career. Just get it in writing … politely, of course.

> May I request a written confirmation of the offer?

And then you can frame it. Years from now, you'll look back at the moment that launched it all, and laugh with your friends and family about the "salaries back then…. But, of course, a dollar was worth something then. A gallon of gas was only $6.50, I remember."

Chapter Summary and Activities:

The job search process requires thoughtful preparation, reflection, and analysis. Careful consideration of yourself, your goals, and the employment market will enable you to make educated choices based not merely on salary offers, but on the true value of the opportunity for you as an individual. These considerations along with targeted actions and strategies in the interview process can increase the likelihood of realizing career success.

Activity 1: Company Culture

- Analyze company Websites and other resources such as product/service brochures and annual reports, for insights into company culture. Share your findings with the class in a brief oral presentation.

- Assess an "office culture" using observation techniques you might employ during an actual interview. With the approval of a department manager, you might conduct these analyses on campus, or perhaps in an actual business in the area. For instance, visit an office and document the following interactions:

  - Are you greeted by the receptionist when you walk in? Note the body language, presence or absence of a smile, and offers of assistance.
  - Sit down in the reception area and observe how others are treated when they walk in. Describe the interactions between employees and customers, and between co-workers.
  - How are the phones managed?
  - Observe the physical space. What impressions does it create?
  - Are there publications available? What insights do they provide into the company's culture?

Activity 2: Job Fit

- Develop a general profile of your ideal job. Then conduct an Internet search and find a job posting in your field. Analyze the job for personal fit. How does it compare to your ideal job? Does it have the potential to help you reach your career goals?

Activity 3: References and Thank You Letters

- With another student, role play an interview situation, with one playing the role of employer, one the role of interviewee. Use a job posting from an employer's Website to set the stage for the activity. At the conclusion of the interview:

  - What insights has the interviewee (or the class, if they are observing the role play) gained about the employer and the company?
  - What types of personal and work-related experiences would this employer value?
  - Based on these observations, what should the candidate communicate to his references to better prepare them for the employer's follow-up call?

    ° Using the guidelines from this chapter, design a thank you letter that references a particular aspect of the interview.

Activity 4: References

- Select a job posting relevant to your career field and your level of expertise. You may find these postings by using a job search engine, visiting employer Websites, or visiting your campus Career Services office. Analyze your personal list of references as they relate to this job posting, and then determine the three best references to pursue for assistance. Explain your rationale for choosing these references.
- Highlight key skills that your references should address with an employer. Provide examples that demonstrate the skill sets.

Activity 5: Compensation

Consider the following packages.

- Assuming that the medical, dental, and vision plans are all of equal value, can you determine which of these packages provides the greatest overall value? Explain your answer.
- How would you rank-order the offers? Why?
- Can you determine which of the following offers provides the greatest earnings potential in the first two years of employment? Explain your answer.

Base Salary	Benefits	Company Car	Tuition Reimburse- ment	Bonus	Average Performance Review Increase	Frequency of Performance Reviews
$34,000	Medical Dental Vision 401K 10% Match	Yes	No	No	4.0%	Annual
$45,000	Medical Dental Vision 401K 2% Match	No	Yes	No	4.0%	Annual
$45,000	Medical Dental Vision 401K 2% Match	Yes	No	No	2.0%	Every 6 months
$28,000	Medical Dental Vision 401K 2% Match	Yes	Yes	Yes – Annual ave. $20K first year, 25K second year	2.5%	Annual

Activity 6: Compensation

- You have just received the offer listed in Row #1 above ($34,000 salary). You ask the employer for some time to consider the offer. That night, as you evaluate your cost of living expenses (rent, food, utilities, gas, car insurance, car payment), you realize that they amount to an average monthly expenditure of $2,000. Can you financially afford to accept this position? Are there other considerations you might include in reaching a decision? What are they?

Activity 7: Compensation

- Use one or more of the following resources:

  ° U.S. Bureau of Labor Statistics
  ° National Association of Colleges and Employers (NACE) Salary Survey
  ° Your college Career Services office

  Determine the average starting salary range for someone with your level of experience in your field of study, and in your geographic area (for instance, northern New Jersey). Compare this range with another geographic region (for instance, southern California). From your research, what factors seem to influence the determination of these ranges?

Works Cited

Bazan, Kathryn Lee. "Job Interview Follow-up." *The Art of the Follow-up After Interviews.* Quintessential Careers. 24 Oct 2006 http://www.quintcareers.com/job_interview_follow-up.html.

Bolles, Richard Nelson. *What Color is Your Parachute?* Berkeley: Ten Speed Press, 2006.

Bureau of Labor Statistics, *Occupational Outlook Handbook 2006-2007 Edition.* "Evaluating a Job Offer." 20 Dec 2005. U.S. Department of Labor. 24 Oct 2006 http://www.bls.gov/oco/oco20046.htm.

Denham, Thomas J. "Salary and Benefits." *Evaluating Job Offers and Negotiating Salary.* National Association of Colleges and Employers. 24 Oct 2006 http://www.jobWeb.com/Resources/Library/Salary_and_Benefits/Evaluating_Job_75_01.htm.

Eyler, David R. *The Ultimate Job Book.* New York: Random House, December 2002

Fein, Richard. *95 Mistakes Job Seekers Make.* Manassas Park: Impact Publications, 2003.

Hansen, Randall S.. "Career Articles." *Job Interview Follow-up Do's and Don'ts.* Quintessential Careers. 24 Oct 2006 http://www.quintcareers.com/interview_follow-up-dos-donts.html .

"Job Searching: Technical." *How to Rehearse Your References.* About Inc. 24 Oct 2006 http://jobsearchtech.about.com/od/interview/l/aa031300_2.htm.

Ojimba, Orisa. *Career.* "What to Look for Before, During, and After the Interview." Salary.com Inc.. 24 Oct 2006 http://www.salary.com/careers/layouthtmls/crel_display_nocat_Ser199_Par297.html.

Williams, Debra. "Job Hunting Advice." *Finding References That Sing Your Praises.* Wall Street Journal. 24 Oct 2006 http://www.careerjournal.com/jobhunting/resumes/19990122-williams.html.

Additional Resources

A host of career resources is available from your local Career Services office, the library, and the Internet. Listed below are a few such resources readily available by accessing the links below. These sites include tutorials, surveys, industry outlooks, and relevant articles.

General Job Search Resources

- National Association of Colleges and Employers (NACE) Website: Career Development and Job Search Advice for New College Grads. http://www.jobWeb.com/default.asp

- U.S. Bureau of Labor Statistics: includes the Occupational Outlook Handbook for 2006-2007, salary guides, and job search advice. http://www.bls.gov/home.htm

Salary Surveys and Negotiation Tips:

- The Wall Street Journal's Executive Career Site: http://www.careerjournal.com/salaryhiring/negotiate/

Thank You Letters:

- Quintessential Careers Website: a comprehensive site for all matters related to the job search, including tutorials. http://www.quintcareers.com/tutorials.html

- About Inc. is part of the New York Times Company. The About.com Website contains a host of information that includes pertinent resources for careers. http://jobsearchtech.about.com/od/thankyouletters/

CHAPTER ELEVEN
Growing Into a New Career
Karen Hanes

By three methods we may learn wisdom: first, by reflection, which is noblest; second, by imitation, which is easiest; and third by experience, which is the bitterest.

– Confucius (551-477 BC)

Chapter Goal:

To help a new employee acclimate, transition, and adjust to a new organization and its corporate culture as effortlessly, skillfully, and quickly as possible.

Chapter Objectives:

- Learn to identify and assess a new organizational culture.
- Acclimate to a new work environment quickly.
- Learn the pitfalls of potential Career Limiting Moves (CLMs).
- Make office relationships work for you.
- Avoid the potential problems of business travel.
- Analyze the legalities of today's workplace.

Reading a New Work Environment

With the completion of a degree program in your chosen field, you are ready to launch a new career – or to enhance an existing one. You want to make the most of this opportunity. Your entry point is either a new company or a new work environment within the existing organization. Though you are new, you want to project the image of a professional. This has nothing to do with your age or even experience, but much to do with applying your learning, intelligence, judgment, and ability to adapt to the new environment. How do you accomplish this goal? Start with some basic considerations – What do I wear to work? How do I act? How do I interact? What is the corporate culture of this place?

Dress

You may want to revisit the guidelines in Chapter Nine on dressing for interviews. These have a lot to do with creating a favorable first impression. As a new employee at your company or in a department, you are also building a first impression that is likely to linger. Your co-workers, as well as your new boss, are still forming their opinions about you. You have a chance to nudge these impressions in a positive direction by the way you present yourself.

If you didn't establish what the office dress code is at the time of your hiring or promotion, try to learn from observing your co-workers. Be selective in this approach, however, since you may also pick the wrong models for imitation. If on your first day of work you do not know what the expectations are, then dress as you did for the interview. Even if you are overdressed, people will understand that you are new, not weird. Likely someone, such as your manager, will bring you up to speed on the daily dress expectations. If in doubt, ask your manager.

Business Casual
In most work environments, business casual means the following:

MEN: Casual slacks, of cotton or khaki material, such as golf pants, would work. Suit pants are not necessary, though these would also be OK. Trousers should be ironed and neat. Jeans are *not* considered business casual. Golf-style or polo shirts would work. These have a few buttons at the top, short sleeves, a collar, and might feature the company logo somewhere. A dress shirt without a tie is another option. Not acceptable are t-shirts, tank tops, sleeveless shirts, and shirts without a collar. Shoes might be casual loafers with socks, or dress shoes. Avoid boots, gym shoes, sandals, or flip-flops of any kind.

WOMEN: Business casual for women provides more options, which can be good or bad. The simplest combination for most women is a pair of khaki or dark pants and the company golf shirt with loafers. If business casual is the norm every day, you may need more options. Skirts that are well fitting and mid-knee or longer are a good choice. Jeans are not an option. Not wearing pantyhose may be an option depending on your office and the season. Blouses with sleeves and with or without a collar are fine. Hair, makeup, and undergarments should all be in good taste.

While there are always exceptions based on the company, type of work, and regional location, the following are *not* good choices for business casual wear for men or women: jeans, sandals, gym shoes, flip-flops, or any open-toed shoe. Neither is any clothing that is revealing, see-through, or meant for the beach, athletic club, or night club. The casual spectrum should also not include poor-fitting, torn, or stained clothing. Good grooming and hygiene still apply.

Casual Fridays
In the days when most companies expected employees to wear suits and ties, Friday was a day of respite when employees could wear business casual. Today, with many companies approving business casual for daily wear, these Fridays have either gone by the wayside or become even more casual, including even jeans, sneakers, and the like. But, be sure to find out what is appropriate at your company before you get *too* casual!

Workplace Etiquette
Perhaps you see the counterpart of casual dress in the spread of bad manners – in our society as well as in the workplace. Certainly, as the form of dress has become more casual, so has the manner in which employees address each other, quickly adopting a first-name basis, for example. Relations are also more casual and informal, but it is important to *distinguish informality from bad manners*. A simple distinction might be that informality can make others feel more comfortable, while bad manners tend to make them feel uneasy.

Bad manners are often a result of careless or thoughtless behavior that does not take into account the effect of one's actions or comments on others. I may launch an occasional cuss word into a group of friends or associates at work, but if I speak the same way to new associates, vendors, or customers, I may be guilty of bad manners. I may also be accused of thoughtlessness if I use swear words for their shock value or to impress people.

The guideline to follow in these matters is to practice your best manners. This does not mean that you should adopt a formality that makes you as well as others uncomfortable. It does mean that you should set a standard of being polite and professional at all times. The standard applies to both words and actions. Here are some specific suggestions:

Punctuality

This is one of the basic ways to show respect for others and their time. It is also one of the most abused and misinterpreted of standards. The point is worth making in a categorical way: As a new employee or a veteran, *be on time,* regardless of the circumstances! As a new employee, remember that you were hired because your employer thought you were a responsible, dependable person. Don't undercut this assumption by being lax about arriving on time for work and being punctual for meetings and appointments. (Consider such behavior also as a CLM – a Career-Limiting Move.) If the traffic is heavy or the weather bad, leave earlier. If the meeting is scheduled for 2 p.m. on another floor, leave your office at 1:50. If you are in another meeting till 2 p.m., ask the group leader for permission to leave five minutes early.

TRUE TALES FROM THE TRENCHES

Sue, a recent MBA graduate, was surprised at how quirky some corporate culture elements could be. Sue had studied corporate culture in the last few years of college, but she had never heard of punctuality being a trait of a company's culture. Shortly after her third week on the job with a Fortune 500 company, she arrived at 7:50 a.m. for an all-day meeting scheduled to start at 8 a.m. The entire department, including her boss, James, was already assembled. They looked as though they had been there for some time. She thought she saw James and some of the others give her a searching look. She checked her watch against the wall clock and found that she was on time. The meeting began at 8 a.m. sharp. When the group took a coffee break at 10, James asked Sue for a private word. In a serious tone, James said, "Sue, the meeting was set to begin at 8 a.m. You will need to be on time in the future." "But I arrived at 7:50 a.m.," Sue politely replied. James continued, "Yes, you did arrive at 7:50, but let me explain something about our company. When a meeting is set to begin at 8, everyone is expected to arrive 30 minutes before that to take care of incidentals. They get coffee, go to the restroom, make phone calls, socialize, and get to their seats by 8 a.m. We like to stay on schedule. Socializing and networking with your co-workers is important, and these meetings are a good chance to do that. As a new employee, you should really take advantage of this. Do we understand each other?" Sue replied, "Absolutely." Sue was always "on time" for meetings after that.

This is a good example of a particular corporate culture trait or quirk. Many companies have unwritten and unspoken rules that are part of their way of doing business. These rules may have developed gradually over time within a stable workforce. They can make it difficult for a new employee to adjust smoothly to the new environment. Other possible examples of unwritten rules: Employees only take 15 minutes for lunch; everyone leaves a little early on Friday afternoon; whenever your boss asks you to go to lunch, you should go. What you can do as a new member of such an organization is to seek guidance from your boss, from friendly co-workers, or from a mentor.

Basic Courtesy and Tone

Within the bounds of basic courtesy, saying *please* and *thank you* should be automatic, including over the phone, in e-mails, and in person. The concept also includes not interrupting others when they are talking or obviously busy. It means listening when someone is speaking and not interrupting. When attending conferences or meetings, wait until the official break to use the restroom or get refreshments. Also, practice good cell phone manners. Turn the unit off when you shouldn't be interrupted (meetings and conferences); talk on the cell phone only where you are not bothering others. These are some of the basic courtesies that you should already practice on a daily basis in any workplace.

The more subtle aspects of office etiquette are just as important. Consider the *tone* of your e-mail or voicemail messages. Do you sound overly aggressive or perhaps vague and indecisive? Are you demanding something or politely requesting it? Are you expressing a positive, optimistic tone or a negative judgment or expectation? Projecting the right tone may be a challenge that takes practice and seasoning within an organization. In the meantime, it is always best to err on the side of friendliness, politeness, and gentle suggestion. You can always get more aggressive in tone later if you need to. It is much harder to soften your tone once it has been set.

TRUE TALES FROM THE TRENCHES

Claude, based in Chicago, serves as manager of a sales team consisting of Americans and South Americans selling all over Latin America. He faces daily challenges in his region – on both the sales and cultural fronts. During one of his monthly conference calls, he asked each of his country sales directors to send him a report on new customers by the end of the day. From the 10 directors, he received only 4 reports. The next morning his e-mail contained no additional reports. Claude was very upset. He needed the information for a meeting with the Vice President of Sales that afternoon.

He began personally calling each of the directors and asked them to e-mail their reports immediately. He explained the urgency of the situation. After he had spoken to three of the directors, his Executive Assistant ran into his office and asked, "What did you say to Jose Carlos in Brazil? He says you yelled at him, and he is afraid he may lose his job!" Stunned at this miscommunication, Claude explained that he had simply called Jose Carlos and requested the report as soon as possible. He had not yelled or threatened; in fact, he thought he had maintained a friendly tone given the circumstances. The assistant reminded him of the cultural differences between the countries, especially with respect to reporting relationships. Many Latin American countries conduct business on a formal basis, using people's titles and last names, and not using the first name of a direct supervisor – even after being asked to do so.

As the case suggests, even a "friendly" tone may be interpreted as demanding by another person. A boss' asking for something a second or third time in a hurried manner can be construed as harsh in some cultures. Additionally, the concepts of time and punctuality are open to varied interpretations around the world. "Right away" and "immediately" can mean very different things in different parts of the world.

Voicemail and E-Mail

At a time when you are agitated, frustrated, or downright angry, leaving voicemail messages or sending e-mails can be a bad idea. Most of us convey our emotions at such times, whether we mean to or not. Such unintended messages can contribute to our CLM account. Often, what we say from emotion is not what we would say when we are calm. If you find yourself upset over something, wait until you have calmed down before you respond. In the case of an e-mail reply, a good technique is to compose the message but not to send it. Sleep on it and the next day revise the message as necessary. Chances are you will be relieved you didn't send it and that you took the time to adopt a more diplomatic tone. Use this approach for voicemail messages as well.

Response Times

In this age of e-mail, instant messages, and cell phones, most people expect to reach someone or get a response within a short time. Be sure to find out what is expected of you in this regard. Are you expected to check e-mail every hour? Are you expected to respond to *all* e-mails within the day? How long should you wait for an answer from your manager? Remember that "right away" has different meanings for people, especially when you are doing business in other countries.

TRUE TALES FROM THE TRENCHES

Denise, an experienced professional, was the VP of Information Technology, managing a team of software engineers. While she was based in New York City, the rest of the team was scattered around the United States and Canada. This dispersion created many problems with logistics and time in particular. Unlike in the New York office she worked from, time was more of a fluid, indefinite element to the engineers in certain locations. For example, when she scheduled a conference call for the team, very rarely were all eight of them on time. Usually, she and one other manager were on the call waiting for the rest of the team, who typically logged in over the next 20 minutes. She found this extremely frustrating when the call itself was only supposed to last one hour!

> Finally, with the help of her administrative assistant, Denise devised a system that worked for everyone and saved them all a lot of time and frustration. She set the time of a conference call 20 minutes prior to when she actually wanted to start. She then asked her assistant to monitor the call and take attendance. Once the entire team was on the call, she would inform Denise, who would join the group then. This approach also sent a subtle message to the team that they were to *wait for her,* and not the other way around.

Company Culture

Much of what is expected in your behavior and how it is interpreted depends on the culture of the company itself. Many of the traits of a company's culture and the reasons you may or may not want to work there need to be examined at the time you consider joining the organization. Some companies are very formal. For example, you must make an appointment to speak with your manager; employees are addressed by their titles. At informal companies, on the other hand, managers have "open door" policies and are on a first-name basis with their employees. Sometimes the company's culture is thought of as *the feel* of the organization.

Here is a formal definition of the concept of corporate culture by the author of a best-selling business text:

> The set of values, beliefs, behaviors, customs, and attitudes that helps the members of the organization understand what it stands for, how it does things, and what it considers important. (Griffin 2004)

How to do things is a common and visible aspect of the company's culture. Thus, behavior that may seem harmless and benign at one company can be discordant at another. There may also be expected behaviors, and others to be avoided, at the company you work for.

TRUE TALES FROM THE TRENCHES

> Aaron was excited to land his first job out of business school as an accountant at an international consumer goods company. He spent his first few weeks getting organized and learning the ropes.
>
> Finally, after a month, it was time to meet the rest of the accounting department at a quarterly meeting. At the start of the meeting, Aaron's boss, Dennis, gave a heated talk about the timing and accuracy of accounting reports. He spoke about the need for compliance with the stricter accounting standards created in the wake of the Enron collapse several years before. "Our internal audit process has not risen to the level required by this legislation," he exclaimed, adding a mild obscenity for emphasis. No one in the group took particular note of his expletive, or thought anything more of it.
>
> After the group returned from a coffee break, Dennis resumed the meeting by apologizing profusely. "My behavior was really uncalled for and unprofessional,"

he said. "That is not the kind of department we are and the kind of example I want to set. I hope I didn't offend anyone and that you all accept my apologies."

Aaron had no idea what his boss was apologizing for. A co-worker informed him that Dennis was upset at himself for swearing earlier. Not only was Dennis a very polite person, but company practice as a whole was quite restrained and formal in this aspect. The lesson for new employees is to be careful and modest in their language.

Consider the opposite extreme. Years later, Aaron accepted a position at a smaller, regional company. He was shocked when his first managers' meeting demonstrated that foul language was not only acceptable, it was almost expected as a way of showing solidarity with the group!

You can see by these examples that acceptable behavior at one company can be a clear CLM at another. Expectations about social and professional behavior reflect the company's culture.

Relationships at Work

All companies have formal procedures for how things are supposed to work, and then there are the ways things really get done. Fostering relationships with your managers, peers, and colleagues can be very helpful in this respect. Being a new employee, you will have to rely on others for information. They can give you good, solid advice or inadequate and inaccurate information. Establishing and maintaining positive working relationships with others will help ensure that such information is accurate and helpful. Also, everyone prefers to work with people they like. *Be that likeable person.* It will help you adjust to and blend in with the organization.

Mentors

One particularly useful relationship to a new employee is the interaction with a mentor. A mentor is a senior employee, usually in a position of responsibility, who is viewed in a positive light by fellow employees and senior management. Because of this successful experience, a mentor should be very familiar with the company's policies, politics, and culture.

A mentoring relationship with such a person can help clear up a lot of the confusion for a new employee. While some managers naturally step into a mentoring role with new employees, just as many or more do not. Perhaps they view it as favoritism and as taking away from their supervisory role. Much of the advice new employees need is on how to deal with their new manager and a new environment without appearing backward or immature. This is where the mentor can be most helpful. If your manager or another senior person does not offer this kind of help, you may want to find someone yourself.

How does one find a mentor? Make a list of managers with at least five years at the company. At the top of the list should be people in or around your immediate area or function. Find out what you can about each. Consider what you would like them to advise you about. Then ask your leading candidate to help you in this way.

Be sure you have answers to the typical reasons for declining your request: "I would love to, but I really don't think I have anything to offer you." "I would, but I just don't have the time." If you have drawn up your list carefully, you know this person has much to offer you. Point out what you're looking for, and the senior person may realize that she does know a lot about such things. Clarify that you are seeking only a lunch or coffee meeting once or twice a month, and the mentor-to-be might realize he can spare the time after all. Most importantly, make this person understand that you are interested in becoming the best you can be as a professional in an area that he already commands and in which he provides a positive example of accomplishment.

An important point about this campaign to "woo" a mentor is that you must genuinely respect the person, and that any attempts at false flattery will quickly become apparent. Choose someone you can learn from, not someone you just want to use.

Dating at Work

Many people spend more time at work today than they do with family or friends. Not surprisingly then, many romances begin at work. Yet workplace romances can create problems. While some may lead to permanent relationships or even marriage, many more do not survive the pressures and may leave the participants with bruised feelings, broken hearts, and looking for a new job.

Though it may seem overly cautious, many companies have a no-dating policy for employees. One of the main types of these policies says no dating of any kind is permitted within the company, and violations will lead to termination. The second kind of dating policy states that people in any kind of reporting relationship cannot date each other.

Even if it is not against the company's policy, in most cases dating one's co-workers is viewed as less than professional, because of its potential for destabilizing the work environment. It is best to avoid this situation altogether.

Why is dating at work such an issue? Isn't this really your own business? Here are two possible consequences that cause companies to take an interest: (a) hurting department morale and (b) sexual harassment lawsuits. Imagine working on a team or in a department where everyone knows that the manager is dating Susie, or Sammy. The upshot is that the person dating the manager is treated differently. S/he is held at arm's length because of the belief that what is said and done will get back to the boss. It is also hard for the manager to remain impartial when disputes must be resolved or appraisals done. Because of the special relationship, everyone is looking for "unfair treatment" with a microscope. Suspected instances lead to damaged morale and complaints of favoritism.

If the relationship is between peers, it is subject to the chance of a complicated breakup that may bring the couple's problems to work. Other employees may take sides and upset normal working relationships. If one of the participants wanted the relationship to end and the other did not, the company may end up in the middle. Most sexual harassment situations begin this way. Very few harassers and their victims are strangers or have a work-only relationship.

Social Situations

Many new employees do not realize that social situations are frequently part of the working environment, rather than something separate and apart. Handling these situations properly can add to their chances of success at work. If the social interaction is handled poorly, a career can be damaged and, with repetition, severely limited.

Food

A lot of business is conducted over food and drink. Food usually means lunch, sometimes dinner. Regardless of the occasion, follow the lead of the senior person. If this is your manager, take notice of what s/he is doing and ordering. For example, if the senior person is simply ordering a quick meal or sandwich, you do not want to be the one who orders a five-course meal. Try not to stand out either by ordering the most expensive selections or being the only one drinking alcohol.

You may also want to consider the ease with which the food can be eaten. It can be very embarrassing to have barbeque sauce trickling down your chin while you discuss your future in the company with a manager or mentor. You might also consider what food agrees with you during the meal and later in the day. This can save you a lot of embarrassment later, especially if you are in an all-day meeting.

Alcohol

Many a career has been damaged or ruined by alcohol. Part of the reason is that alcohol is a social lubricant that loosens people up and lowers their inhibitions. Many companies intentionally serve alcohol at events to see how their employees handle it. Who drinks too much and acts badly because of it? Who doesn't drink at all? Whom can we trust to take an important client to dinner, have a drink or two, and still get the business done?

The key in these situations is moderation. One may think that not having a drink at all would be the best or safest course. Actually, in social settings, such as cocktail parties or receptions, the drink is almost an expected feature – a prop. If you don't drink alcohol, order a club soda with a lime. The idea is to avoid making others feel uncomfortable, particularly customers or clients. If you do drink, but feel a pressure to drink more than you wish, simply hold on to the glass you are sipping and nurse it along. Be sociable but know your alcohol tolerance, and stick to a limit.

TRUE TALES FROM THE TRENCHES

Jennifer was hired as a product manager by a leading consumer electronics firm soon after graduation. Apparently her company has an open-bar Happy Hour every month. Sometimes it is held in the company boardroom and other times at a local restaurant. The idea behind these gatherings is for employees to network and socialize internally to bridge the gaps in a large company. These occasions are also a chance for the Senior VPs and department managers to mingle with the employees, particularly the new ones.

At one of the events early in her tenure at the firm, Jennifer took full advantage of the open bar! Not only did she drink more than she could handle, she began to yell at the bartender to "Keep that tequila bottle handy!" Next, she challenged others, in a slurred voice: "Who wants to do tequila shots with me?" This performance was widely observed but failed to impress the VPs and managers. In the end, she didn't stay with the company long. Reasons were found to let her go. In this company's conservative work environment and culture, Jennifer's lack of judgment and control identified her as unsuitable for meeting important clients and customers.

Traveling for the Company

Travel can be one of the perks of your job, or it can be one of the most challenging requirements. If your company is investing time and money to send you out for business purposes, try to enjoy it and make the best of it regardless of where you are sent. But prepare for and avoid the potential pitfalls.

Language

If you are traveling to another country and speak the language, great! You can use the opportunity to brush up on your language skills while you are abroad. Be sure also to research or inquire about customs and tone of conversation in addressing superiors, peers, and clients. You may be able to speak fluently to your friends from that country about what kind of wine to order, but business conversations are generally more formal in tone the world over. Confirm this before you travel. It is better to err on the side of being too formal than too informal. People may correct you if you are too formal. They usually will not correct you if you are too informal; they will just be offended.

If you do not speak a word of the language of the country you will visit, you can at least rely on the status of English as the international language of business. You may still want to pick up a phrase book or pocket dictionary for reference. It is also wise to learn the following five terms, *no matter which country you visit.* Some samples:

English	Spanish	Portuguese	French	German	Italian
Please	Por favor	Por favor	S'il vous plait	Bitte	Per favore
Thank you	Gracias	f. Obrigada, m. Obrigado	Merci	Danke	Grazie
Excuse me	Perdon	Desculpe	Pardonnez-moi	Entshuldigen mich	scusilo
Yes	Si	Si	Oui	Ja	Si
No	No	Nao	Non	Nein	No

Fill out your own list for the country you're traveling to, and make sure you are pronouncing and using these words correctly. Even if your hosts speak to you in English, using these key terms will convey your effort to meet them halfway.

Using these terms also shows your basic good manners. For example, you may bump into someone accidentally. If you say nothing, you will be judged to be rude. If you say "Excuse me" in the local language, you will draw a friendly response. Learning a little of another language also shows you have an interest in the people and culture of the other country. It counters the "Ugly American" myth – that Americans do not respect other people or cultures and think of themselves as the most important people in the world.

Culture

It can take a decade of living in a foreign country to begin to understand a culture and some of its nuances. How will you learn these in just a few days or weeks before a business trip? Try instead to speak with a native of that country or someone who has lived there a while. Ask about the important issues and the differences between your country and his. Ask specifically about how business is conducted, how women are regarded, what the business dress is, and what you should be careful about. There are also a number of good business travel books that address these issues specifically. For example, the *Kiss, Bow and Shake Hands* series (Morrison and Conaway) is very thorough and divided up by regions of the world. (See references at the end of the chapter.) But do not simply go to another country blind – not knowing any of the customs or greetings. You may be inviting trouble otherwise.

Women and Travel

Women in North America and parts of Europe may indeed have "come a long way" from the days of male domination. Their status may be very different in other parts of the world. You will need to be aware of how women are viewed and treated when you travel abroad on business. Speak to a foreign national, if possible, about women in business or find an experienced colleague at your company (preferably another female), or check a business travel reference book.

TRUE TALES FROM THE TRENCHES

Jessica, a consultant for a large international company working out of a Boston office, is sent to Brazil to conduct an audit in the company's Sao Paulo office for two weeks. Jessica is a single, confident 30–year-old used to going where she wants, when she wants. She speaks very little Portuguese and, unfortunately, has not done any research on Brazilian culture and women in the workplace.

On Jessica's second night in Sao Paulo, her audit team, consisting of four local Brazilian men and herself, go to dinner together. Dinner runs quite late because, by local custom, it begins at 9 p.m. The meal has been productive in breaking the ice with all the team members. After dinner, the rest of the team plans to go to a local club to continue the festivities. Wanting to fit in, Jessica accepts their invitation.

At the club, after a few rounds of drinks, she is shocked when one of the men begins to make advances. She hasn't anticipated this because he, along with the others, is married. She wards off his attentions but remains uncomfortable. By the end of the evening, each of the men has made a pass at her or expressed a strong interest in her. Even though she has turned them away, one man sends her a gift the next day at the local office.

Aside from feeling uncomfortable and seeing the morale of the team bruised, Jessica did not expect the reaction she received at the local company office, where gossiping is a very active pastime. Within a day or two, everyone was talking about her "affair" with one of the men in the team. When Jessica returned to Boston at the end of the two weeks, her manager pointedly inquired about her "situation in Sao Paulo."

What should Jessica have done to avoid these problems? If she had been more familiar with local customs and the role of women in this country, she would have known that dinner was probably OK. However, going to a club late at night with men and drinking alcohol were signals to avoid. In this particular situation, the men were probably as confused as Jessica by the end of the evening. They did not read her "signals" properly. Sexual harassment, by the American definition, in this kind of environment is almost never recognized or reported because women and their role in business are viewed very differently. Unfortunately, Jessica had not done her homework and the results could be harmful to her career.

What about *men* traveling overseas? Their actions may also be misconstrued in countries with different customs and cultures. Men traveling alone may also be targeted for confidence schemes, theft, or other illegal activity that a foreigner may be vulnerable to. There are the reports of men who went on dates with local women only to wake up days later, dazed, confused, and robbed, or worse! Yielding to the temptation to indulge in illegal activities in the seeming anonymity of a foreign country may lead to severe consequences – personal harm, jail, and dismissal from one's company. The best policy for men traveling on business is to remember that they are still at work and not traveling as tourists.

The Logistics of Business Travel

The devil can indeed be in the details of business travel, especially for those with little or no experience. Larger companies may have their own meeting and travel planning departments that will make all of your travel arrangements with just a phone call. Usually they use lists of hotels the company has used before and found to be satisfactory both in price and amenities. These are most likely your best bet if you are traveling somewhere for the first time. If you have no such service and have to make your own arrangements, ask an experienced colleague to recommend routes and hotels.

Also, if traveling out of the country, be *sure to notify your credit card companies in _advance_ of your plans* and of which cities and countries you will visit. The reason for this is that many credit cards have security systems in place that are triggered by use out of the country or by frequent use. (The card is frozen and cannot be used.) This can cause a business traveler a lot of problems.

Corporate Credit Cards

Companies may issue their frequent travelers a corporate credit card to be used for business travel and other business expenditures. The usual procedure is that the employee later submits a report of expenses and is reimbursed to pay the credit card bill. Some companies pay the credit card bill directly.

These cards are issued for business and business travel purposes, and are usually meant to be used *only* for these purposes. Most companies have detailed written rules and procedures about the limits of such use because of the potential for misunderstanding and abuse. Many employees have received written reprimands and/or terminations because of misuse of the corporate credit card and the reimbursement procedure.

Remember that all your expenses need to be accounted for so they can be reviewed. This means that your manager, her manager, and the accounting department will all see your expenses and ask for clarification from time to time. You do not want to claim questionable expenses (large bar bills, in-room movies, discretionary purchases, etc.) or stand out as the employee who consistently overspends.

Human Resources and Legal Issues

Regardless of where you work within your new company, the rights and requirements of the workplace will affect your status as an employee. Learn these regulations, and stay informed about them as they change. Most companies will train you on some of the key provisions, but you cannot count on complete coverage through this means alone. It is your own responsibility to be informed and current. Reading your employee handbook, including its coverage of policies and ethical guidelines, will be a good start. Ask questions about these matters, and discuss them with your manager or a Human Resources staff member.

Sexual Harassment

One of the regulations your company will be enforcing concerns this sensitive topic. You may have heard about the lawsuits and the damage awards to victims and the fines levied on companies for the harassers they failed to control. Aside from the potential financial losses, companies are also concerned about the effects on morale and the bad publicity that these allegations and lawsuits generate.

The sexual harassment training most companies provide for new employees and managers focuses on three primary kinds of cases.

Quid pro quo (from the Latin phrase "this for that"). A person in authority, e.g., a supervisor or manager, states or implies that if an employee performs certain sexual acts or favors, he or she will receive favorable treatment or benefits such as a raise or promotion. The converse may also be true: the employee will *not* receive unfavorable treatment if favors are granted.

Unwanted touching or grabbing by one employee of another. The key idea here is *unwanted* contact. In some countries and cultures kissing or hugging someone in greeting would be considered normal behavior and not sexual harassment.

Hostile workplace. The most difficult to define or prove, this category includes situations in which employees find a workplace "sexually charged" or uncomfortable. What makes this difficult to establish is that everyone has a different threshold of comfort. Some people have no problem with jokes about sex or with mild flirting, while others may be offended by such activities.

The key here is that the offended party must make clear that s/he is offended. For example, a calendar with women in bikinis may offend one person and not another. Also, if someone is offended by the work environment *before* hiring on, that person cannot make the complaint after joining the firm. For example, a woman who accepts a job as a bartender at an "exotic" dance club cannot later claim that the sexually charged environment offends her.

How does dating in the workplace tie in with these policies? With respect to the three main categories above, there could be an overlap between a couple dating and a broken-up couple in which one is "harassing" the other. For example, say a female co-worker has broken off a relationship with a male co-worker. He is hurt and is trying to get her back. In doing so, he crosses the line of "unwanted touching" and also creates a "hostile workplace" for her because these advances are no longer welcome. Most sexual harassment cases began as romantic relationships that went sour. If the issue is unclear, ask your direct manager. Also, keep in mind that women can be the harassers and there can be same-sex harassment as well.

Confidentiality and Proprietary Information

Today most companies ask their employees to sign agreements regarding confidentiality and use of proprietary or privileged information. Usually new employees are given an explanation prior to being asked to sign these agreements. Remaining questions include the following:

- Are these agreements legitimate?
- Are they enforceable in a court of law?
- Have employees (and former employees) been sued or prosecuted successfully over these agreements?

The answer to all three questions is yes! So take these agreements seriously and stay informed about them.

A confidentiality agreement is a promise made by an employee to an employer. The promise is to not discuss, divulge, or sell confidential, privileged, proprietary, competitive, or trade-secret information to anyone outside the company during and after the person's employment. Often the period of compliance includes a specified number of years after the employee has left the company.

Even when an employee does not intentionally reveal a secret, the action may still be considered a violation and can be acted upon with termination or prosecution. Here is an example:

TRUE TALES FROM THE TRENCHES

Sanjay, the vice president of a medium-sized software company, was shocked to overhear two of his department managers discuss current company strategy and a confidential upcoming layoff at the local coffee shop. The conversation was taking place at an open coffee bar, where anyone could overhear, just as he had. Imagine the surprise of the two managers on returning to the office, where they were summoned to the Human Resources office and immediately placed on a final written and oral warning by the VP!

Non-Compete Agreements

- What is a non-compete agreement?
- Is it enforceable?

Answers to these questions depend on the particulars of the agreement and the state in which a person is employed. Generally, a non-compete agreement is arranged for a person in sales or someone who has clients or customers. Employers are concerned that when such employees leave they will take clients with them.

If such an employee leaves the company, the terms of the separation, the details of the agreement, and the location of the company all decide if or how the contract will be enforced.

TRUE TALES FROM THE TRENCHES

Two software product managers who were terminated at different companies had the same job descriptions and had both signed the same non-compete agreement. One manager had been based in Florida, and the other in California. After both had left their companies, they each pursued a software management position with a new company in the same industry as their former employer.

The Florida manager and his new company ended up in court and were instructed that he was in violation of his non-compete agreement with the old company. His new company was forced to dismiss him by court order!

The manager in California received the same threats from her old employer, but was told by an employment attorney that the non-compete agreement had no merit. It could not be enforced because of the way it was written and because of California employee laws.

Illegal Activity

In today's world of corporate scandals and ethical breaches aired in the media, companies are more sensitive than ever to their employees' behavior.

Be aware that when you are at work, you are using the company's time and equipment. The company has access to and can scrutinize everything you do, say, or write. To a large extent, you check your privacy at the door when you join, including when you are traveling on business. Phone calls, e-mails, and Internet sites visited are all open to scrutiny. Any abuse in these areas is normally grounds for reprimand or even dismissal from the company and possible prosecution, depending on the offense.

If you are unsure about which activities are illegal, the company will educate you during your new employee orientation and via the employee handbook. Some activities may also be legal but still grounds for dismissal, such as an ethics violation.

One multinational company takes the task of maintaining an ethical work environment very seriously. They require all of their employees, contractors, consultants, and suppliers to attend an ethics training course and sign off that they understand and will abide by the principles taught. In addition, participants receive a 20-page booklet to consult if they have questions. They also agree to report all ethics violations to a 24-hour hotline and are guaranteed no reprisals or reprimands. In fact, if they are found to have failed to report a violation, they are subject to immediate termination. The company wants to send the message that ethics is everybody's business.

In adapting to a new position at a new company, remember that information is your most valuable guide. Even if this is your first job out of college, you can minimize the number of your missteps and CLMs by using the resources that are available for the asking. These include mentors, managers, co-workers, and the many kinds of printed guides to a successful transition into an exciting new opportunity.

Chapter Exercises:

1. You are traveling alone to a foreign country on business for the first time. What are some of the things you can do in preparation to make your trip a success?

2. You are having problems with a new manager. It seems s/he does not like you or your work. You really like the company and do not want to leave. What should you do?

3. You feel lost and uncomfortable at your new company. An experienced co-worker suggests that a mentor might be able to help you. How and where do you find one?

4. You were at your old company for five years and felt very comfortable with the way things were done. Your former boss gave you a lot of feedback on a regular basis, so you always knew where you stood. Now at your new company you feel uncomfortable and unsure of yourself. Your new boss is always traveling and when you get to speak with her, she is rushed and barely listening to you. You are afraid to take initiative lest you make a mistake. How should you proceed?

5. You recently attended a Happy Hour sponsored by your company. You noticed that there was heavy drinking and felt out of place because you do not drink. Do you have to drink to fit in?

6. You were recently given a corporate credit card for use when traveling. You have been feeling financial pressures as you adjust to the new job in a new city. You are tempted to use the card to pay your bills until you can catch up. You reason that there would be no harm done if no one knows. What should you do?

7. You recently attended an off-site conference with the rest of your sales team. During Happy Hour and then into the next day at the meetings, a number of your co-workers kept making off-color, sexually explicit jokes. At first this seemed harmless fun, but after a while the persistence and intensity of these comments began to make you feel uncomfortable. Being a new employee, you are cautious about your next step. What should you do?

8. While walking into the office of a Senior VP, you overhear him making racist comments about a fellow vice president. You pretend you didn't hear these comments, but the Senior VP repeats them in your presence and asks what your personal opinion is about members of the racial group he is attacking. You are not sure how to answer, because this person hired you (and can fire you), but you are also very offended by his comments and attitude. What should you do?

Works Consulted

Ameche, Kathleen. *The Woman Road Warrior: The Expert's Guide to Domestic and International Business Travel,* 2nd ed. Agate: B2 Publishing, 2007.

Bowman, Judith. *Don't Take the Last Donut: New Rules to Business Etiquette.* New York: The Career Press, 2007.

Carte, Penny, and Chris Fox. *Bridging the Culture Gap: A Practical Guide to International Business Communication.* Kogan: Page Publishing, 2004.

Dale, James. *The Obvious: All You Need to Know in Business. Period.* New York: Hyperion, 2007.

DeCenzo, David A., and Stephen P. Robbins. *Fundamentals of Human Resource Management,* 8th ed. Hoboken, NJ: John Wiley & Sons, 2005.

Griffin, Ricky W. *Management,* 8th ed. Boston: Houghton Mifflin Company, 2004.

Morrison, Terri, and Wayne A. Conaway. *Kiss, Bow or Shake Hands: How to do Business in Sixty Countries,* 2nd ed. Holbrook, MA: Adams Media, 2006.

Morrison, Terri, and Wayne A. Conaway. *Kiss, Bow or Shake Hands: Asia.* Holbrook, MA: Adams Media, 2007.

Morrison, Terri, and Wayne A. Conaway. *Kiss, Bow or Shake Hands: Europe.* Holbrook, MA: Adams Media, 2007.

Morrison, Terri, and Wayne A. Conaway. *Kiss, Bow or Shake Hands: Latin America.* Holbrook, MA: Adams Media, 2007.

CHAPTER TWELVE
Planning a Career Journey
Monty Stanford

Career development by definition is a long journey.

– W. Scott Cameron

Chapter Goal:

To help you formulate effective strategies for maximizing long-term career advancement and professional growth.

Chapter Objectives:

- Apply the principles of career development to design a personal long-term career plan.

- Develop a plan for improving your core professional and interpersonal communication and leadership skills.

- Develop a system for updating your career plan and supporting materials.

- Prepare for and manage career transitions.

Looking Forward by Looking Back

Congratulations! If you have followed the guidance offered in previous chapters of this book, you have already done a lot of planning and preparation toward the goal of advancing your career. Most of your work has been directed toward getting a job or improving an existing position after you graduate. Fortunately, this work also provides the foundation for developing a plan for continued career advancement and professional growth throughout your career. This chapter will help you formulate that long-term plan.

This is your chance to start creating the life that you want. The planning that you do now can have a significant impact on how you live in the years to come and on how much you enjoy life. You have many choices and you are the one who controls what you choose and what you don't. Long-term planning will help you make choices that move you in directions you want to go.

You may feel that you cannot really make plans that will stand up over the long term. You will probably make many changes in your working career and may even change careers entirely. Circumstances besides your work will also change: your family situation, your interests, the economy, and other critical factors. Nevertheless, starting your long-term planning now is not only possible, it is one of the best things you can do for yourself.

Developing your long-term career plan and a system for implementing that plan on an ongoing basis also helps you take advantage of opportunities as they arise, sometimes unexpectedly. Having a plan and system in place is also the most efficient way to collect and organize your career resources in a busy working life. It's just the best way to make it easy on yourself.

Right now is an especially good time for developing a long-term career plan. First, you have already invested a lot of time and energy in preparing your resume, portfolio, networking contacts, and other such tools. You don't want to waste that baseline investment. Second, just as research and planning were necessary for your initial job search or career transition, so they are for your future advancement. Rather than starting all over every time you seek a promotion or better job, it makes sense to build on what you have already developed. And, as is true for achieving short-term goals, reaching goals for the long term works best if you have those goals planned so that you know where you want to go.

Note: Whether you are seeking your first professional job, or are a seasoned professional making a career transition, or just trying to advance in your present career track – a long-term strategy can make a difference. You may be starting from a different career stage, but the same principles apply to realizing each of these goals.

Your Personal Long-term Plan

Let's get started by defining the components of a long-term career plan. Later we will examine a system for developing and maintaining that plan.

- Your Personal Career Plan: This is your long-term plan for progression through a series of positions, from college graduation through your career to retirement.

- Your Skills Assessment: This is an analysis of your strengths and weaknesses matched against the skills needed at various stages of your Personal Career Plan.

- Your Improvement Plan: This is a plan that parallels your Personal Career Plan. In the Improvement Plan you specify activities needed to keep you growing professionally by improving your abilities. With these improvements, you can achieve the full potential of your Personal Career Plan.

From college graduation to retirement! This may sound like an unmanageable span to cover. When you think of the details and preparation that went into your first job interviews, the prospect of planning for 20-40 years of career activities may seem impossible. But relax. You don't need that kind of detail in your career plan. Nor do you need to know that in exactly 19 years you will be interviewing for a vice-president's position. All you really need are some reasonable milestones that provide the framework or main steps in your career progression.

Look at the example of a career path in Figure 1 below to see the kind of planning you need to develop. (These are generic charts drawn from many different job descriptions. Your own individual charts will likely include more details specific to your current or desired positions.)

Developing Your Personal Career Plan

If you are following the guidelines of this book, you have already gathered some of this research information. (You may have developed a personal mission statement after working through Chapter Three. Some of that information will be useful in developing your personal career plan.) If not, review Chapters Five and Seven for guidance on how to research positions in your career track through library research and informational interviews. Then develop a table or chart that shows the positions you expect to progress through, along with the skills needed at each position (see Figures 2-4 below).

You may not be able to fill in the details for every position. You will learn more about successive positions as you advance. For now, complete as much of the detail as you can, at least for the next two positions after your first, or about five years into the future.

Do a "reality check" on the timeline of your career track by reviewing employment forecasts. Perhaps your career field is showing slow growth potential with predictions of increasing numbers of graduates and job seekers in a crowded field. In that case, the number of years you spend in each position of your career track will be greater than in a fast-growing field that has fewer people training to enter that field. More traditional industries, such as manufacturing, tend to have slower career tracks than high-growth industries, such as health care. The Software Engineer example of Figures 1-4 is an example of a relatively mature industry that still has room for development and produces moderate rates of advancement.

The typical steps on a career ladder for a software engineer who succeeds in management are shown in Figure 1. There are many variations to this path, of course, and your own career path chart will be different. But you should develop a chart similar to this one so that you have a base-line idea of your career potential.

Years 1-3	Junior Programmer
Years 4-5	Senior Programmer
Years 6-8	Lead Programmer
Years 9-11	Project Manager
Years 12-14	Assistant Software Manager
Years 15-18	Software Manager
Years 19-23	Director of Software Engineering
Years 24-27	Engineering Vice President
Years 28-30	Senior Vice President
Years 30 +	President and CEO

Figure 1. Career Path Chart for a Software Engineer

Now develop more detailed knowledge of the essential duties of your first position after graduation as shown in the example in Figure 2. Get this information from your research on job postings and interviews with people who have done the job in which you are interested.

First job after college graduation – Years 1-3 – Junior Programmer:	
Essential Duties and Responsibilities	**Position Requirements**
1. Reviews, analyzes, and modifies programs to design specifications.	1. Must have demonstrated proficiency in coding C++.
2. Code, debug, unit test, and document program routines.	2. Experience coding on Windows OS platforms
3. Write scripts necessary for implementing or testing program routines.	3. General experience in working with a programming or scripting language such as PERL and JavaScript.
4. May contribute to creation of functional specifications.	4. Familiarity with Visual Studio 6 or other development/design software.
5. Maintains code in configuration management system.	5. Knowledge of word processing software.
6. Works under immediate supervision.	6.Good communication, interpersonal skills, and organizational ability
7. Other duties as assigned.	7. Bachelor's degree in Computer Science or IT related curriculum.

Figure 2. Career Plan Chart for a Junior Programmer

You also need to plan ahead. So, do the best you can to develop the details for the next two positions that you are likely to achieve as shown in the examples in Figures 3 and 4.

Senior Programmer: Years 4-5	
Essential Duties and Responsibilities:	**Position Requirements**
1. Creates or modifies programs to design specifications.	1. 3-5 years programming experience.
2. Code, debug, unit test, and document program routines.	2. Experience working on system-level development, assembly language, and device drivers.
3. Write scripts necessary for implementing or testing program routines.	3. Experience coding on multiple OS platforms (Windows, handheld devices, etc.)
4. Integrate with other programs/systems in accordance with published APIs.	4. Excellent analytical, planning, and organizing skills, detail orientation, self-motivated, creative, able to prioritize work.
5. Prepares system flow charts and logic diagrams to describe existing and proposed programs.	5. Ability to manage multiple assignments and meet deadlines on a timely basis with a high degree of accuracy.
6. Works independently under general supervision and as part of project teams.	6. Bachelor's degree in computer science or related field.

196

| 7. Contribute to creation of functional specifications. | 7. Strong interpersonal, oral, and written communication skills. |
| 8. Assists and trains junior programmers. | 8. Solid understanding of network protocols (TCP/IP) |

Figure 3. Career Plan for a Senior Programmer

Lead Programmer: Years 6-7	
Essential Duties and Responsibilities	**Position Requirements**
1. Manages project teams effectively to meet quality criteria and schedule deadlines.	1. Excellent analytical, planning, organizational, and leadership skills, ability to prioritize work in accordance with business needs.
2. Performs integration testing and maintains code base in CMS.	2. Thorough knowledge of CMS and testing suites and environments.
3. Writes functional specifications to meet approved marketing requirements.	3. Thorough knowledge of documentation systems.
4. Participates in system testing.	4. Strong proficiency in using project management tools, including MS Project.
5. Writes or compiles documentation according to full documentation standards; maintains documentation in CMS.	5. Ability to manage multiple assignments and meet deadlines on a timely basis with a high degree of quality.
6. Designs programs in accordance with architecture specifications; may contribute to program architecture.	6. A good working knowledge of the software life cycle.
7. Monitors and reports on adherence of projects to quality criteria and schedule deadlines and on team productivity.	7. Proficiency with any of the following reporting tools: Crystal Reports, Oracle Reports, MS Access Reports, SQL Reporting Services.
8. Tracks bug severity, manages bug fixes, and reports on work progress.	8. Excellent interpersonal, oral, and written communication skills.
9. Assists with scheduling and milestone definitions.	9. Bachelor's degree in computer science or related field; master's degree preferred.
10. Recognizes staffing needs and participates in hiring new talent.	10. Ability to evaluate candidates and probe qualifications.

Figure 4. Career Plan for a Lead Programmer

Assessing Skills and Developing an Improvement Plan

After charting your career plan, the next step is to assess your skills in relation to those required for the positions identified in your career plan. The easiest way to do this is to make a Skills Assessment Chart such as the one shown in Figure 5.

First job after college graduation: Junior Programmer: Years 1-3	
Position Requirements	**My Qualifications/Skills**
1. Must have demonstrated proficiency in coding C++.	1. Good proficiency from class projects in college.
2. Experience coding on Windows OS platforms	2. Good proficiency from class projects in college.
3. General experience in working with a programming or scripting language such as PERL, JavaScript, VBScript, or Prolog.	3. Some experience with JavaScript done on my own. ***Do some reading about PERL; take a class in JavaScript.***
4. Familiarity with Visual Studio 6 or other development/design software.	4. Somewhat familiar with Visual Studio. ***Do some reading, or take a class, or see if ACM has a workshop.***
5. Knowledge of word processing software.	5. Good proficiency in MS WORD.
6. Effective communication, interpersonal skills, and organizational ability	6. Excellent organizational skills developed in college courses and projects. Very good writing skills. Fairly good oral communication skills - ***Could improve by joining Toastmasters.***
7. Bachelor's degree in Computer Science or IT related curriculum.	7. Done - Graduation next semester.
8. Will probably need teamwork skills.	Good teamwork skills demonstrated through senior project.
	Joined ACM as a student member. ***Need to upgrade to regular membership when I start the job.***

Figure 5. Example of a Skills Assessment Chart with Notes

Start with the column that shows required skills and add a column beside it for your qualifications. (If you have not already done a self-assessment, you may want to refer to Chapters Three and Four.) Decide whether a skill is one in which you are already strong or one in which you need to develop more capability. Then identify what you need to do in order to develop your weaker skills.

As you review the requirements for a particular position, you may modify your original skills description. The description might say, for example, "Good oral and written communication skills required." But, if this is for a marketing position, you might want to add, "Strong creative and persuasive writing skills needed." You may also want to add skills to the list for a position. As you reflect on the work that you would likely do in a position, you may decide that your initial research on the position did not include skills that you think would be necessary or, at least, useful to have in that position. (See Figure 5 for an example.)

Core professional skills are almost always listed as requirements for jobs. You may also want to consider interpersonal skills that are important in business but may not be listed in typical job announcements, such as these:

- Communication skills
- Leadership skills
- Teamwork skills

Planning for Improvement

Once you have finished analyzing your qualifications, summarize your strengths and weaknesses. Then develop your time-based improvement plan as shown in the example in Figure 6. Choose the skills that you wish to improve first and determine how you will strengthen them. For some skills, you may want to seek on-the-job training either through specific work assignments or company sponsored seminars or training programs. You might also become active in professional or other organizations to improve your skills as well as to build network contacts. For each case, develop a workable plan with a realistic timeline.

Of course, you can educate yourself through reading books and professional publications related to your career field. In addition, most companies are interested in enhancing the core professional skills of their employees. Consequently, you may find encouragement and even financial support for pursuing company training programs and attending professional association conferences, seminars, and workshops or taking college classes. Some companies sponsor college courses at the company workplace or provide tuition support for employees to take classes at a local college. Be alert for these opportunities and include them in your review and revision of your career and improvement plans.

1. In the first month of my new job, I will upgrade from my student membership to regular membership in the ACM.

2. I will enroll in a college night class in JavaScript when new term begins.

3. After I feel well established in my new job (probably 3-6 months), I will join Toastmasters.

4. After I have finished the JavaScript class, I will decide whether to learn more about PERL or Visual Studio.

5. I will also investigate ACM workshops and junior college classes.

Figure 6. Example of an Improvement Plan

Continue developing your interpersonal skills also, as well as your core professional skills. Most employees today work as part of a group or team, so companies want employees who have the interpersonal skills to be effective team members. Consequently, there are a growing number of opportunities offered by companies and professional associations for continuing education in communication skills, leadership, and management.

Another way to develop your interpersonal skills is to volunteer for tasks at work that will give you practice at sharpening these skills. Offer to write a group report, deliver a report at a meeting, or take leadership responsibility on a special project. Remember too that you have a life outside of work. You can improve your communication and leadership skills in recreational activities and volunteer work in your community. Sports require teamwork and leadership just as much as business teams, and a scout leader exercises many of the same managerial skills as a business manager. Your business skills can contribute to your community and, in turn, help make you a better business person.

You should also consider the role of networking and mentoring in your Improvement Plan. Building a relationship with one or more mentors is discussed in more detail in Chapter 11. A mentor can provide guidance, point you to valuable resources, and give you specific training. As you grow into your career, think about becoming a mentor yourself. As many have recognized, one of the best ways to learn something is to try teaching it. You may find that mentoring and teaching hone your own skills and abilities as much or more than those of your students.

You may have a number of skills that you want to improve, and that realization may begin to make the process seem onerous or even overwhelming. Here again, learn to take things one step at a time. Learning and growth are activities that contribute energy to a well-led life. In a few years, you may see them as activities that keep you young. For the time being, focus on first things first, secure in the knowledge that you will get to other things later.

Your career plan and associated improvement plan will be two of your primary tools for career advancement in the coming years. These are dynamic documents, however, that you will change over time as you learn more, become more skilled, and progress through your career. You will also need to have a system to keep these tools and others up to date.

Reviewing and Renewing

Periodically you should review your career plan and other career materials. You can do this quarterly, semi-annually, or, at the least, annually. A checklist, such as the example in Figure 7, can be helpful. The items that you should review include:

- Your Personal Success Strategies (see Chapter Two)
- Your Career Plan
- Your Skills Assessment
- Your Improvement Plan
- Your Portfolio – including your Resume and Reference Sheets (Chapter Six)
- Your Marketing Plan (Chapter Seven)

As you review your Career Plan, ask yourself if your career goals have changed. Have your job priorities changed? You may need to adjust your timeline depending on how you are progressing. Check or add the job requirements for the next step in your plan. Make any necessary changes and then consider whether these changes also affect your other plans.

Add to your Skills Assessment plan by matching your skills against the job requirements for the next step in your career plan. Remember that self-assessment is an ongoing process. You may need to re-calibrate your qualifications.

- **Personal Success Strategies**
- **Career Plan**
  - ° Have my career goals changed?
  - ° Have my job priorities changed?
  - ° Does my timeline need to be adjusted?
  - ° What are the job requirements for my next position?
  - ° Are there any other changes necessary?
  - ° How do these changes affect my other plans?

- **Skills Assessment**
  - ° Add the job requirements for my next position.
  - ° How do my skills match up against these job requirements?
  - ° Improvement Plan
  - ° What items have I completed?
  - ° What needs to be added based on the additions to my skills assessment?

- **Portfolio**
  - ° Resume
  - ° Reference Sheets
  - ° Recognition Awards, Letters, etc.
  - ° Performance Reviews
  - ° Work Samples

- **Marketing Plan**

Figure 7. Career Plan Checklist

When reviewing your Improvement Plan, decide what changes you need to make. What items have you completed? You may want to delete completed items, or mark them as done and leave them in your list as a reminder of what you have accomplished in the past year. This will be useful for your annual employee performance review that most companies conduct. At the same time, you may find it useful to synchronize your personal Improvement Plan with your company plan.

Finally, what needs to be added based on your additions to your Skills Assessment plan?

Update your portfolio, especially your resume and reference sheets. These typically get out of date quickly. If you do not update them at least once a year, you may lose track of references or forget information that should be in your resume. Don't wait to add material to your portfolio until your annual update, however. If you receive special recognition, such as an employee award, add it (or a copy) to your portfolio right away.

If you want to add samples of your work, in either hard copy or computer file form, be sure that you have the right to take them. Your work may include confidential information, such as financial records, client or patient information, or computer source code. If you do have the right to show them to people outside your company or if you get written permission to do so, add them to your files as soon as possible. In the event of a layoff or job termination, many companies will no longer allow you access to your work files once you have been notified of the termination. It is also best to keep your career files in a well organized manner at home. Even if you cannot keep samples of your work, recognition of your accomplishments is usually included in your performance reviews. You should be able to get copies of these for your personal records.

Review and update your Personal Marketing Plan also, even if you are not looking for a new job. You can use it to sell yourself for a promotion, as well as to apply for a new job. As you progress through your career, you will be going through several transitions, including promotions and, very probably, job changes. What effect might these changes have on your career plan?

Career Transitions

Prepare for change. Change is always a factor in the business environment. Companies that you work for may grow, contract, merge with other companies, or go out of business. Any of these developments could affect your employment. You may be promoted faster than you expected. You may have to seek another job. Whenever you experience a significant transition or change in your employment, take time to review your career plan and other career materials.

The career materials and planning system presented in this chapter will help you prepare for many transitions in your career. Promotions or seeking a new and better job are natural parts of your career planning. Are there other ways to prepare for these transitions? And what other transitions can you prepare for?

One of the best ways to prepare for positive career transitions is to continue your education. Education, or learning, is a life-long process, whether formal or informal. In today's rapidly changing technology and business environment, none of us continue to work and do business in the same ways for very long. People who learn the new techniques, tools, and processes are always in demand and move ahead in their professions. Those who resist learning relegate themselves to more static jobs that offer few, if any, salary or advancement rewards. Eventually, their knowledge and skills become obsolete along with their jobs.

In addition to education, networking is another great way both to prepare for transitions and to expand your horizons. As noted in Chapter 8, networking is an essential career success strategy to build business relationships over time, within your company as well as externally. Your networking contacts will help you stay informed about new developments in your field and possible opportunities both inside and outside your company.

You can build your network through membership in professional and volunteer organizations that put you into contact with people outside of your company. Over time, you will gather an ever-growing list of contacts. Be sure to keep information about these contacts organized and easily accessible. A folder of loose business cards or even the classic Rolodex is not as useful today as a computerized database. You can use software that you probably already have, such as Microsoft Excel. Or, you can use software specifically designed for maintaining contact information, such as customer relationship management (CRM) software.

Another transition that you may experience is a change in corporate culture. Social culture naturally changes over time. Corporate culture change may be more abrupt when a company is bought, when companies merge, or when you change jobs. This is true even if you are just moving to a new department within the same company. Keep up to date on etiquette and legal issues, as discussed in Chapter Eleven. Your company may institute new training programs for some of these changes. For example, changes in the law, such as new environmental or safety regulations, may be cause for the new training.

But corporate culture changes can be more subtle. Different companies or departments may have different communication styles, for example. One company may rely primarily on e-mail, while another may use primarily voice mail. Be sensitive and alert to such differences during times of transition to help you make the conversion from one corporate culture to another.

Mark has been working at his company for several years now. He's been able to manage his workload, his personal life, and the changes in the organization. Recently, however, the executive level of the company has undergone significant turnover, and the new leadership is refocusing the mission and vision of the company. Mark finds himself at odds with the new directions and has gotten into some debates with his boss about the effects of the new policies on employees and customers. Mark tells his wife Ginger that he still enjoys his work, but is not sure the job meets his expectations anymore.

What are some of the options available to Mark? Should he pursue additional education? Consider changing careers? Look for another company but stay in his present line of work? Does networking offer some options for Mark in this situation?

Transition Shock

A worst-case scenario of change is losing your job through "involuntary separation" or "downsizing" or some other unsought process. This kind of change almost always feels bad. But if you are prepared for change and have your career materials updated, you can make the best of the situation. Even CEOs and company founders face these changes. In his commencement address to the 2005 Stanford University graduating class, Steve Jobs said:

I didn't see it then, but it turned out that getting fired from Apple was the best thing that could have ever happened to me. The heaviness of being successful was replaced by the lightness of being a beginner again, less sure about everything. It freed me to enter one of the most creative periods of my life (<u>Stanford News</u> 2005).

Few of us have had the remarkable career of a Steve Jobs, of course. But a positive attitude and good preparation can help any of us improve our situations in looking for a new job at a minimum. Then too, being "separated" may provide the time to get another college degree, finish training for a certification, or do something else that brings us further along to a more satisfying position.

Steve Jobs was eventually re-hired by Apple and, as has been apparent in media reports, brought the company to the highest levels of success in its history. Many others have used the separation from a prior job to take their lives in quite different directions. Whether you make a slight change or a major one, you can use your long-term plan as a guide to maintain the balance in your life and make the change a productive one.

The Ultimate Transition
One of the positive transitions that you can make in your career is the transition to retirement. That stage may seem to be a long way off, but your actions now will ultimately affect your retirement as well.

Retirement is arguably the most significant psychological and financial transition you will make in your career. Many people reach retirement and find that their financial preparations have been inadequate. The tax-deferred growth available in a 401K plan doesn't accrue to very much if it is started too late or your contributions have been too small. On the other hand, contributions made at the beginning of a 30- or 40-year career will have grown significantly. Planning for retirement from the beginning of your career can pay big dividends.

You can benefit from early retirement planning in more than financial ways. An old cliché is that many men retire from work only to die a year or so later. These men made their jobs the purpose and meaning of their lives. When the jobs ended, so did their lives. But you can avoid that pitfall by developing your other interests in life at the same time as you progress in your working career. As you grow in the pursuit and development of non-work interests, you will most likely find that you grow in the enjoyment and satisfaction of those interests. Retirement can then be a time when you fulfill some of your other dreams.

As noted above, changes will happen throughout your career. Some will be positive and some not so positive. Preparing for change will help you make changes as constructive as possible. And preparation will help you know when it is time to change. When you leave a job, your colleagues, or a company, leave with an affirmative attitude and a positive departure. In today's mobile workforce, it is likely that you will meet some of your colleagues again and they may be in a position to help you. Don't burn any bridges behind you.

Conclusion and Summary

This chapter has presented strategies to help you maximize career advancement and professional growth. These strategies consist of developing and maintaining planning documents and preparing for changes and transitions throughout your career. Developing long-term career plans is an effective and efficient method to collect and organize your career resources and help achieve your long-term goals.

The planning documents discussed in this chapter include:

- Your Personal Career Plan – A chart of your long-term plan for progression through a series of jobs or positions in your career from college graduation through your career to retirement.

- Your Skills Assessment – An analysis of your strengths and weaknesses matched against the skills needed at the various stages of your Career Plan.

- Your Improvement Plan – A written time-based plan in which you specify activities that will keep you growing and improve your abilities so that you can achieve the steps in your Career Plan.

These are dynamic planning documents that you should review and update at least once a year. Other plans discussed in previous chapters should also be included as part of your annual review. These plans include:

- Your Personal Success Strategies

- Your Portfolio

- Your Marketing Plan

This chapter also discusses other activities that can help you enhance your career. One of these is continuing your education through personal reading, company training, professional associations, and college classes. You can also improve your communication and leadership skills in recreational activities and volunteer work in your community. You should continue networking both within and outside your company. Be alert also and sensitive to changes in corporate culture, especially in times of transition, such as when you start a new job. Finally, don't put off planning for retirement; early investments in retirement pay the biggest dividends.

Remember to maintain a balance in your life among your interests other than your work career. And, keep a positive attitude, especially in times of transition. Your good preparation will help you make the most of your career.

Enhancing Your Career (and Life) Planning

You may have interviewed people about the specific job and career that you are currently interested in. (If you have not done this, you probably should do it now!) But have you considered your working career as part of your whole life? Many of our decisions about work depend on our other interests in life. You might want to consider the following activities:

- Talk to someone in the older generation – for example, a family member, older work colleague, college professor – about her work choices and the factors that influenced them.

- Read a book that discusses work in the context of life choices. The books listed below are examples that many people have found helpful and inspiring.

  o *What Color Is Your Parachute?* by Richard Nelson Bolles

  o *Do What You Love, The Money Will Follow: Discovering Your Right Livelihood* by Marsha Sinetar

  o *The Pathfinder: How to Choose or Change Your Career for a Lifetime of Satisfaction and Success* by Nicholas Lore

  o *The Renaissance Soul: Life Design for People with Too Many Passions to Pick Just One* by Margaret Lobenstine

- Imagine that you have just retired and write your own brief biography for *Who's Who*. What does the biography say about your career? What about your non-work life? What have you not had time to finish? What gives you the most pride?

Chapter Mini-Case:

Margaret has been receiving glowing reviews for her work, and has taken on growing responsibility for her department's projects. Valuing her work, her manager has allowed her to leave early for her kids' school events or to work from home when the children were sick. Some of the other employees have taken advantage of this flexibility, however, and one of them was recently placed on probation after a confrontation with the HR department. Margaret's manager announces that work schedules will be strictly enforced from now on. The crackdown hurts morale; many department members come to Margaret to voice their complaints, since they know how important the issue is to her. One day, department members arrive to learn that their manager has resigned.

What are Margaret's options now? Should she pursue the department manager's job, given that she has performed well and her colleagues respect her? How might a promotion affect her time with her kids? What are Margaret's life choices?

A Career Planning and Development Bibliography

Arden, Paul. It's Not How Good You Are, It's How Good You Want to Be. New York: Phaidon Press Limited, 2003.
Barry, Nancy. When Reality Hits: What Employers Want Recent Graduates To Know. Dallas: Brown Books, 2007.
Berens, Linda, and Dario Nardi. The 16 Personality Types: Descriptions for Self-Discovery. Huntington Beach, CA: Telos Publications, 1999.
100 Best Companies. Working Mother Magazine. 29 Jun 2007 http://www.workingmothermediainc.com/web?service=vpage/575.
"Best Employment Interviewing Tips - Interview Questions and Questions to ask the Employer." Career Consulting Corner. Career Consulting Corner. 20 Nov 2006 http://www.careercc.com/interv3.shtml.
Bolles , Richard Nelson. What Color Is Your Parachute? 2007: A Practical Manual for Job-Hunters and Career-Changers. Berkeley, CA: Ten Speed Press, 2007.
Boone, Mary. Managing Interactively: Executing Business Strategy, Improving Communication, and Creating a Knowledge-Sharing Culture. 1st ed.. New York: McGraw-Hill, 2000.
Chicago Fitness Express. 29 Jun 2007 http://www.chicagofitnessexpress.com/.
Collegegrads.com. 2006. 15 Aug 2006 http://www.collegegrad.com.
Contract Employment Weekly. Contract Job Hunter. 29 Jun 2007 http://www.ceweekly.com/.
Covey, Stephen. Seven Habits of Highly Effective People. New York: Simon & Schuster, 1989.
--------. The Eighth Habit. New York: Free Press, 2004.
Digitial Directory. Switchboard. 29 Jun 2007 http://www.switchboard.com/.
Dikel, Margaret F. "How to Use the Internet in Your Job Search." The Riley Guide: How to Job Search. 01 Mar 2007. The Riley Guide. 02 Apr 2007 http://www.rileyguide.com/jobsrch.html.
Dikel, Margaret, and Frances Roehm. Guide to Internet Job Searching. 2006-1007 ed. McGraw-Hill, 2006.
"Duke HR - Professional Development Institute (PDI)." Duke Human Resources. 08 Dec 2006. Duke University. 28 Jun 2007 http://www.hr.duke.edu/pdi/interviewing.html.
Enelow, Wendy, and Louise Kursmark. Cover Letter Magic: Trade Secrets of Professional Resume Writers. 2006. Indianapolis: Jist Works, 2006.
Engineering Enterprises, Inc.. 29 Jun 2007 http://www.eeiweb.com.
Evers, Frederick, James Rush, and Iris Berdow. The Bases of Competence: Skills for Lifelong Learning and Employability (Jossey Bass Higher and Adult Education Series). 1st ed. Jossey-Bass, 1998.
Forbes. 29 Jun 2007 http://www.forbes.com.
Fortune. CNN Money. 29 Jun 2007 http://www.money.cnn.com/magazines/fortune/.

Goodall, Jr., H. L., and Sandra Goodall. <u>Comunicating in Professional Contexts</u>. 2nd ed.
Belmont: Thomson Higher Education, 2006.

Goulet, Tag, and Catherine Goulet. <u>Jobs.aol.com</u>. 2005. FabJob.com. 08 Aug 2006
<u>http://jobs.aol.com</u>.

Graber, Steven. <u>The Everything Get-A-Job Book</u>. Holbrook, Massachusetts: Adams Media
Corporation, 2000.

Gross, Kim, and Jeff Stone. <u>Chic Simple Dress Smart for Women: Wardrobes that Win in the
Workplace</u>. Grand Central Publishing, 2002.

Hamlin, Sonya. <u>How to Talk So People Listen: Connecting in Today's Workplace.</u> Rev. ed.
New York: HarperCollins, 2006.

Hansen, Julie. <u>I Don't Know What I Want, But I Know It's Not This: A Step-by-Step Guide to
Finding Gratifying Work</u>. New York: Penguin Books, 2003.

Hansen, Katharine. "Ten Surefire Ways to Organize Your Job Search." <u>QuintCareers.com</u>.
QuintCareers.com. 02 Apr 2007
<u>http://www.quintcareers.com/printable/organize_your_job-search.html</u>.

Heim, Pat, and Susan Murphy. <u>In the Company of Women.</u> New York: Tarcher/Putnam, 2001.

-------. <u>Hardball for Women</u>. New York: Plume, 2005.

Heller, Robert, and Tim Hindle. <u>Essential Manager's Manual</u>. New York: DK Publishing,
1998.

"Hidden Job Market." <u>University of Minnesota</u>. 2005. Regents of the University of Minnesota.
06 Apr 2007 <u>http://www.stpaulcareers.umn.edu/jobsearch/find_positions/
hidden_market.html</u>.

Hoovers a D&B Company. 29 Jun 2007 < <u>http://www.hoovers.com</u>>.

IBIS World. 29 Jun 2007 <u>http://www.ibisworld.com</u>.

<u>Inc. 500</u>. Inc. Magazine. 29 Jun 2007 <u>www.inc.com/resources/inc500/2006/</u>.

<u>Industry Link. 29 Jun 2007 < http://www.industrylink.com></u>.

Investor Relations Information Network . 29 Jun 2007 <u>http://www.irin.com</u>.

"Job-Hunt.Org: Networking to Your Next Job - Push Techniques." <u>job-hunt.org</u>. 2007.
NETability, Inc.. 06 Apr 2007 <u>http://www.job-hunt.org/hiddenjobmarket.shtml</u>

"Job interviews: Qualities employers look for." Workforce2.org. 26 Sep 2006
<u>http://www.workforce2.org/qualities-employer-look-for.htm</u>.

Jobs, Steve. "'You've got to find what you love,' Jobs says." <u>Stanford News</u>. 14 June 2005.
Stanford University. 23 Oct 2006 <u>http://news-
service.stanford.edu/news/2005/june15/jobs-061505.html</u>.

<u>Jobs.aol.com</u>. 2005. CareerBuilder.com. 08 Aug 2006 <u>http://jobs.aol.com</u>.

<u>Jobs.aol.com</u>. 2006. Robert Half International. 08 Aug 2006 <u>http://jobs.aol.com</u>.

Johnson, Spencer. <u>One Minute for Myself.</u> New York: William Morrow and Company, 1985.

----------. <u>Who Moved My Cheese?</u> New York: G.P. Putnam's Sons, 1998.

Kador, John. <u>201 Best Questions To Ask On Your Interview</u>. New York: McGraw-Hill, 2002.

Krannich, Ron, and Caryl Krannich. <u>Campus Career Center's The Job Hunting Guide</u>.
Manassas Park, Virginia: Impact Publishing, 2003.

----------. Nail the Job Interview. Manassas Park, Virginia: Impact Publishing, 2003.
Land's, End. Land's End Business Attire for Men: Mastering the New ABCs of What to Wear to Work. Clarkson Potter, 2004.
Levinson, Jay, and David Perry. Guerrilla Marketing for Job Hunters: 400 Unconventional Tips, Tricks, and Tactics for Landing Your Dream Job. New York: Wiley, 2005.
Lewicki, Roy, David Saunders, and Bruce Barry. Negotiation. 5th ed. New York: McGraw-Hill/Irwin, 2005.
Littauer, Florence. Personality Plus: How to Understand Others by Understanding Yourself. Rev. ed. Revell, 1992.
Lobenstine, Margaret. The Renaissance Soul: Life Design for People with Too Many Passions to Pick Just One. New York: Broadway Books, 2006.
Lore, Nicholas. The Pathfinder: How to Choose or Change Your Career for a Lifetime of Satisfaction and Success. New York: Simon & Schuster - Fireside, 1998.
Lorenz, Kate. Jobs.aol.com. 2005. CareerBuilder.com. 08 Aug 2006 http://jobs.aol.com.
Mayer, Robert. How to Win Any Negotiation: Without Raising Your Voice, Losing Your Cool, or Coming to Blows. Career Press, 2006.
Meyer, Paul J. Attitude is Everything. 1997.
Miller, John. G. Flipping The Switch. New York: The Penguin Group, 2006.
--------. QBQ! The Question Behind the Question. Denver: Denver Press, 2001.
Mitchell, Mary. The First Five Minutes: How to Make a Great First Impression in Any Business Situation. Wiley, 1998.
Morin, William J. "The 25 most difficult questions." The 25 most difficult questions you'll be asked in a job interview. 05 Jan 1983. Focus Magazine. 20 Nov 2006 http://www.datsi.fi.upm.es/~frosal/docs/25mdq.html.
Nelson, Bob. 1001 Ways to Take Initiative at Work. New York: Workman Publishing, 1999.
Niven, David. The 100 Simple Secrets of Successful People. New York: HarperCollins, 2002.
Niznik, J. Steven. "Hidden Job Market." About: Tech Careers. 2007. About.com. 60 Apr 2007 http://www.jobsearchtech.about.com/library/weekly/aa090897.htm.
Plunkett Research, Ltd.. 29 Jun 2007 < http://www.plunkettresearch.com>.
Quast, Lisa. Your Career, Your Way. Livermore CA: Wingspan Press, 2007.
Sanders, Tim. Love is the Killer App. New York: Three Rivers Press, 2002.
SARK. Inspiration Sandwich. Berkeley, CA: Celestial Arts, 1992.
--------. Make Your Creative Dreams Real. New York: Simon & Schuster, 2004.
Simon, Linda. New Beginnings: A Guide for Adult Learners. 2nd ed. Englewood Cliffs, NJ: Prentice-Hall, 2001.
Simon, Mary. Negotiate Your Job Offer: A Step-by-Step Guide to a Win-Win Situation. New York: Wiley, 1997.
Sinetar, Marsha. Do What You Love, The Money Will Follow: Discovering Your Right Livelihood. New York: Dell Publishing, 1989.

"Six degrees of separation - Wikipedia, the free encyclopedia." Wikipedia.com. 21 June 2007. About.com. 27 June 2007 http://www.en.wikipedia.org/wiki/six_degrees_of_separation.

Stebleton, Michael, Michael Henle, and Connie Harris. Hired! The Job Hunting/Career Planning Guide. 3rd ed. Upper Saddle River: Pearson, 2006.

Stein, Marky. Fearless Interviewing: How to Win the Job by Communicating with Confidence. New York: McGraw-Hill, 2002.

Swanson, Richard W. The Smart People's Guide to Job Hunting. Premier. Denver: Buck Jones Books, 2001.

Troutman, Kathryn. Federal Resume Guidebook: Strategies for Writing a Winning Federal Electronic Resume, KSAs, and Essays (Federal Resume Guidebook: Write a Winning Federal Resume to Get In). 4th ed. Indianapolis: JIST Works, 2007.

Turner, Harry. You Can Do It: A Guide for the Adult Learner and Anyone Going Back to School Mid-Career. Merrit, 1997.

U.S. Securities and Exchange Commission. 29 Jun 2007 http://www.sec.gov/edgar.shtml.

Vashistha, Atul, and Avinash Vashistha. The Offshore Nation: Strategies for Success in Global Outsourcing and Offshoring. New York: McGraw-Hill, 2006.

Vault. 29 Jun 2007 < http://www.vault.com>.

Whitcomb, Susan. Resume Magic: Trade Secrets of a Professional Resume Writer. 3rd ed. JIST Works, 2006.

Whitmore, Jacqueline. Business Class: Etiquette Essentials for Success at Work. St. Martin's Press, 2005.

Yate, Martin. Knock 'em Dead 2007: The Ultimate Job Search Guide. Avon: Adams Media, 2006.

Index